Sisters and Brothers for Life

Sisters and Brothers for Life

Making Sense of Sibling Relationships in Adulthood

Suzanne Degges-White

ROWMAN & LITTLEFIELD
Lanham • Boulder • New York • London

Published by Rowman & Littlefield
A wholly owned subsidary of
The Rowman & Littlefield Publishing Group, Inc.
4501 Forbes Boulevard, Suite 200, Lanham, Maryland 20706
www.rowman.com

Unit A, Whitacre Mews, 26-34 Stannary Street, London SE11 4AB

British Library Cataloguing in Publication Information Available

Library of Congress Cataloging-in-Publication Data

Names: Degges-White, Suzanne, author.
Title: Sisters and brothers for life : making sense of sibling relationships in
    adulthood / Suzanne Degges-White.
Description: Lanham, Maryland : Rowman & Littlefield, [2017] | Includes
    bibliographical references and index.
Identifiers: LCCN 2016057630 (print) | LCCN 2017022304 (ebook) | ISBN
    9781442265950 (electronic) | ISBN 9781442265943 (cloth : alk. paper)
Subjects: LCSH: Brothers and sisters. | Interpersonal relations. | Families.
Classification: LCC BF723.S43 (ebook) | LCC BF723.S43 D44 2017 (print) |
    DDC 155.44/3—dc23
LC record available at https://lccn.loc.gov/2016057630

∞™ The paper used in this publication meets the minimum requirements
of American National Standard for Information Sciences—Permanence
of Paper for Printed Library Materials, ANSI/NISO Z39.48-1992.

Printed in the United States of America

Contents

Acknowledgments

Thank you to all of the study participants around the globe who shared their adult sibling relationship stories of triumph, tragedy, and everything in between. Family relationships can be messy, and I appreciate all of the individuals who let me peek inside their family systems.

I offer heartfelt appreciation to my brother, Andrew, who taught me a lot about conflict, resolution, sibling loyalty, and love.

Lastly, I acknowledge the enthusiastic support of my editor, Suzanne Staszak-Silva. Her continued belief in my ideas has been a gift.

Preface

While no one is likely to love you more than your own mother, no one is likely to know you as well as your siblings. Growing up in the same home, sharing mealtimes, playtimes, and disciplinary experiences, you and your siblings became intimately acquainted with one another in a way that is seldom experienced in life. Many people erroneously equate *intimacy* only with feelings such as love and support. Unfortunately, intimate family relationships are not always the picture of peace and harmony one might hope. Some siblings begin life as the best of friends, grateful for the presence of a companion. Other siblings may argue and fight throughout childhood, only learning how much they appreciate one another's presence in their lives in adulthood. This book is designed to provide assistance and suggestions to help readers better manage, or even reestablish, their adult sibling relationships.

ORGANIZATION OF THE BOOK

Multiple large-scale research studies have used existing data sets to predict attitudes, behaviors, and experiences of siblings and parents. This current study explores the responses of more than four hundred adults to a set of open-ended questions relating to sibling relationships and their development and transitions in adulthood. The survey questions and demographic data of the online respondents are found in Appendix A. For the purposes of clarity and consistency, pseudonym first names are used throughout the book. These names have been chosen for convenience by the author and are not knowingly the actual names of any of the respondents, as no identifying information was collected in the online survey. Face-to-face interviewees' names have also been changed to respect their privacy.

Hundreds of adults shared about their relationships with siblings. Women and men described their relationship conflicts, challenges, turning points, and regrets. People learn about negotiation, compromise, winning, and losing from their siblings. The lessons learned in youth can shape the roles we play in adult relationships as well as the expectations we place on friends and romantic partners. The old saying that "the apple doesn't fall far from the tree" speaks to the power of parental influence, but siblings are just as genetically similar to one another as they are to either parent. Though temperaments and personalities can differ markedly between siblings, evolution and socialization encourage the desire for an enduring bond with our sibs.

Unfortunately, past interactions can forestall attempts to maintain a warm and supportive sisterly or brotherly bond. The closest there is to a one-size-fits-all magic solution to relationship problems is effective communication. Using real-life examples of sibling battlegrounds or stand-offs, suggestions are provided for approaching time bomb topics in such a way that no one is left feeling emotionally assaulted and the relationship isn't sacrificed in the fray.

Siblings in Family Context

The first section of this book is titled "Family Constellations, Culture, and Communication." The first chapter explores the role that birth order may play in childhood and into adulthood. The constellation of a family refers to the size and shape of the family—number and gender of siblings, presence or absence of parents or stepparents, and so on. Family constellations shape our childhood experiences and the choices we make regarding our own nuclear families in adulthood. The next chapter explores the ways in which culture and family heritage can influence sibling relationships. A wide lens is used to capture many forms of diversity, including ethnicity and culture. One event that can permanently alter family constellation and functioning is the death of a child. The third chapter presents a developmentally structured examination of the ways that this loss can influence surviving siblings. In the fourth chapter, we explore communication pattern development between siblings and family members.

Baggage from the Past

The second section of the book is titled "The Effects of the Past on the Present," and it includes four chapters that address the earliest appearance of specific family dynamics or sensitive topics that often defy open discussion in families-of-origin. The first chapter focuses on the potential for sibling rivalry to remain active into adulthood. Addressed in the following chapter is the potentially lasting influence of favoritism or family roles, such as the "black sheep" or the "favorite." The next chapter takes aim at potentially painful family secrets such as abuse and addictions. The final chapter focuses on taboo topics such as sex, politics, religion, and money.

Right Here, Right Now

The third section of the book is titled "Focus on the Present." In this section, we explore topics that can be difficult for siblings—or even good friends—to discuss. Siblings' lifestyle choices and shortcomings are covered as are siblings' romantic relationships and caring for siblings facing health and wellness challenges.

Preparing for the Future

The final section, "Making Changes for the Future," opens with a chapter that addresses the realities of caring for aging parents and coping with their deaths. The next chapter explores ways to enhance adult sibling communication. The final chapter, "Siblings for Life: Closing the Gaps in the Family Circle," addresses the ways in which our sibling relationships affect other adult relationships—friendships and romantic partnerships—and ways to bring closure to residual conflicts from the past and build the foundation for positive, long-lasting sibling support.

CONCLUSION

There's a valuable directive that is helpful in challenging situations: "Control your controllables." This is a good reminder that we all face circumstances beyond our control; being born in a particular family to particular parents with particular siblings is one of those things. What *can* be controlled are the ways in which you orchestrate difficult discussions or communicate with others. This book provides information about the role that early family experiences play in shaping sibling relationships, the ways in which family secrets can influence us long past our childhoods, and the power of challenging topics to disrupt relationships, as well as suggestions for undoing past damage and preventing future discord to the greatest extent possible. It is hoped that this book will also provide encouragement and the necessary tools for readers to strengthen their adult sibling relationships.

Introduction

The list of legendary siblings stretches throughout earliest recorded history, mythology, and literature. Complex sibling relationships abound in these realms—from Cain and Abel in the Bible to Cersei and Jaime in the wildly popular television series *Game of Thrones*, which was based on the books by George R. R. Martin. Siblings seem to bring out the best and the worst in one another. Jumping into contemporary news stories, siblings celebrities include the Kardashian sisters; Venus and Serena Williams; Eli and Peyton Manning; George and Jeb Bush; John, Robert, and Ted Kennedy; and Andrew, Owen, and Luke Wilson; just to name a few. Fictional families are everywhere in the movies, television, and in books. Which family most resembles your own? Some parents may try to re-create the warmth and humor portrayed in shows like *Modern Family*, *Parenthood*, and *This Is Us*. Others may be living out the adventures of a real-life Homer Simpson and family.

Depending on your own family history, brothers and sisters may feel like built-in playmates, full-time rivals, or something in between. Sometimes siblings are described as partners in the longest relationships you will ever experience in life. Because children have no say when it comes to determining who will be sharing their parents or sharing their toys, they often feel fully justified in harboring resentment for a sibling's presence in their lives. For most brothers and sisters, sibling rivalry begins to wane as the external world exerts a greater pull on young adolescents and they move beyond the family circle to establish their individual identities and measure their developing self-worth.

All this maturity and independence, however, can disappear in a heart-beat when family members get together and childhood dynamics are reactivated. Brothers may engage in intense computer and video game battles; sisters may compare partners, children, wardrobes, hair, and careers; and they all might argue about superficial decisions, such as who sits where or who chooses the music, or more elemental topics such as who is doing better than whom in life. Depending on old family scripts, parents may stand back and let siblings sort things out on their own or jump in to settle the squabbles as they might have done when the children were young.

If you're wondering what "normal" sibling behavior looks like, you will have a hard time finding a definitive answer. As children learn early, every family system is unique and governed by different expectations and different rules. Some families let kids have a lot of freedom and little guidance; other families have strict rules and significant consequences for misbehavior. Most families fall somewhere in the middle. Thus, the concept of "normal" family life is hard to pin down. As a further complication, and as every successful family counselor knows, there are multiple realities within each family system.

Every family member undergoes unique experiences that shape the relationships and exchanges within the family. Ask two siblings to recall a single shared experience, and the memories of the event can be markedly different for each of them, regardless of the seemingly shared history. Whether the two siblings argue vehemently about whose version is more accurate, the truth is that whatever a person remembers about an incident from childhood becomes their own de facto truth. In effect, there really cannot be a single universal family truth. Learning to accept that each of your siblings has their own unique family narrative may make family gatherings more peaceable. Even without a unifying, incontrovertible family truth, there still exist a few uniform expectations about how most sibling relationships play out over time.

A BRIEF OVERVIEW OF SIBLINGSHIPS OVER THE LIFESPAN

All relationships change over the years, even those between children and their parents and between siblings. There are some relatively predictable shifts in most long-term relationships, and when it comes to siblings, individual development and maturation can be harbingers of relationship changes to come. In addition to the long-lasting nature of siblingships, the intensity of the relationship may be heightened in families today due to the smaller number of children being born in any given family.[1] Another relevant cultural shift includes the loosening of family bonds through divorce, separation, non-permanent parental cohabitation, shared custody, split custody, and so on. With the potential for so many changes in the location and the composition of the nuclear family, sibling relationships may be strengthened or severed, depending on factors far beyond children's control. The once somewhat predictable path of sibships may be anything *but* predictable; nonetheless, following is an overview of the developmental tasks accomplished through the sibling relationship, according to Ann Goetting.[2]

Youth

When adults are asked about their earliest childhood memory of sibling interactions, they typically share a story that includes childhood play. Siblings are usually our first playmates; even when we don't get along, their presence can be as a distraction or a layer of protection from the adult world. Middle or older children often have early memories of the day a new sibling arrived in the home, or memories of being assigned to babysit or care for the new sib. The developmental tasks that transpire during this period include 1) companionship and emotional support, 2) delegated caretaking, and 3) aid and direct services.[3] Siblings can be good friends or rivalrous enemies, depending on the individuals and the family dynamics involved. Resentment between siblings can arise from perceived unfair treatment by parents—whether the facts bear out the inequity or not.

Emerging Adulthood and Midlife

The bond between siblings may be emotionally close throughout their lives or it may reflect estrangement, residual discontent from childhood, or deepened devotion as past wrongs or resentments fade with age. The developmental tasks that occur between siblings during the bulk of the adult years include 1) companionship and emotional support, 2) coopera-tion in the care of elderly parents and ultimately in the dismantling of the parental home, and 3) aid and direct services.[4] While not every sibling remains emotionally present for another as years pass or priorities shift, parental well-being and family crises are critical incidents that may draw siblings back together as adults. There's a saying that "the older you get, the more like yourself you become." It's also common for family-of-ori-gin relational issues to spring up full force when far-flung siblings gather together during stressful events—whether these occur around the table at holiday dinners or around a parent's hospital bed at the end of life. Find-ing a way to manage knee-jerk or childish reactions that can occur at times like these can provide a path for deepening, age-appropriate relationships to develop between sibs.

Older Adulthood

Invited to reflect on her sibling relationships, an elderly woman shared her grief at being an only child. She plaintively confided, *"My parents have been gone for almost forty years; they were both the youngest of their families, and they didn't have me until they were in their late thirties. They lost a second child to a miscarriage shortly after my first birthday. Now, there's no one left to remember me as I was . . . when I was a child."* The desire for siblings in life is likely strongest during our early years and, even more so, during our later years. As we face a declining social circle with age, the longing for strengthened bonds with family members tends to deepen. The developmental tasks of siblings that Goetting[5] assigned to this period include 1) companionship and emotional support, 2) shared reminiscence and perceptual validation, 3) resolution of sibling rivalry, and 4) aid and direct services. Only children may feel the absence of sib-lings the most acutely at this stage of life.

Throughout this book, we will explore a variety of sibling constella-tions that may reflect the traits and patterns found in your own sibships, for good and for bad. Ideally, readers will gain new insights about their own relationships as well as support for making the changes they desire. In some cases, the descriptions may help readers simply come to terms with the status of their relationships with their brothers and sisters.

CONCLUSION

Just as a person cannot choose his parents, siblings cannot be chosen either. Learning to maneuver the path from childhood to adolescence with siblings is a daunting challenge, depending on family composition, temperamental predisposition of its members, and the family's ability to balance transition against chaos. As adults, however, you have the opportunity to choose the perspectives through which you view and interact with siblings. It is hoped that the anecdotes and suggested practices in this book will provide tools that help you deepen your sibships from just sibs to good friends for a lifetime.

Part I

FAMILY CONSTELLATIONS, CULTURE, AND COMMUNICATION

Chapter One

Birth Order and Family Constellations

Are you an independent firstborn? A forgotten middle kid? Or maybe the admittedly spoiled baby of the family? There are many stereotypes used to describe children based on their birth order. The research is split on whether or not birth order makes much of a difference in innate characteristics such as intelligence or disposition, but there is every indication that your place in the family constellation affects the way you are treated within the family and how you finesse your way through family relationships and family engagement.

FAMILY CONSTELLATIONS

Alfred Adler was the most influential psychology scholar to emphasize the role that our early familial circumstances play in our development.[1] Adler described the construct of the *family constellation* as a singular system inclusive of all of the varied family members, nuances, and interrelationships among family members. When Adler began building his theory, most families consisted of the traditional lineup of biological parents and their offspring. Adler believed that each member of an offspring group had a uniquely individual experience of identity development within the family constellation. According to Adler, personality development was the product of this unique experience and one's birth order.

Contemporary family constellations often exhibit markedly more complex relationships due to divorce, remarriage, and other factors. Some statistics indicate the divorce rate is actually declining and others suggest it is holding steady, if not climbing. Unfortunately, trying to pin down the exact likelihood of a marriage ending in divorce is not an easy calculation.[2] In fact, two decades ago, the government ceased collecting data related to prior marriages when couples applied for new marriage licenses. Although the states may no longer be interested in this data, the impact of entering a new marriage with children from previous relationships can be immense for all involved. Shifting family constellations can wreak havoc on a young person's identity development and sense of place within the family system.

A young man, Art, in his mid-twenties, described an experience of a seismic shift in his own family constellation when he was younger. Art's parents divorced when he was six, and a couple of years later, his father remarried a woman with two sons of her own; one was older and one was younger than Art:

> *I'll never forget how angry I felt the first night that Candy's [his step-mother] kids spent the night at Dad's house when me, my brother, and my sister were there, too. Candy's older son was fourteen and I was only nine, and I was terrified of him. He cursed, he threatened to beat me and my brother if we didn't do what he said, and he watched television shows and played video games that me and my brother weren't allowed to. When we complained to our dad, he just said, "Jake's the oldest, so he gets more privileges than you and your brother and sister do. I went from feeling confident and good about myself as the "oldest son" in my "real family" to feeling like a second-class citizen in the "new family."*

Art went on to share that this new family constellation didn't last too long; by the time he was twelve, his father's new marriage was falling apart. Desperate to save his marriage, Art shared, his father demanded that all the kids go to counseling with the couple, but Candy's boys refused, Art's sister refused, and his dad finally gave up. Art said that when his dad announced that he and Candy were splitting up, it was one of the best days of his childhood. He knew that he would no longer have to compete in that family hierarchy for his rightful place in his father's eyes.

This anecdote clearly illustrates the power of the *family stage* to shape a sibling's sense of self and competence. The construct of self-esteem is often misunderstood. It is often assumed to describe how a person feels about herself. Actually, one's level of self-esteem is determined by how she believes *others* perceive her. Your own self-esteem is tied directly to how you believe you rank in the esteem of others. In our earliest years, there is a limited group of individuals from whom to gather data as we seek to gain competence in life. For children with no siblings, it is typically their parents to whom they look for feedback and approval. For children with siblings, they may measure their self-worth by their ability to master the skills their older siblings possess. Older children with younger siblings are often able to gather positive feedback regarding their accomplishments due to the relative inexperience of younger brothers and sisters. The family constellation creates a family stage on which many of our earliest power struggles and mastery moments play out.

Taking this broader perspective of the family system and reflecting on your own personal family experiences might provide a fair amount of anecdotal evidence to support the belief that birth order influences our adult identities. While Adler felt it necessary to incorporate all aspects of the genetic and environmental/cultural components of the family system as potentially influential on birth order effect, many pop-psychology books today want to simplify the equation and typify adult development based on birth order alone. When it comes to human development, however, this type of streamlining is seldom sufficient.

BIRTH ORDER

Nearly seventy years after Adler's[3] first forays into the role of family constellation and birth order, Sulloway published a book titled *Born to Rebel*[4] in the mid-1990s. This book provided an exploration of the role that birth order played in the way that siblings' personalities developed in more contemporary times. Many of the strong claims that were made in the book have been examined more closely through research studies and found to be less static and more obscure than first hypothesized. However, the desire to ascribe sibling differences in traits and characteristics to birth order persists. Following is a brief exploration of the variables that have been studied.

Birth Order, Intelligence, and Income

The first stereotype that needs to be broken is the one that addresses birth order and brains. Firstborns are likely to assume—and broadcast—that their *chronological* superiority also yields them *intellectual* superiority to their younger siblings. While there is some evidence that a slight difference does exist, the most recent research does not bear this out as convincingly as firstborns might like.[5] In fact, the difference in intelligence, as measured by a standardized IQ test, was only one point.[6] With a standard deviation of fifteen points, the "one-point advantage" likely has little significance in the real world.

The IQ component that actually showed any measurable difference was verbal skills, which makes intuitive sense given that parents likely spend more time engaging in verbal stimulation of their firstborns due to the greater time available to focus on the first child. After the second child arrives, unless there's a significant age gap, parents are seldom able to replicate that intensive focus on parenting an infant as they exhibited the first time around. Clearly, squabbling or negotiating with older siblings doesn't provide the same level of intellectual stimulation that adult interaction does. It has also been shown that siblings who are born earliest (first- or second-born) into a family and siblings from smaller families will have a better episodic memory system from adolescence into older adulthood.[7] This can definitely influence academic performance.

In addition to the slight difference in IQ and the stronger memory, there is also a tendency for the oldest to be better educated, overall, than any subsequent siblings.[8] This is not necessarily due to inborn potential, but is likely a function of parental influence and parental expectations. Parents may be less likely to react as punitively to poor school performance in their later-born children, thus allowing those children the opportunity to choose their own career paths more freely than firstborns. There is also research pointing to the firstborn as the sibling most likely to succeed financially in life.[9] This is likely a result of the additional education or perhaps stronger negotiating skills learned through sibling interactions.

Beyond using birth order to identify the family genius or the family tycoon, there are other physiological fortunes that might be related to birth order, such as physical traits like height, weight, and health. Empirical research does give credence to inherent differences between siblings for a few of these factors.

Birth Order and Physical Characteristics

Height

The oldest child in a family—regardless of gender—will typically enjoy being the tallest and the strongest for at least a few years due to the way physical maturation unfolds. However, this physical dominance may actually be consistent across firstborns as a group. Researchers found that a child's birth order actually affects childhood height.[10] Firstborns tend to be the tallest sibling among the group. In families of three siblings, middle children are taller than third children. While gender plays a significant role in adult height, looking up to your older same-gender siblings might be a fact of life due to birth order, not necessarily personal achievements.

Weight

If firstborns are taller, it might seem logical that they are heavier, too. Contrary to what many later-born siblings might prefer, however, firstborns actually weigh less than their younger siblings in childhood.[11] As adults, many people long to be taller and slimmer than they are due to the cultural influence on views of attractiveness. In fact, one study showed that adults who were taller and thinner than average, both of which positively influence attractiveness, married individuals who had higher than average incomes as well as higher levels of education.[12] At first glance, firstborns may seem to hold an advantage in the long-term relationship market due to inherent genetic factors, but there are also some downsides to being the oldest. While firstborns weigh less in infancy and childhood, by the time they reach adulthood, their likelihood of being obese is higher than that of their siblings. For reasons that have not yet been identified, obesity is more common among oldest children, regardless of gender.

Health

Birth order appears to play a role in a person's metabolism.[13] Firstborns are more likely to develop some serious illnesses in later life than their younger siblings. In fact, two very significant health issues that they are more likely to face are metabolic diseases, including Type 2 diabetes and cardiovascular disease.[14] Firstborns also have higher daytime blood pressure levels. These findings may seem a bit surprising since these individuals start out longer and leaner in life. Beyond being a little surprising, these findings are concerning, as well. With smaller families and more firstborns overall, there is growing concern that these diseases will become widespread health crises.

Beyond the potential threats to metabolic health, there are also some positive health aspects to being the oldest. A recent large-scale study of the effect of birth order on health and well-being turned up some interesting findings, no matter where a person falls in the family.[15] Firstborns were found to be less likely to smoke than their siblings. Not only are kid brothers or kid sisters smoking more, they are also reporting lower levels of both physical and mental well-being than firstborn sibs. When it comes to being happy in life, older siblings are more likely to have an advantage there, as well. In a study that utilized a large-scale Swedish data set,[16] it was found that the risk for early mortality in adulthood was greater for later-born siblings, with the relationship being stronger for women than men.

It cannot be denied that there are many known and unknown factors that contribute to a person's health over a lifetime. Birth order, as a factor, reflects a slew of other bits and pieces of confounding variables and circumstances. Family size, maternal age, economic status, family dynamics, and family expectations all play some role in determining maturational paths. However, the desire to find connections between birth order and personality type invites speculation and additional research studies that are designed to prove or disprove these relationships.

Birth Order and Personality

A great deal has been written about the role of birth order in personality development, as noted earlier in this chapter. Researchers have attempted to find a predictive link between birth order and career choices, marriage partners, temperaments, negotiation styles, and so on. Adler's original work[17] on birth order and personality development became the basis for much of the research being completed today. Adler believed that we are born into our families wrestling with a sense of inferiority due to the helplessness that all infants experience in terms of self-sufficiency and independence. We are driven to master the world and to gain competence in the tasks necessary to provide a sense of superiority in life, which Adler believed was all for the greater good. As children strive to develop as individuals, they are also working within a complex family system. It is this system that creates the stage and circumscribes the roles that family members must navigate amid the larger cast of family members. Adler described five unique birth order categories that heavily influence the way family engagement, or roles, takes shape. These are the firstborn, the second-born, the middle child, the youngest child, and the only child. Following are brief overviews of the hallmark traits that are stereotypically assigned to each position.

Firstborn Children

The firstborn child is often the only child in a family to have a complete record of his childhood; the baby book usually has several entries already completed regarding preparations and celebrations prior to the child's actual arrival in the family. The firstborn enjoys the full attention of parents and basks in their encouragement until a subsequent child arrives on the scene to dethrone the "reigning monarch," as Adler described a family's firstborn.

According to Adlerian theory, the firstborn is the child most likely to understand the value of personal power and how best to wield it.[18] Often this dynamic is unwittingly encouraged when parents place the oldest child in the role of caretaker of younger siblings. Directing the oldest child to look after the little ones can force the oldest to take on a quasi-parental and managerial role that he might not be temperamentally inclined to assume. Some oldest children relish being known as the responsible one, but others would prefer to be free to be followers rather than leaders. Adler suggested that with maturity, the oldest are likely to become more conservative, nostalgic for the past, and highly organized while hewing to the status quo. Firstborns are expected to be responsible, and this expectation can be worn as a badge of their superior maturity within the family constellation.

Second-born Children

There was an advertising campaign that was in use for over fifty years for a car rental service. The company used a now-iconic slogan: "We're number two so we have to try harder." That slogan pretty much sums up the life of a second-born child. No matter how quickly the second child learns to walk or talk, there's another child in the house who's already "been there, done that." Second-born children may feel like they are spinning their wheels behind the pace car, and the first two siblings in a family are likely to manifest a genuine case of sibling rivalry.

Never having been a soloist on the family stage, the second child doesn't resent the sharing of parental attention the way the usurped first child might. Second-born siblings are also assumed to be even-tempered, easygoing, and willing to achieve in areas different from those a firstborn has already claimed as his own. Some second-born children, however, may continue to present an inadvertent threat to their older siblings, and the relationship may be a little rocky until late into adulthood.

Middle Children

Children who end up in the middle of the family may have once known the world as a second-born and the youngest; they may resent having lost their special place as they become squished between siblings. The stereotypical middle child feels left out and forgotten amid his multiple siblings. Some middle children use this circumstance to create a unique identity that differs markedly from what the other siblings have developed. Middle children may also be easier going than their siblings as they display a laissez-faire attitude toward life. Some resent the injustice that they feel "middlehood" represents for them, and some use this persistent grudge to spur them on to protest other forms of injustice or become the whistleblower when needed. Some middle children become peacemakers as they learn to act as diplomats between the two sides of the sibling age spectrum.

Youngest Children

The child that lands in this spot often appears to be the anointed one. Adler described this sibling as potentially being treated like the family pet. Younger brothers may become the family prince and younger sisters the family princess. These positions can be strongly solidified when the youngest child is also the only child of a particular gender. If a second-born received a great deal of spoiling by his parents, a firstborn may harbor a great deal of resentment toward his sibling; however, when it comes to the "baby" of the family, when there is at least one child between them, even the oldest child is often drawn to spoiling and petting the baby. Children also recognize that aligning with their parents in recognition of the youngest as "the baby" elevates them to a higher status. If Adler's supposition that feelings of inferiority drive individual development, then any desire of the baby to excel over her siblings makes sense. Another expectation of the youngest is for him to be free-spirited and willing to challenge the rules. A recent study exploring the identities of the players in the U.S. Supreme Court who supported the application of the Bill of Rights to the states revealed that this shake-up of the status quo was not led by firstborns, but by those in subsequent birth order positions.[19]

The Only Child

Only the oldest child in a family will ever fully understand the world of the only child, another position that is assumed to be a favored one due to the undivided attention from parents. Adler suggested that only children may be less competitive than those with siblings, but it was also remarked that this speaks more to the absence of the need to compete due to their unchallenged sovereignty in a family.[20] Sharing with others may be a challenge in relationships for the only child due to lack of practice, not necessarily lack of willingness. Only children are also likely to behave in a more adult manner due to lack of experience interacting with siblings.

Does Birth Order Predict Your Future?

Even Adler believed that many more factors were involved in the development of individual identity and life trajectory than birth order alone. Other researchers have explored birth order as a way to develop a specific family niche that will provide access to specific parental resources.[21] There are lists of firstborns who became president, firstborns who became senators, and firstborns who became astronauts. These lists have met their match via lists that detail all of the youngest children who became writers, artists, and comedians. If there is a way to bolster a claim to ownership of a particular predilection for a career or a skill set, substantial evidence can be turned up just by typing into the Google search bar or asking Cortana, Alexis, or Siri. While birth order cannot lock in your future career, it may lock in some of the dynamics of your adult sibling relationships.

When invited to reflect on the role that birth order played in their sibling relationships, some individuals were quick to note that it was gender, not birth order, that had the greatest effect on their roles within the family. Whether or not it is surprising, it was typically women who voiced their belief that gender had a larger influence on their siblingships.

The Youngest

Youngest males noted that they felt their older siblings continued to receive greater respect than they did from their families. One youngest boy, in his early sixties, admitted that he felt birth order played a significant role in his family and concluded, "*I think that my opinions as the youngest were never really honored.*"

One woman, the youngest of several siblings with her only brother being the oldest of the group, expressed regret at believing that she and her sisters felt they were not supposed to beat their brother to any developmental milestones. She shared, "*[The oldest always] have to do things earlier and be a role model in some way.*" When she moved out and got a job before her brother, she "*always felt bad for it, like I had to hold back so he wouldn't feel bad.*" Another woman shared that the cultural expectations of the older son, her brother, created challenges for her when "*his failure to meet [parental] expectation caused them to focus on me, and I'm rarely told I 'act like' a youngest.*"

Some youngest children were also quick to express frustration about being last in the family hierarchy even into adulthood. Comments such as "*My sister, the oldest, takes over telling the two of us what to do as if she is the parent*" and "*My older sister expected me to follow her way of doing stuff because she was older to the point of thinking that she was my second mother*" suggest that some patterns are difficult to undo. One woman recalled the childhood nickname given to her by her older siblings—"Tap"; she said that name was chosen "*because they could make me cry so easily, just like a tap turns on the water.*" Another youngest sister, Teri, said that when she was a young teen, her older sister revealed that she had been excited at the prospect of a younger sister until she found out that watching the baby would increasingly become her responsibility. The older sister still blames Teri for having missed out on social events in adolescence. Teri admitted being dumbfounded by her older sister's revelation that she was so resentful, even decades later, that she had shared this concern with a psychologist during a counseling session.

Younger siblings don't intentionally want to create more work for their older brothers and sisters, but they certainly want the status the oldest holds. Georgie, a twenty-eight-year-old big sister, recounted a story about her youngest sibling, Thomas, which occurred when she was eight and her brother was three. Their grandmother was visiting and asked the children what they wanted to be when they grew up. The classic baby-of-the-family's response was quick to bubble up from Thomas as he shouted, *"The OLDEST!"* Younger siblings see the privileges and the skills that maturity brings, even in childhood, and it's only human nature to long for what one doesn't yet possess. While the youngest sibs are clamoring to grow up, some middle siblings may feel that they are out of sight and out of mind due to their middle lane position.

The Middle

The famous columnist Ann Landers has a column titled "Middle Children," in which she highlights their strengths and acknowledges their difficulties in life. The middle children in this world are often painted as a group that is almost misplaced in a family somehow. One middle child, now in her twenties, lamented that she *"did feel squeezed and, at times, sometimes left out."* She countered these feelings by focusing on the things she enjoyed rather than trying to compete with her siblings. This provided her with a highly individual path to follow, and she felt it made up for her occasional feelings of not fitting in.

Another female middle child, around thirty, responded enthusiastically to a question as to what type of role birth order played in her early sibling experiences: *"Huge! I am a counselor and I can tell you I am textbook middle child in terms of birth order. I am the peacemaker. I hate conflict. I am flexible to accommodate the high maintenance needs of my siblings. My brother is treated like the baby and is super spoiled and my sister is incredibly driven, outspoken, and in charge."*

Another happy-go-lucky middle child in her thirties shared that she resented being tacitly expected to step into the traditional role of the oldest in her own family due to her older brother's inability to take on any familial responsibility. She preferred lying low, as she had for most of her life, rather than stepping up and taking on the firstborn's responsibility within the family-of-origin. A middle-aged man felt that the middle child position had indelibly, and unfavorably, influenced his childhood and adolescence. When asked about any effects that he felt birth order had caused in his family, he responded, *"Parental favoritism. My parents never hid the fact that my older brother was of greater value as the firstborn and as the male namesake. My younger sister was clearly their precious baby and I was their scapegoat."*

As humans, we love to categorize people and things due to the sense of control and understanding that labels provide. Understanding the nature of things and the ways that relationships work are goals for many of us. Just like organizational charts help employees know who is in charge, using birth order to conceptualize a family system is equally helpful for many. When it comes to the top of the family hierarchy chart, the oldest sibling often ranks just below the parents.

The Oldest

In terms of the roles people ascribe based on birth order, it seemed that many firstborns were being classified and described by their siblings as to how well they did or did not accept the responsibilities that younger siblings expected them to carry. One older brother was applauded by his middle child sister for willingly taking on the emotional burden of being the oldest more often, now that they were in their thirties, especially when it came to making decisions related to care for their aging parents. Another middle child was sorely disappointed when she was forced to step into the role of the oldest in place of her sister due to her sister's health problems. *"When I realized that shift in responsibility, even as an adult, I felt resentment and anger."*

Nathan, a middle born now in his thirties, has one older brother and one younger sister. He related, *"I believe that birth order played a significant role in our lives growing up. There is also an inherent level of respect that my brother receives from my sister and I. [Even as adults], we often acquiesce to him and show him respect."* The willingness to offer respect that is earned isn't especially surprising, but some firstborn brothers were not hesitant to state that solely their status as males and eldest children warranted deferential treatment. James confessed that in his family, he was favored; however, this privilege brought expectations that he would take responsibility for his younger siblings, as well. Another oldest son shared that he believed the oldest should be respected as the decision-maker among siblings, but that he also was accountable for guiding his younger siblings as they matured. Another young man shared, *"I have always been quieter than my brothers as I have always felt responsible for their safety and well-being as the oldest. I tend to observe and react more than jump right in and speak, which I think translates to how I am now."* In describing how they were viewed by their parents growing up, the birth order differences were evident: *"I would be the intellectual, responsible one. [T]he middle would be the fun, energetic one. [T]he youngest would be the cool, musical one."*

Oldest sisters may also be highly aware of the power differential between themselves and their younger siblings. As one woman recalled, *"I was definitely the dominant one in the relationship as the eldest. Even growing up, I determined when we got along or when we conflicted. I decided when we would play together and so on."* An oldest brother revealed an even darker side to the position of oldest as he noted, *"My parents were not married when they found out my mom was pregnant, so I believe my father takes it out on me that he had to marry my mother. My sister is the golden child."* When the oldest child is also perceived as the reason for an unplanned and unwelcome marriage, the lingering resentment from parents can create a permanent rift between parents and child. Unfortunately, this resentment can bleed over into the next generation so that any subsequent children develop disconnects with their older sibling.

Being the leader comes easily for many eldest children, and although there is entitlement to take a leadership role in relationships, this can play out in an unexpectedly disappointing way for some siblings. As one young woman complained, *"With my sister being the youngest of us two, she feels more entitlement to* her needs *being met, and she makes me feel like I need to take care of those needs, because I'm the oldest."* Another woman, in her sixties, still recalls the unfair treatment that her mother meted out to her, merely because, as she described, *"My mother thought the oldest child had an unfair advantage and always did her best to see that I received less than my brother and sisters."*

Being the oldest proved to be an emotionally distressing barrier between Svetlana, around fifty, and her younger sisters. When one member of a family is intentionally isolated from the others or when communication patterns are altered to exclude a family member, this refers to the concept of an emotional cut-off[22] within Murray Bowen's family systems theory. While Bowen considered a cut-off the result of conscious decisions by family members, he also noted that individuals who no longer see themselves as part of the system will either try to change the others or simply withdraw from the system. Svetlana shared her experiences growing up in her home in the Netherlands: *"My two younger sisters bonded early on and are friends today. I'm happy for them. I felt cut off as I had huge pressure as the eldest, as a teenager, when our mother was widowed, to be the serious one, to never be irresponsible. But we each learnt from each other in life, over time. No, today I think we can laugh now at some misunderstandings and be together without judging and rating each other as badly as we were taught to growing up."*

Svetlana hopes that she and her two siblings will be able to live out the rest of their lives as friends and equals, although she acknowledged, *"We honestly waste too much time watching each other to see who does the most to please our mother. My middle sister takes on too much. My younger sister keeps busy when she is upset. Confidences come in outbursts, rather than a confident sharing of knowledge. I hope we all mature without hurting each other."*

"Being oldest," shared another woman, *"put me in a caretaking position early on . . . Cooking dinners for the whole family from when I was thirteen made me learn how to take care of them all. As an adult, I have provided living space in my home to many of my siblings more than once."* The caretaker role is often naturally assumed to be a woman's job, and for many older sisters, the ability to provide assistance to their siblings is a way to show they care while providing evidence of the strength and resources that the eldest is expected to possess.

DOES GENDER MATTER?

The role of gender in family relationships was mentioned multiple times by individuals explaining the dynamics between siblings in their families. In some family cultures, parents expect their sons to take care of their sisters, regardless of age. One woman rejoiced that *"being the eldest and living in a society where elders are given great respect, I feel like a queen amongst [my siblings]."* Another woman shared that she has stepped up as the matriarch in her family and that this is how her siblings perceive and treat her. A young man noted that birth order played a role in sibling relationships, *"but maybe also gender. My sister looks up to me as a leader."* In his family, it is a gendered expectation that men lead and women follow. An eldest daughter noted that in her Latino family, gender was as influential as birth order in family roles. Whether gender is viewed by traditional U.S. society as a binary construct or a fluid category, many families still strongly adhere to cultural gendered expectations of the roles of their sons and daughters in the family system.

CONCLUSION

Stereotypical traits ascribed to birth order are well known across cultures, and if siblings engage with one another in stereotypically expected ways, birth order labels might implicitly invite less-than-ideal behavior. Middle siblings complain about bossy older siblings and helpless younger siblings. Babies of the family gleefully demand extra attention from parents and readily admit to tormenting older sibs knowing that they can "get away with it" due to their place in the sibling hierarchy. Older siblings often enjoy being at the top of the sibling cluster, but also regret some of the inherent responsibilities embedded in the rank. In the next chapter, we will explore the ways in which other family cultural influences affect sibling relationships.

FINAL TAKEAWAY: Birth order may shape you and your sibs' behavior as a function of the family environment, but stereotypes are not mandates—especially once you and your siblings reach adulthood.

Chapter Two

Cultural Influences on Sibling Relationships

[My only brother is] a firstborn son, which caused my parents to treat him much differently growing up [because of] our Asian culture. At the same time, his "failure" to meet their expectations caused them to focus on me, and I'm rarely told I "act like" a youngest.

—Leah, an Asian woman in her late twenties

Gender roles also intersect birth order. From a traditional Latino family, we all felt specific obligations to care for our family as a whole.

—Melanie, a Latina around forty

CULTURAL VARIATIONS ON SIBLING RELATIONSHIPS

Who are the people you count as your siblings? Depending on your family culture, the categories of individuals you claim as your siblings may vary greatly from the list that someone from another culture might create. Here in the United States, most European American families consider only the biological or adopted children of the parents to be siblings. These children might be full siblings, sharing both biological parents; half-siblings, sharing only one biological parent; stepsiblings, sharing neither biological parent; and adopted siblings, who typically are not the biological child of either parent, although extramarital relationships or artificial insemination might result in a parent "adopting" a biological child, depending on the circumstances.

In a review of sibling relationships around the globe, Cicirelli[1] provided a look at the multiple configurations that sibling connections can take depending on the culture and the community. He noted that in some locations, the individuals we call cousins, the offspring of our parents' brothers and sisters, are considered siblings. Another culture only extends the label of sibling to the cousins born to a parent's cross-sex siblings. In another Oceanic culture, it is gender that determines siblings: Your same-sex cousins, the same-sex siblings of either of your parents, and your same-sex grandparent are all considered siblings. In Kenya, there is a culture in which all of the age mates in a village are considered siblings. Not only does it take a village to raise a child there, but the children actually comprise a good part of the village!

In contemporary U.S. society, the average number of children under eighteen in a household is slightly under 2.0, down from the once frequently quoted "2.3 kids per family" from the mid-1960s.[2] Growing up in the 1970s, I envied the neighborhood families with station wagons filled with tons of kids. I was one of two sibs, and I felt our family never had as many adventures or as much fun as my friends with two or more sibs. My parents were clearly ahead of the times when they decided two kids were enough. Since 2010, the birthrate has slowed down, and the prevalence of couples having only one or no offspring has increased. Demographics of our country have shifted so significantly that more babies born today are non-white than white. In fact, when looking at household size, the children most likely to have siblings in a family are, in descending order, Hispanic, African American, Asian, and, finally, Caucasian.[3] This growing shift in population composition invites a closer look at the ways in which family and sibling expectations may differ across cultures.

BIG ONES HELP THE LITTLE ONES

In many nonindustrialized nations, older children are raised to care for their younger siblings. In one Melanesian society, children begin taking some level of caretaking role around age three—an unbelievably young age to Westerners![4] In countries where there is little time for the leisure that more industrialized countries work to manufacture, sibling responsibilities to the family are much greater than are common in the United States. Many of us might scratch our head and wonder how a young child can be much help caring for even younger siblings, but there are several sibling education practices that are used around the globe. Methods described in the literature[5] include modeling, giving feedback for siblings' efforts, repeating directions, and paraphrasing what they are communicating. Younger caregivers know to question the younger siblings they are trying to train, to repeat directions, and to explain themselves. Not surprisingly, our modern culture has been criticized for missing out on the potential socialization and informal education that older children can provide to younger siblings.[6] Many contemporary parents may be more concerned with equal treatment than with leveraging the skills and desire to take on responsibilities that normally developing children demonstrate. While many oldest U.S. children, especially daughters, might claim that they were tasked with looking after their siblings, it is unlikely they were given the same weight of responsibility that firstborns are given in other countries.

PREDICTABLE TRENDS IN FAMILY SIZE?

Ethnicity

Families that immigrate to the United States bring with them customs and cultural expectations from their countries of origin. Upon arrival, some immigrants are committed to creating a family structure in which cherished traditions are honored and maintained. Others might be eager to embrace the "American way" and let go of ties to the past that they see as barriers to progress and success here. Regardless of their mind-sets, family size and birthrates still differ from the shrinking majority of Caucasian residents. Siblingship size is predicted by family ethnic identity, to some extent. Looking at the number of women forty to forty-four years of age who had three or more children, the following statistics were found: 34 percent of white women, 28 percent of Asian women, 40 percent of Black women, and 51 percent of Hispanic women had three or more children.[7]

Geography

Large families were once necessary to ensure survival and are still prevalent in most nonindustrialized societies.[8] Children are appreciated as sources of inexpensive labor who actively contribute to a family's economic success. Whether it is another body to help with the "hunting and gathering" or "sowing and reaping," children are productive resources, not simply resource consumers. With the high infant mortality rates that once prevailed,[9] large families also provided a form of "survival insurance" against insufficient family labor. In contemporary industrialized economy, there are few economic benefits in having large families. In a Pew Research Center report on "ideal family size," the number has dropped from 3.6 kids in 1936 to two kids today.[10]

Religion

Even before we were able to understand the deeper meaning of the arrival of multiple siblings in a family, kids in my 1970s childhood neighborhood were making jokes about the large Catholic families on our street. The kids didn't understand the deeper connection between religious beliefs and birthrates, but they recognized the tendency for the three-child norm in the neighborhood to be bested by the four- and five-child Catholic families that lived there, too. Another religion, Mormonism, also figured prominently in determining family size for young females during that time. The country idolized the handsome and entertaining Osmonds, especially Donny, and their Mormon faith became one of the valuable pieces of information that *Tiger Beat* magazine provided about the hunky family. Current research indicates that the Catholic faith, along with most other Protestant faiths, is shrinking in size and losing members; however, the Mormon faith bucks that trend.[11] It may be of note that fewer individuals raised in the Catholic Church continue to identify with that denomination than do Mormons who were raised in that faith. As far as fertility stands today, Mormons have 3.4 children, Black Protestants have 2.5, Evangelical Protestants have 2.3, Catholics have 2.3, and Jews round out the top 5 with 2.0 children. Mainline Protestants don't break the 2.0 barrier, with a statistical 1.9 average children in the household.[12]

Education

What is your first thought about the relationship between education and family size? Many people assume that well-educated women might show shrinking interest in parenthood and thus experience diminished fertility. The prevalence of reliable forms of birth control and menstrual control,[13] along with later ages for marriage and first childbirth, do suggest a steadily declining interest in motherhood. This may have been true back in the 1990s when glass ceilings were being shattered and there was still a great momentum to focus on career over family. But since then, there's been a dramatic shift in the link between higher education and family size. Compared to a decade or so ago, highly educated women are definitely having larger families than before.[14] Data also indicates that the less education a mother has, the greater the number of children she has. Thus, there appears to be a U-shaped curve to family size and education.[15] There have been discussions about the dumbing down of America that may be due to a host of factors, from shortened attention spans to the "Googlization" of complex knowledge. One fervent expert, Jonathan Last, wrote a book about his cataclysmic predictions regarding, in part, the inverse relationship between education and fertility; it was titled *What to Expect When No One's Expecting: America's Coming Demographic Disaster.*[16] However, the current census data suggests that fewer educated women are childless than in decades past.

SIBLINGS IN FAMILY-OF-ORIGIN

Research shows that a mother's current parenting practices are associated with her childhood sibling experiences in a couple of positive ways.[17] First, women who experienced conflicts with their own siblings are able to promote more peaceful relationships between their own children. Whether they redirect children during tension-building interactions or develop an enduring climate of peaceable relations, moms are able to positively influence the relationships between their own children. Another "wrong" that moms are also successful in "righting" in their own nuclear families has to do with favoritism. Moms who reported having been raised in families in which children were unequally treated or unfairly favored by a parent are effective in ensuring that their children are treated equally and fairly in measurable ways. Although past patterns of failed relationships and poor parenting practices are often assumed to be repeated in subsequent generations, it is clear that destructive patterns can be broken and new models of family engagement enacted.

Is there any predictive power in the size of a family-of-origin in terms of the number of children an adult produces? Most of us have heard someone state an opinion about this relationship from their own personal perspective. I have two only child friends who both intentionally chose to limit their own families to a single child. On the other hand, I had always wished that I had more than one sibling, so I vowed to have at least three children. Another friend, Anne, who was one of five children in her family-of-origin, regretted the decision her parents had made to space their children's births so close together. Anne shared that she intended to have "*no more than two kids who will be at least five years apart in age.*" When asked about the specific five-year gap, she explained, "*Research shows that children born five or more years apart are considered developmentally 'only' children. That lets me be a better mom.*" In some cases, family size appears to be a lot like hair color or body shape; we want what we don't have. In other cases, we may want to try and re-create what we felt was the perfect family size for ourselves.

While we have just reviewed a good amount of data that clearly indicates family size is related to a host of demographic factors, only one recent study has explored family size in subsequent generations at a significant depth. Robert Francis Lynch carefully reviewed the very well-kept and comprehensive census data for an entire country, Iceland, which spanned two centuries.[18] It turns out that the more siblings an individual has in her family, the fewer children she is likely to have as an adult. Lynch crunched the numbers and developed a mathematical formula that suggested that each additional sibling had a direct negative effect on the length of an individual's lifespan and family size. This is traced back to the fact that parental access to resources are limited and the more children they must care for, the smaller the portion of resources each individual receives. Maybe the idea of the value of raising "developmentally only children" has some merit, in terms of resources that parents can offer their kids.

ARE ONLY CHILDREN REALLY *THAT* DIFFERENT?

Although having siblings is related to a smaller share of parental resources (time, attention, economic, and so on), there are a variety of benefits that accrue to kids who have siblings in their lives. It makes sense that some skills grow stronger for children when they are sharing their living space with another child, but competition may have a negative influence on social behavior, as well. Learning to negotiate shared living space and parental attention can be difficult processes for children, but the benefits of developing effective skills of persuasion and debate can serve a child very well throughout his life.[19] Following are some findings regarding the differences between only children and those with sibs in the home.

Sociability

There have been many conflicting studies reporting the benefits of being a sibling versus being an only child in terms of social skills development. Some researchers claim that only children engage predominantly with adults and this enhances language acquisition and communication skills. Other research suggests that having full-time playmates can significantly increase the social skills of siblings. Large-scale data sets have provided evidence that kindergarteners with siblings display stronger social skills than their only-children peers.[20] A follow-up study that explored the social skill development of eleven thousand children between kindergarten and fifth grade indicated that the only children did not show the same level of skill development as expected based on their school attendance and engagement with peers. The authors expressed concern for the development of effective social skills due to the growing number of one-child families.

One of the most dreaded conversations in families of multiple siblings occurs when loading up the car for an outing. If you have more kids than window seats, the protestations about being stuck in the middle can be surprisingly intense. A British automobile manufacturer conducted a market research study to explore the role of car seat position and adult personality and career outcomes.[21] According to the survey of 1,000 adults with more than one sibling, almost all, fully 90 percent, of the individuals who held director-level positions had occupied the middle seat position as a child. Even more intriguing is the finding that 80 percent of the adults who had been relegated to the middle seat believed that this position had contributed to their work-life success. Whether the seating position gave them more time to engage with the adult(s) in the front seat or just the opportunity to practice their skills of mediation and diplomacy by taking the position that their siblings found objectionable, the skill set they developed or enhanced through the experience included such traits as being easygoing, reasonable, patient, level-headed, and adaptable. Many of these mirror the adjectives that frequently are used to describe the upside of the middle child birth order position.

Creativity

Some parents would argue that only children have to learn how to make their own fun and be more creative than children in other families who have multiple siblings to play with. Other mothers might believe that having children at different stages of development can spur creativity as their children learn how to communicate and participate in mutually engaging shared activities. From results of a recent study, it appears that only children may have an edge on the creative side as compared to children with siblings. Scientists utilized both behavioral and anatomical measures to explore the levels of creativity and agreeableness among kids.[22] Their findings confirmed that children from multi-sibling families had higher levels of agreeableness while singletons had higher levels of flexibility, a measure of creativity. Brain scans verified that brain development was structurally different based on family composition. Our early environment actively shapes our brains from the get-go, underscoring its early malleability and resilience.

Loneliness

Most people who have positive sibling relationships may imagine that only children might be lonely with no one in the home to entertain them. Fortunately, research does not support this stereotype to any significant degree. In interviewing a few adult onlies for this book, the feelings about loneliness were pretty much split fifty/fifty. When asked about the positive and negative aspects of having been an only child, one woman in her sixties shared, *"Nothing positive or negative. I didn't even think about it . . . for me, it was normal."* Another woman shared that she did feel different from other children who had siblings: *"As an only child I was always giving to others. I enjoyed family gatherings. Friendships were a lot of work because I couldn't understand their behaviors. I felt totally alone at home and longed to always have the house busy on the weekends."*

Although inherent shyness or a family's tendency to keep to themselves may be more influential on how engaged with others an only child actually might be, an interesting research finding regarding only children and weight has emerged.[23] Whether it is more the lack of a playmate rather than outright loneliness, there may be reason to encourage more peer interaction for even very young only children. It has been revealed that there is almost three times the risk for obesity by first grade for children who do not have a younger sibling born before they enter school.

Unfortunately, there are also later life ramifications that might heighten or awaken a feeling of loneliness for adult onlies. In studies of this demographic group, the presence of siblings is viewed as an asset when it is time to care for aging parents.[24] Solo caregiving and decision-making is a lonely business.

Although the number of people who believe that bigger is better when it comes to family size has been on a downward slide since the 1930s, only 3 percent believe that the perfect family size is one child.[25] Only 2 percent believe that no children are ideal. Although the national economy is one of the most often cited reasons for preferring smaller families, babies are still being born, and the presence of siblings is a fact of life for the majority of kids and adults. So, whether you choose to be one of the 3 percent of families who choose one or the ninety-some percent who choose two or more to fill your home, remember that it is effective parenting and strong family networks that are most important in raising healthy and well-adjusted kids.

CULTURALLY SPECIFIC RESEARCH ON SIBLING RELATIONSHIPS

There have been many studies exploring sibling relationships across cultures. Some studies are comparative in nature, and others focus only on a single aspect of cultural identity. While sibling squabbles are universal, researchers have isolated some notable cultural differences regarding sibling interactions.

African American Siblings

Much of the foundational knowledge that offers support to the assumption that cultural differences between sibling groups exist reflects earlier research that provided evidence of the strong communal and socially connected culture present in African American family systems.[26] This structure provides children the opportunity to take on familial responsibilities at an early age and to gain an integral understanding of the value of each family member's role in the functioning of the household. This allowance for flexible family roles[27] can build the "sibling esteem" or "daughter/son esteem" of offspring. Feeling good about the role played in the family can provide a sense of meaning and purpose that provides protection against emotional or social assaults beyond the home.

In addition to the level of responsibility that siblings are given early in life, they also benefit from the transference of a strong sense of family loyalty and honor. This strong family-centric perspective is similar to the familism found within the Latina culture, but also reflects the indigenous African beliefs regarding respect, responsibility, and reciprocity.[28] These experiences give rise to a unique perspective and approach to task completion. For instance, elementary-aged siblings in African American families are more likely to collaborate on problem-solving tasks than European American siblings.[29] African American siblings look to one another to help figure out solutions rather than assigning task-specific responsibilities. In short, sibling relationships in African American families tend to reflect a strong sense of loyalty and responsibility to the family and its greater good.

Asian American Siblings

While there is an expanding body of research regarding sibling relationships over the lifespan,[30] overall there still seems to be a paucity of research addressing the relationships between Asian American siblings. This may seem surprising given the level of filial piety (which involves caring for parents and respecting their wisdom) and collectivism associated with Asian cultures.[31] For over 150 million residents of China, however, three decades of the One Child Policy left these citizens bereft of siblings and large extended family networks. Although the rule has been relaxed to a Two Child Policy, significant emotional damage has already been inflicted.[32]

Four Asian American ethnic groups that are often studied are the Chinese American, Filipino American, Korean American, and Japanese American. In terms of values and relationships, there are definitely a number of similarities, although Filipino Americans have been noted to share additional similarities with individuals of Hispanic origin.[33] Also of note regarding Filipino American family relationships is that this ethnic group actually may place a higher value on family and connectedness than other groups;[34] this suggests a stronger sense of familism, a benchmark trait within the Latina culture that is further explored in the section on Latina/Latino siblings.

In a study of Korean and Vietnamese siblings in immigrant families, it was found that the older siblings were more likely to be loyal to cultural values and mores than their younger siblings.[35] It was proposed that the higher family ranking of firstborn siblings placed them in a position that supported hewing to the traditional values, whereas younger siblings found little benefit in remaining true to their cultural heritage. Sibling relationships consequently suffer from the acculturation clash, and younger siblings are often considered "black sheep" for rejecting traditional values and behaviors. The shrinking degree of value differences between later born Asian American siblings and the typical European American child may also be attributed to the greater educational opportunities and potential occupational mobility that are available in the United States.[36]

European American Siblings

As with most areas of psychological and sociological research, the vast majority of participants in sibling studies have been European Americans. Thus, the majority of what we know to be "true" about sibling dynamics and relationships is based on the majority culture. European American children reflect the values of the greater Western civilization in which they live, and sibling relationships and interactions are no different. For the most part, sibling engagement noted by researchers among this group reflects the individualism and independence that are prized by contemporary U.S. culture. Competitiveness is often found among siblings in situations where scarce resources (tangible or intangible) are present or when parents encourage competition or favor one child over another. Not only are they less collaborative, preferring to work on shared tasks through division of labor rather than collaborative efforts,[37] they also spend less time with one another than siblings from other ethnic groups.[38] And, unlike other groups, adolescent European American siblings do not tend to feel guilt regarding conflict that they generate within their families.[39]

Latina/Latino Siblings

Reflecting on Latina family systems, the concept of *familism* often springs to mind as a defining characteristic. Familism is all about the importance of putting the family's best interests above one member's interests. This facilitates close and supportive family bonds.[40] This value has been suggested as an influencing factor in a slew of different sibling outcomes and relational variables. Conflict resolution among siblings is one area that has been explored. According to one study, however, siblings were no more likely to use collaboration in conflict resolution than controlling behaviors by older siblings or nonconfrontational strategies by younger siblings.[41] However, it is worth acknowledging that family patterns do exist for young adult Mexican American siblings and romance.[42] If an older sibling is involved in dating relationships, cohabitation, engagement, or marriage, the younger sib was likely to follow in the older sib's footsteps within the next two years. The role of an older sibling as a model cannot be overestimated—in both pro-social and adverse behaviors.

Sibling communication is another area of focus for researchers interested in the role that familism plays in sibling interactions. Young adult Mexican American siblings who reported sibling relationships characterized by negativity reported more frequent interactions with these siblings if they also reported higher levels of orientation to their Mexican cultural identity.[43] The stronger the orientation to Anglo culture, the more likely the negative relationship qualities would overshadow the desire to maintain contact. As expected, too, this study gave evidence that sisters are much more consistent and frequent communicators than their brothers are. For the college-aged participants in this particular study, texting and face-to-face conversations were more frequent than phone calls or e-mails. This makes sense given this age group's definite preference for texting.[44]

IS IT THE "SAME DIFFERENCE" AFTER ALL?

When it comes to cultural influence on sibling relationships, it appears that the U.S. cultural norms that emphasize individuality and achievement are growing more common among immigrant populations. Individual family dynamics and parenting practices will always hold the greatest influence in shaping sibling relationships, of course, but as increasing geographical mobility occurs and children grow more assimilated into U.S. culture, it is likely that ethnic differences in sibling relationships will become less striking over time.

CONCLUSION

Although the likelihood of having multiple sibling relationships to navigate is smaller for children being born in the twenty-first century, the need to successfully maintain the sibling relationships they do have will grow in importance. The metaphorical pendulum has finally reached that place in its arc in which children ages five and younger are about to be outnumbered by adults ages sixty-five and older.[45] Sharing the caring for aging parents as well as providing social support are two important ways in which siblings can positively influence the well-being of one another over time. Learning to optimize your sibling relationships in adulthood is a worthwhile investment of energy. In fact, the role your siblings play in your life in adulthood may far outweigh—and carry greater significance than—the role they played in your childhood and adolescence.

FINAL TAKEAWAY: Cultures are built on tradition, but if the traditional expectations of your family's culture do not make sense for you and your siblings in adulthood, you are free to create a different culture for yourselves—for your own family, too.

Chapter Three

Sibling Loss in Childhood and Adolescence

Statistics surrounding childhood mortality indicate that more than forty thousand children die each year in the United States.[1] While over half of these deaths occur during the first year of a child's life, this fact does not necessarily lessen the impact of the loss over the lifespan for their families. Losing a child at any time in life can be insurmountably heartbreaking for parents and permanently alter the course of a parent's life. However, the loss of a sibling during childhood or youth can leave an indelible mark on surviving siblings, as well. Losing a sibling can be as emotionally disruptive as the loss of a parent might be; in fact, one study indicated that girls suffer more when a sister is lost than when a parent dies.[2] More generally, siblings are assumed to be a child's lifelong companion, or "forever friend," so it is only natural that the loss of a sister or brother is a traumatic event.

The immediate impact of a sibling's death may be difficult for a young child to articulate, but an increasing amount of empirical evidence indicates that the impact is not necessarily a temporary setback. Research suggests that adult psychiatric disorders can develop when grief over the loss of a sibling is not resolved effectively.[3] A group of researchers analyzed two large-scale longitudinal data sets to explore long-term outcomes for individuals who have lost siblings.[4] One fact that stood out in their report was the finding that 7 percent of young adults have experienced the death of a sibling in childhood. Another finding was that surviving siblings complete fewer years of schooling than those who have not experienced such a loss and this deficit in schooling can result in lower earnings overall.

A further finding is that sisters are more tangibly affected by the death of a sibling. When a sister loses a sibling to a chronic illness or if she loses an infant sibling, she is less likely to marry in adulthood. If she has lost a sibling unexpectedly, she is more likely to live with her parents through adulthood and to have less schooling than those who experienced other types of loss. The intangible emotional toll is poignantly expressed through the words shared by a thirty-five-year-old woman about the unexpected childhood loss of her own sister: *"We all continue to miss her; she's always missing from our lives and her loss is always felt, and because it was a sudden death, we are all aware of the fragility of life."*

THE EXPECTED ORDER OF THINGS

It is never expected that a child will die before his parents. Children are typically perceived as parents' link to the future and the means by which their influence will reach across generations. Loss of a child affects both parents and siblings. For parents who lose a child, depression and compromised well-being can turn from acute consequences into lifelong challenges.[5, 6] Unfortunately, surviving children are often left alone to work through their grief responses at an age when they are unprepared to effectively make sense of the size, shape, or meaning of the loss. It has been estimated that approximately 83 percent of children who die leave behind a surviving sibling.[7] Depending on the age of the surviving child, the loss can have significant developmental effects that endure over time.

USING ERIKSON'S PSYCHOSOCIAL DEVELOPMENTAL THEORY AS A FRAMEWORK

While there are multiple frameworks through which to view childhood development, the Eriksonian model of psychosocial development[8] is often the best choice for exploring the ways in which traumatic events influence adult development. According to Erikson, there are eight chronological stages that span life from birth through older adulthood. These stages reflect the progress of an individual's development of both personal identity and relationships with others. Each of the hypothesized stages harbors a unique *developmental crisis*, as Erikson termed these challenges.

The period in which a significant critical incident, such as significant loss or crisis, occurs can be predictive of how the event will be responded to by an individual and its influence over time. Following is a summary of the first five stages of Erikson's model, which cover development from birth through late adolescence, as well as a discussion of potential challenges that may be embedded within each developmental stage related to sibling loss.

Developmental Crisis: Trust versus Mistrust

Birth to Eighteen Months

Erikson postulated the first stage of psychosocial development as one in which infants learn whether or not it is safe to trust others to help them meet their basic needs. The initial relationship between an infant and his primary caregiver is first established and solidified in this stage. The development of a stable bond during this period is viewed as essential to the development of trust in others. The successful navigation of this developmental period provides a child with the ability to *feel hope*, which is the basic virtue associated with this stage, according to Erikson. This is a period in which the first efforts to connect to a social and relational world begin.

Typical Developmental Response to Death

As expected, infants do not have the cognitive complexity to understand that the death of a sibling is anything more than a separation, such as the type that gives rise to the experience of separation anxiety. The manifestations of this discomfort can include irritable, prolonged crying, disrupted eating and sleeping routines, and even weight loss.[9]

Potential Challenges Associated with the Loss of a Sibling during this Period

The early years of a person's life are typically subject to something called *infantile* or *childhood amnesia*. This refers to the inability to recall events that occurred during the first two or three years of life. For some time, it has been assumed that our first memories of childhood begin around three and a half years of age; however, more recent research suggests that we do have memories of earlier events, but due to the way in which our brains work, we postdate these memories to later ages.[10] If a sibling dies during this earliest developmental period, whether the loss is remembered or not, the surviving child's own developmental progress can be affected if parents are unable to manage their own responses to the death.

While a child may have no conscious memory of a sibling's death, the effect the loss has on the child's parents potentially can negatively influence a child's ability to establish trust in others. When parents are preoccupied, emotionally overwhelmed or absent, or wrapped up in their own sense of loss, they may be unable to provide the consistent care and engagement that a child needs to successfully negotiate the development of trust in the goodness of others and the world in general. Not unexpectedly, given the intensity of parental grief, researchers have noted that parents themselves report an inability to attend to their surviving children's needs after the death of a child.[11] A crying child can be a heartbreaking reminder of a child who has died, and parents may avoid tending to the needs of their infant due to clinical depression or even resentment of the surviving child. Thus, even such an early loss can shape the developmental trajectory of a child.

Developmental Crisis: Autonomy versus Shame and Doubt

Toddler Years (1½ to 3)

The next developmental stage that children encounter revolves around the developmental crisis that Erikson termed *autonomy versus shame and doubt*. This is the stage toddlers must experience en route to a sense of personal independence that will carry them through later challenges. Research findings have suggested that a strong and secure parental attachment, a task that is typically worked out in that first year, resulted in less conflict in three-year-olds.[12] Not surprisingly, the basic virtues of *willpower* and *self-control* are associated with this stage's developmental conflict.

The toddler years are marked by enthusiasm and activity. As toddlers assert their individuality and their will, they inevitably run up against authority figures (parents, caregivers, older children) who may block their efforts to get their way. When limits are put in place and enforced by caring and supportive adults, children learn that their desires cannot always be met, but that their identity as an autonomous individual is worthy of respect from others.

Typical Developmental Response to Death

Children this age still are unable to comprehend the finality of death and may respond to news about a sibling's death with questions about when the sibling will return home. Toddlers are acutely aware of the moods of others in the home, recognize the changes to the household routine, and notice the absence of a familiar presence with anxiety-related reactions.[13] They may throw tantrums as a way to engage preoccupied parents; experience nightmares; or engage in regressive behaviors. All of these are manifestations of their anxiety.

Potential Challenges Associated with the Loss of a Sibling during This Period

Because this period of development is still considered to be within the bounds of childhood amnesia, the family's response to the death of a child will play as big a role for a toddler as the memory of the sibling's death. This period of individual development is marked by a testing of wills between a child and the adults in her world. By pushing limits and testing her willpower, a toddler tries to conquer her world. Effective parents spend a great deal of time creating safe boundaries, reigning in overreaching behaviors, and providing discipline in a warm and supportive manner.

When a parent is unable to be physically and emotionally present, the toddler may have difficulty learning how to respect limits or, alternatively, how to test their powers of self-control. Growing up in a home where parents allow a toddler to have the run of the home without supervision can contribute to the development of an adult who has difficulty building relationships that incorporate healthy boundaries and mutual respect. When children are not taught the meaning and significance of the word *no*, for instance, they may have a difficult time respecting other adults or authority figures as well as the boundaries and needs of potential partners.

On the flip side of unbridled freedom is the risk of overprotecting the surviving child. Some parents may react to the loss of one child by placing a high value on the containment of a surviving child. If this child becomes the sole focus of the parents' energy and attention, the parents may keep him under such watchful eyes that he is never allowed to test any limits or exert his will to contradict his caregivers' wishes. Rather than engaging in the expected behaviors of a spirited toddler, the child may be kept under constant parental vigilance where every effort to assert his independence is met with parental control. This may create negative repercussions that follow a child long into adolescence and adulthood. If children are never allowed to make mistakes, they also are deprived of the opportunity to learn from their mistakes. A fear of the unknown or trepidation about unfamiliar situations may develop, which inhibits a young person from trying out new ideas or new activities or establishing new relationships and friendships. The toddler years ideally provide a safety net period in which children learn how to move beyond the safety of what is known and test limits in controlled environments. As noted previously, willpower and self-control are the personal competencies that are the goals for this period. When young children are held back from developing into autonomous individuals during this period, they may doubt their own sense of self or agency in the world as they move into adulthood.

Developmental Crisis: Initiative versus Guilt

Preschool Years (3 to 5)

The next stage of development sees children move into a wider social world in which they are given opportunities to interact with a broader range of people. As their roles in social relationships increase and they become increasingly responsible, they now face the conflict of *initiative versus guilt*. Aware of the need to be their own little person, they also begin to understand that there are consequences for unacceptable behavior. Thus, *purpose* and *direction* in life are the basic virtues that children should begin to develop during this period.

If a young child resides in an environment in which she is not allowed to practice making individual choices or testing out new behaviors, or if these efforts are met with negative caregiver responses or punishment, the child's drive and initiative may be compromised. At the opposite end of the disciplinary spectrum, however, children who are allowed too much freedom without adequate adult guidance may fail to develop a sense of purpose and may lack direction in later pursuits.

Typical Developmental Response to Death

Young children in this stage are learning about cause and effect in relationships, as noted by their focus on pleasing others and the guilt and remorse that they feel when they have displeased others. Due to this cognitive processing development, children may assume that they perhaps did something to cause a sibling to die. They may also still believe that death is a temporary state, and that if they do the "right thing," they may be able to bring a sibling back to life.

To cope with their own mourning, children often utilize the medium of play to work through their feelings, which may include sadness, anger, and confusion, among others. Play therapy is an excellent outlet for young children coping with experiences and feelings for which they do not have the vocabulary necessary for verbal articulation. Reenacting or playing out an event can provide children with the opportunity to gain a sense of control over the overwhelming loss and all that it represents.

Potential Challenges Associated with the Loss of a Sibling during This Period

Losing a sibling during this period can be devastating for children, as they are now old enough to be cognizant of the sibling's absence from the home. The reaction of the family to the loss can either exacerbate or mitigate the lasting impact of the child's death. If a sibling has been ill for a time, the surviving child might have grown to be jealous or resentful of the time and energy that parents invested in the care of the sick child. He may have wished that the sibling would *"get better or go away,"* as one interviewee recalled having experienced as a young child himself. Young children may also react to parental requests for good behavior with tantrums, arguments, and boisterous activities in intentional opposition to parents' directives. When a child dies and siblings exhibit any of these normal, age-appropriate behaviors, they may also feel a crushing sense of guilt for their willful misbehavior. This is a normal response, as well, but if parents do not anticipate this or do not appropriately respond to this self-deprecation, surviving siblings may internalize a feeling of responsibility for the death that may linger throughout their lives.

In cases of accidental or sudden death, young siblings may believe that their unrelated activities may have somehow caused the tragedy. If a parent has scolded a child for a particular behavior that occurred around the time of the loss, the child may be fearful of a causal connection between the behavior and the death. Parents who are absorbed in their own grief and unable to step back into their parenting roles may not recognize their surviving children's needs for assurance and age-appropriate explanations of the sibling's death. Parents who are able to contextualize the loss for a child of this age, by placing it into perspective and weaving it into a part of the fabric of the family's history, can ensure that surviving children do not take on an unwarranted mantle of guilt or responsibility for the loss. An example of how this can be successfully accomplished was shared by an interviewee in his late thirties or early forties: *"I was three when [the death] occurred, and the only way it affected us is that our mother would occasionally talk about our sister's death [that happened when she was] three days old. Plus, we would stop by her grave every once in a while."* By adding the events surrounding the loss to the family history and openly addressing the loss, the surviving sister did not grow up harboring feelings of guilt or misguided notions that she had the power to have prevented her younger sister's death. Losing siblings in infancy—even as young as a few days old—may affect siblings throughout the lifespan.[14] Researchers have revealed that there are three major themes that describe the influence of this type of loss: personal loss/unacknowledged loss, continuing bonds/memory keeping, and sense-making.[15]

In terms of psychosocial development, parents play a strong role in their children's self-perceptions. Typical four- and five-year-olds are working hard to achieve the twin virtues of purpose and direction. Thus, the death of a sibling can leave them feeling cast adrift, just as it might do with older siblings or adults. When children's efforts to develop a sense of initiative are compromised by a parent's response to grief, the fallout can persist for decades. For adults who recognize their own stories of sibling loss in this description, it may be of value to acknowledge the likely implausibility of their own responsibility for a sibling's death and to find opportunities to gain control of their life stories in a way that accurately reflects the powerlessness that children have in altering the path of others, including themselves, in many ways.

Developmental Crisis: Industry versus Inferiority

Primary School Years (5 to 12)

The elementary school–aged child should now have a growing sense of self-confidence and competence to master the challenges faced during these years. If development has taken a normal course, children are eager to dive into the learning process with an enthusiasm that is seldom matched at any other point in life. The virtue associated with successful mastery of this stage is *competency*, and Erikson labeled the crisis of this stage *industry versus inferiority*. Children enter this period hungry to increase their knowledge and understanding of the world, but they also face the potential for a sense of public and private failure.

The risks of feeling inferior to others in the classroom, social settings, and at home are daunting. Because a child's self-esteem is contingent on her perceptions of how others perceive her, this period can be instrumental in building and maintaining self-confidence. If a child is unable to develop a strong sense of competence during this stage, it may be difficult for him to participate in activities that are not easily mastered or to show persistence when faced with tasks that are challenging. Avoidance is commonly the method of coping with the fear of failure for individuals who fail to master a sense of personal competence. In addition, feelings of competence and self-worth are essential for successfully managing the subsequent psychosocial crisis that revolves around identity and friendships.

Typical Developmental Response to Death

In the earliest years of this stage, children still believe that death will not happen to anyone in their own family—it happens "out there" or to others. They need to believe that it happens because someone is frail or old and that it cannot happen to healthy young people. Therefore, the loss of a sibling can be especially difficult to handle, as a young person's death does not fall within children's limited understanding of how the universe works. Children between seven and nine may see death as some sort of punishment.[16] Children may also be very curious about the details of death and the ceremonies associated with a death due to their natural interest in learning at this stage.

Emotionally, school-aged children are better able to cope with the loss than preschoolers, although they may still use vestiges of play to make sense of death. They may use mental imagery or fantasy to play out strategies for preventing future deaths. It has also been suggested that children may take on the roles previously held by the deceased person as a way to step up and assist the family, whether it's trying to take on meal preparation, caring for younger siblings, or trying to keep the peace by avoiding arguments or tending to the emotional needs of younger children. As children move toward puberty, their responses increasingly reflect adult behaviors or concerns. They may ask how the role played by the now deceased sibling will be filled in terms of contributions to the household chores, income, or emotional functioning of the family, if relevant.

Potential Challenges Associated with the Loss of a Sibling during This Period

At this age, children are greatly aware of their own growing competence in the world, and they are eager to follow the rules and succeed in the classroom and at play. Knowledge about death is usually limited and still unsophisticated. Children have a hard time accepting that young people, especially family members, can die. When a sibling does die, their sense of order in the world can be shaken. As competency is the virtue associated with this age, if a child feels somehow responsible for the loss of a sibling, a sense of personal competence may be difficult to achieve.

The need to strive for industry as a way to avoid feelings of inferiority can create a barrier to healthy development, as well. Children may believe that their parents would have preferred that the lost child had lived and the surviving child had died in his place. Tragically, there are some parents who not only have thought such a thing, but have also verbalized this wish within earshot of the surviving child. This type of remark can have a heartbreakingly traumatic and lasting effect on a child's self-esteem and sense of worth. With the stage-related focus on avoiding inferiority, when a parent leaves a child feeling "less than" or unwanted, she can struggle with feelings of inadequacy well into adulthood. It is important that parents and older family members be aware of any overt or covert comparisons between a sibling who has died and her surviving siblings. As one interviewee in her early twenties shared, *"Sometimes I think my sister might wish it had been me who died, and not her twin sister who did."* The negative feelings between the two surviving sisters are likely to continue unless they are able to address the lingering doubts and hurt still present between them.

Developmental Crisis: Identity versus Identity Confusion

Heading toward Adulthood (12 to 18)

As puberty begins, significant changes are afoot physiologically, emotionally, and socially for young adolescents.[17] These developments are driving behavior as adolescents seek to manage the developmental conflict of *identity versus identity confusion*. This conflict tends to play out its drama most frequently within the parent-child relationship, as the goal for this stage is individuation through the development of an identity separate and distinct from the family. There is a highly charged allegiance to peers, and this is the springboard to the solidification of the virtues of *fidelity* and *devotion*.

As an adolescent increasingly looks to his peers, rather than family, as his primary reference group, parents experience a diverse range of emotions; few reactions are positive at the outset. Biologically driven to take risks, adolescents try on new behaviors and take on new identities. Although not all adolescents use the same force to push against parental restraints, these years can generate intense battles that are reminiscent of the iconic toddler temper tantrum. Keeping a child too close will hinder development, but allowing too much freedom may provide peers with too much control over the teen's behavior and burgeoning identity.

The optimal developmental goal for this period is to strike a balance between freedom and responsibility. Adolescents who are able to discern the difference between calculated risks and foolish risks fare best as they enter adulthood. Being able to assess when it is better to play it safe is a valuable skill that is gained during this period. Skills that require risk management and assessment, such as driving, have been shown to be more highly developed in adolescents who are more psychosocially mature,[18] an example of how significant the development that occurs during adolescence can be as a child becomes an adult.

Important Aspects of Adolescent Psychological, Social, and Emotional Development

Five unique aspects of adolescent development directly or tangentially affect their decision-making and emotional responses to external events.

1. **The imaginary audience at play.** Teens often feel as if everyone is watching and judging their behaviors and picking apart their faults.
2. Standing alone on that imaginary stage, a teen is acting out her own **personal fable.** This is the narrative that shapes a teen's behavior and by which she shapes her personal story.
3. **A trusting belief in personal immortality and invulnerability.** Teens are able to acknowledge the risks in a behavior, but are unable to cognitively intuit that the risk may result in harm to them; for example, driving a car around a sharp curve at ninety miles per hour isn't too risky for their skill set—it's just a way to have some fun.
4. **A strong sense of uniqueness.** This is that potentially endearing quality that unfortunately motivates every teenager to affirm to adults, *"This is my life—you wouldn't understand!"*
5. **Omnipotence.** This is a teen's belief in her power to accomplish whatever she sets out to do, no matter how seemingly improbable.

Each of these five beliefs can affect an adolescent's response to the death of a sibling.

Typical Developmental Response to Death

Most adolescents have experienced the death of someone they knew, or knew of, and have accepted that death is another aspect of reality. Adolescents are likely to turn to their friends, rather than the family, as support networks to help cope with their grief. Some teens may reject their close families' offers of support through their denial of any suffering or depression-related symptoms. Adolescents may use denial as a coping strategy as well as self-medication through the use of illegal substances. Teens may also show signs of regression or neediness that may surprise adults. Alternately, some may try to take on greater responsibilities in the household, either to pick up the chores that the deceased sibling once completed or as a way to help grieving parents who are having difficulty coping with the loss themselves.

Potential Challenges Associated with the Loss of a Sibling during This Period

Difficulty coping with the loss of a sibling may manifest through difficulties with peer groups or social behaviors. Teens may either abandon their families-of-origin as they spend increasing amounts of time with their social groups, or they may isolate themselves away from friends and hide out in their bedrooms as they try to cope with or run from their feelings of loss. The personal stage may be too much, emotionally, for the teen, and this may motivate the choice to hide out from others. Just as younger children do, teenagers have difficulty conceiving of death happening to someone young. With regard to the grieving process, the adolescent sense of omnipotence is a double-edged sword in some ways. When teens feel unable to control the world around them, or if they feel some sort of responsibility for the death of a sibling, the blow to their sense of power and control can be devastating. Further, the divergence between their perceived control and their actual control creates an inner imbalance, as well, as they try to make sense of events in their lives over which they have no control, such as death and dying. This awareness conflicts with their own personal feeling of immortality. Unfortunately, if teens are using risky behaviors as coping mechanisms, they may be unable to recognize the danger in which they are placing themselves.

Depending on the cause of a sibling's death, some teens may feel "different" from their friends in a manner that detracts from the teen's age-appropriate sense of uniqueness that is present during these years. If a sibling was stricken by a terminal illness, the grieving process may be less eventful or less traumatic than if the sibling died as a result of homicide, accident, or suicide. When an adolescent's personal fable gets rewritten through a family tragedy, it may have significant repercussions. As one interviewee shared about the loss of a brother during her and another brother's late adolescent years, "*When I was twenty, my eight-year-old brother was killed in a school tragedy. It changed the dynamics entirely in our family and caused my seventeen-year-old brother to head down the wrong path in life.*" Now that she was around fifty, she revealed that the fallout from the loss had continued into adulthood for her brother: "*My brother used this tragedy as a reason for everything that has gone wrong in his life. He began using alcohol in his twenties and thirties, then on to prescription drugs and now heroin in his forties.*"

Research shows that when parents are less successful in processing their grief, children may be negatively affected by their parents' unavailability.[19] The influence and modeling of a parent's mourning play a strong role for children and teens. In some cases, adolescents may feel that they must step into the parental role with their siblings or in the running of the household, if a parent is unable to continue functioning effectively. This may cause teens to avoid friends or extracurricular activities, and grades can also suffer. Teens may feel that as the family composition has changed, so, too, have their own personal identities. This can be one of the most significant impacts of sibling loss, as adolescents are working hard to develop and gain acceptance of their personal identities. When this process is impeded or altered by the death of a sibling and the reconfiguration of a family system, their progress toward healthy individuation can be temporarily—or permanently—obstructed. For adolescents, as for all age groups, a healthy mourning process can be fostered by family members and close significant others who step in and support the surviving sibling and encourage the sibling to feel safe in asking for support in whatever form is most needed.

CONCLUSION

It's been noted that childhood and adolescent bereavement can be summed up as a three-step process.[20] These three steps include 1) understanding that death is a final good-bye, 2) being given permission and space to mourn the loss in age-appropriate ways, and 3) being allowed and supported in returning to "normal," in whatever new form normal now takes. One interviewee, around thirty years old, shared the following description of how her family acknowledged the early loss of her sister and how they continue to celebrate the place the child held in the family: "*My family still celebrates the birthday of my sister who passed and honors the anniversary of her death, some thirty-plus years later. [I] and all my siblings have educated our children of our sister's presence in the family and we still share stories of her. My oldest sister buys flowers on these two days for both my parents. The rest of us siblings buy flowers for our own houses in honor of our sister.*"

Regardless of the age at which a sibling met her death, a relationship with the lost sibling endures for a lifetime. As Kempson, Conley, and Murdock termed it, even if surviving siblings never knew the brothers or sisters who died before they were born, there is often a "ghost" of the lost child that resides with the family for generations.[21]

FINAL TAKEAWAY: No matter the age of the child who died, siblings may be forever affected by the loss. Acknowledging the loss and taking the time necessary to grieve can be as important for children as they are for adults.

Chapter Four

Family Communication and Engagement

Effective communication is essential to any healthy relationship—whether it is between married couples, parents and children, friends, or siblings. It is within the family that our communication skills are first shaped and developed. As we develop within our own unique family environment, communication is typically role-driven. We learn how to be a member of the family through the feedback communicated by other family members. Communication in families is also formative and involuntary.[1] Communication between family members serves multiple purposes and provides the vehicle through which the family's culture and expectations are transferred to its members. Beyond family roles, the culture of the family includes its rituals, such as giving thanks before meals or completing specific activities at holidays, for instance; family stories, such as oral histories or narratives of significant events in the family; and family secrets, which can vary widely and are further addressed in chapter 7.

Scholars have developed and refined two main theories related to family communications. One is aptly named the Family Communication Patterns Model;[2] it has been subject to consistent revisions as new information and schema were revealed that improved its fit with contemporary families.[3] The second theory is the Circumplex Model of Family Interaction,[4] and it provides a slightly different focus on the interactions between family members.

FAMILY COMMUNICATION PATTERNS MODEL

The Family Communication Patterns Model addresses the interaction of two specific facets of engagement intensity between family members, *conversation* and *conformity*.[5] The level of conversation reflects the encouragement given to family members to discuss any topic—not just family-approved topics—within the group. The level of conformity describes the level of emphasis present in the family for embracing uniform values, attitudes, and beliefs. These two vectors of intensity can be seen as intersectional in their influence on family communications. To better understand the model, it helps to visualize two lines that are perpendicular to one another and that cross each other at their midpoint. The horizontal line, or vector, would represent expectations of conformity, and the vertical vector would represent conversational openness. The intersecting vectors would create four equal quadrants, each of which would include both scales of reference, as illustrated in the model in figure 4.1.

High Conversation Low Conformity	High Conversation High Conformity
Low Conversation Low Conformity	Low Conversation High Conformity

Figure 4.1. Family Communication Patterns Model

Source: Fitzpatrick, M. A., Ritchie, L. D., & Koerner, A. F. (1994). Communication schemata within the family: Multiple perspectives on family interaction. *Human Communication Research, 20,* 275–301.

In the upper right quadrant are high levels of conversation and high levels of conformity. This type of family is termed *consensual*. While the family is open to discussions, everyone is required to follow the family rules and reflect similar perspectives. Conflict is typically seen as a threat to the status quo, so while conflict is to be avoided if at all possible, it is also something that must be resolved to ensure that the status quo is maintained.

In the bottom right quadrant are low levels of conversation and high levels of conformity. These families are labeled *protective*, and there is little room for alternative ideas and no room for alternative behaviors. The old expression "Children should be seen and not heard" would be very fitting to describe how parents view their offspring within a protective family. Open communication is not encouraged, and, due to the lack of experience the members have in discussing diverging ideas, there is little opportunity for siblings to gain expertise in communication skills.

In the bottom left quadrant are low levels of conversation and low levels of conformity. These families are termed *laissez-faire* families. In this type of family, no one's voice is given space for listening, and little concern over anyone's behaviors is evident. There are likely few rules and little care on the parents' part as to whether the children exhibit a willingness to follow the parents' leads in terms of values, beliefs, or attitudes. While children are trusted to make their own decisions, they may long for more visible support and involvement from their parents.

Lastly, in the upper left quadrant are high levels of conversation and low levels of conformity. *Pluralistic* is the term used to describe these families. Here, dissenting voices are accepted, and if individuals can provide strong rationales for their dissenting behavior, this will also be accepted. In these families, offspring are perceived as capable of developing their own identities, but discussion and verbal communication are expected. Each family member's ideas are viewed as worthy of being heard; parents do not feel the need to always be right.

Every family has its own unique "climate" regarding tolerance for nonconformity and open conversations, and each climate is likely to support the development of different traits among siblings reared within it. For instance, families that expect high levels of conformity from children are likely to produce siblings who are shyer and have lower self-esteem than those with less emphasis on conformity.[6] Since there is no real modeling of ways to discuss differences or conflict, siblings who grow apart as they mature may have a more difficult time managing their disagreements or differences as adults due to the early prohibition on conflicting perspectives. On the other hand, children from families in which conversation is highly encouraged reported higher levels of sociability as well as possessing stronger self-images.[7] When siblings from families in which discussion of diverse ideas was encouraged disagree or need to make joint decisions later in adulthood, they may be able to generate innovative ideas and the potential for creative solutions and resolutions due to their early training in debate and consideration. Although broad sweeping generalizations seem easy to make based on the two limited areas of assessment within the Family Communication Patterns Model, the Circumplex Model is a bit more complex, as it addresses the interactions of three discrete dimensions.

CIRCUMPLEX MODEL OF FAMILY INTERACTION

This model of family interaction focuses on the dimensions of *cohesion* and *adaptability*, and the role of *communication* in the shaping of the first two dimensions.[8] Cohesion describes how well the members of a family are emotionally bonded to one another. Adaptability addresses how well a family can "flex" in response to change. Family communication is the trait that weaves between cohesion and adaptability and is considered to be the most critical aspect of family engagement.

Family Cohesion

Olson and his colleagues developed a four-level division of both family cohesion and family adaptability that produced sixteen distinct family types. The four levels of cohesion are *disengaged* (little closeness, little loyalty, and high independence), *separated* (low-moderate closeness, some loyalty, and interdependent), *connected* (moderate-high closeness, high loyalty, and interdependent), and *enmeshed* (very high closeness, very high loyalty, and high dependency). The mid-range types, separated and connected, allow for more effective family functioning across life stages. Disengaged families show evidence of significant autonomy among members, but few avenues for seeking or receiving support. Enmeshed families are extremely self-contained and have little desire for seeking external support or connections to non-family members. There is little room for "private space," literally or metaphorically.

Family Adaptability

Being adaptable to change is an extremely valuable quality in terms of family functioning. Within this model, adaptability would include changes in these areas: family leadership, role relationships, and relationship rules. The levels of adaptability developed by Olson and colleagues include *rigid* (very low levels of flexibility), *structured* (low to moderate levels), *flexible* (moderate to high levels), and *chaotic* (very high levels).[9] In rigid families, there is too little change; structured families change when it is demanded of them; flexible families change as it becomes necessary; and chaotic families undergo too much change.

With four levels of cohesion and four levels of adaptability, there are sixteen possible typologies within this model, as illustrated in figure 4.2.

Chaotically disengaged	Chaotically separated	Chaotically connected	Chaotically enmeshed
Flexibly disengaged	Flexibly separated	Flexibly connected	Flexibly enmeshed
Structurally disengaged	Structurally separated	Structurally connected	Structurally enmeshed
Rigidly disengaged	Rigidly separated	Rigidly connected	Rigidly enmeshed

Figure 4.2.   Circumplex Model of Family Interactions Typologies

As might be expected, the four types highlighted in the center of the chart are located in the "sweet spot" of family organization; families in these types are considered to be balanced because they are able to maintain healthy functioning even as they move through transitions. As Olson and colleagues noted, families with high levels of rigidity are typically controlled by a single individual within the family system and change is difficult for the family. In families with high levels of chaos, there is typically too little leadership. Functioning suffers from a lack of planning and owned responsibility. Balanced families are much more likely to weather crises successfully and to remain functional even in the most challenging circumstances.

If you were fortunate to grow up in a family with open communication, strong cohesion, and optimal flexibility, it is likely that you enjoy positive relationships with your adult siblings and are able to handle disagreements or conflicting desires in an effective and mature manner. Much of what a person learns regarding interpersonal give-and-take and personal expression is determined within the family-of-origin. If you experience difficulty communicating with your adult siblings, perhaps it is time to gain new skills that will enhance sibling communication.

DO EARLY COMMUNICATION PATTERNS
PREDICT FUTURE BEHAVIORS?

In many families, caregivers and parents feel that the caregiver/parent-child communication pipeline is not as effective as they would prefer. Parents complain that their kids never listen and express surprise at the amount of selective hearing that their children exhibit. Between siblings, though, there are a variety of communication breakdown types. Some siblings take pleasure in annoying their siblings through insults and teasing. Other sibling pairs may just have to throw the right look and the fighting begins in earnest—with no verbal exchange even taking place.

Many of the patterns of behavior that you practiced in childhood and increasingly mastered through adolescence and young adulthood are likely part of your behavioral repertoire well into adulthood. This is especially true when it comes to what you learned through family dynamics and family interaction. Sibling relationships are frequently described as the lengthiest personal relationships that an individual is likely to experience. Whether or not this is true in all cases, what *is* true is that the lessons you learn at the hands of your siblings may shape all of your relationships for decades.

THREE CULTURAL FORCES AFFECTING
SIBLING RELATIONSHIPS

A few decades ago, three cultural shifts were identified as being highly relevant to the quality and value of the sibling relationship over time. These shifts, or forces, represented significant changes in the family structure over the prior century.[10] The first force is the shrinking size of the typical U.S. family. With fewer children entering the family system, each sibling's value, or potential value, to the others becomes greater in these smaller families.

Second, the increasingly peripatetic nature of families today is quite different from earlier generations in which hometowns were where people *lived*, more than just where people were *from*. The rise in divorce and separation as well as cohabitation also contributes to relocation and reconfiguration of family systems. Moving between neighborhoods or towns can be equally disconcerting to children, and when they say good-bye to friends, the constancy of siblings may be extremely important to children's acclimation to new homes and schools.

The third force reflects the increasing absence, real or virtual, of parents in their children's lives. This can be due to divorce or separation; the need to work long, late, or inconvenient hours; self-absorption that comes with long hours spent on the Internet at home or on smartphones out and about; or simply the inability to be a "good enough" parent.

Panning out toward an international view, many concerns have been raised, and numerous studies are in the works to assess the fallout of the three-decades-long ban on having more than a single child in China.[11] There are macro-effects such as population, health, and economic conse-quences as well as individual, "only child"–specific consequences. One of the basic human needs is social support within a community; when the family's size is on the lower end of the spectrum, with few uncles, aunts, cousins, and so on, there can be an isolation or sense of separation from others. Older adults, too, worry about the consequences of having only one child to care for them as they age.[12] Having siblings to share the care and to share your memories can be a reward for all the childhood bicker-ing or rivalry that may have been endured.

Learning to get along as well as possible with your siblings can be the ultimate self-help gift as you grow older, too. While not every sibling relationship is going to blossom into friendship in adulthood, developing a better relationship can pay off when you need it most.

DO BIRDS (OR SIBLINGS) OF A FEATHER FLOCK TOGETHER?

If you have more than one sibling, it is likely you feel closer to one of your brothers or sisters and would likely have an easier time jumping in to assist that sibling if needed. According to the siblings who shared their stories for this book, most siblings feel that if it came down to it, family obliga-tion would outweigh personal animosity in the vast majority of cases. An intriguing research study, however, revealed something that may cause you to reflect on your own "favorite sibling" and even encourage you to reflect on your own image in the mirror. Recent research has revealed

that the more your sibling looks like you, the more willing you are to offer support.[13] In fact, when study participants felt a strong resemblance to
their siblings, they were willing to invest more in terms of money, time,
affection, and communication. Sadly, although research has indicated that
while macaques in the wild treat their half-siblings closer than non-kin,[14]
human beings aren't quite as open or accepting. Dutch researchers found
that individuals were much less likely to know whether a half-sibling was
still alive than a full sibling, and compared to full siblings, half siblings
were much less likely to receive support from one another.[15, 16]

While every set of siblings is unique, it may be useful to reflect on
your own patterns of mutually supportive behaviors with your brothers or
sisters. In adulthood, family constellations can mutate and transform as
marriages, divorces, births, and deaths occur. As people age, the transitory
nature of life grows more evident and relevant. As will be explored more
fully in chapter 14, the need and willingness to overcome communication
barriers also grow as social circles increasingly shrink.[17] As the need for
support grows, so too may the willingness to provide support.

DOES GENDER INFLUENCE
COMMUNICATION PATTERNS?

Women have long had a reputation for talking too much or being too
solicitous of others. It does appear that women, in general, actually use
a wider variety of communication methods with their siblings than their
brothers might use.[18] Sisters are more likely to communicate affection to
their brothers than brothers to brothers or brothers to sisters. Women are
also more likely to communicate messages of inclusion to their sisters
than any other dyadic pairing. Women learn early the values of community and harmony;[19] thus, it makes sense that sisterly communication
would tend to be more relationally focused than communication originated by males. Same-gender siblings have been found to get along better
overall than mixed-gender siblings during childhood and adolescence,[20]
but family dynamics can greatly affect how close siblings are once they
leave the family home. As Linda, a woman in her sixties, shared, "*My
sister and I live cross country from each other . . . we are not very much
involved in each other's daily life but there is much affection . . . my*

brother and I are very close, agree on just about everything, speak to each other multiple times a week . . . as I told him at his birthday, he is the person I have loved the longest in my life!"

DOES BIRTH ORDER INFLUENCE COMMUNICATION PATTERNS?

Although birth order does not necessarily predict communication patterns between siblings, it's been revealed that middle children feel closer to their friends than their siblings do.[21] Not only is closeness lacking between middle children and their families, but they are also less likely to offer assistance to family members when needed. They may feel like the last person in the "telephone game," which possibly may be due to their own sense of being something of a family outsider. As one twenty-six-year-old male middle child complained, *"I'm always the last to know about anything happening with my family. They don't tell me what is going on until after it's already happened. Not only that, but I still swear that they got a new cat to replace me in the family when I went off to college."*

Within each unique set of family dynamics, it is individual perception that predicts basically 100 percent of a person's reactions. It may also be interesting to note that the oldest sibling is more likely to communicate for purposes of control, such as making arrangements or decisions, whereas the youngest siblings tend to instigate communication with their siblings for purposes of relaxation or having fun. Not only do their communication goals differ, but firstborns also tend to be significantly less prosocial than their younger sibs.[22]

As noted in chapter 1, birth order is not the best classification system for sorting out siblings' personality traits. However, birth order can definitely influence the parenting and parental communication that children receive. Older children often receive messages from parents and are asked to carry the information to their siblings. Older children also are frequently given tasks to assist with the care of siblings, from something as simple as "give the baby her pacifier" or "play with your brother" to tasks such as preparing meals, picking up younger siblings from school, and getting younger children to bed. The older child will always have experienced more time with a parent than his younger siblings, and the relationship may be closer due to longevity and focused time spent together. This can lead to challenges in later life when difficult caregiving decisions must be made and siblings vie for or shrink from the implied responsibility. This topic is explored further in chapter 13.

CONCLUSION

Some siblings take peculiar pleasure in efforts to intentionally annoy one another, whether they are children, teens, or adults. When parents or caregivers allow these behaviors to become the accepted mode of sibling communication, the family system also likely exhibits compromised communication patterns. Learning new ways to relate can be difficult, but recognizing that sibling relationships come close to being lifelong investments, the long-term payoff of honest, trusting, loyal, and supportive siblings can make middle and older adulthood a lot more pleasant overall. Brothers, especially, stand to gain a lot by working to maintain sibling relationships in adulthood, as research shows that women tend to have much stronger social support networks, overall, than men do.[23] Keeping lines of communication open between you and your sibs can positively influence your physical and emotional well-being throughout the lifespan.

FINAL TAKEAWAY: Families develop individual patterns of communication that follow spoken and unspoken rules regarding content, audience, and timing of discussions. You and your siblings might need to break some of those outdated rules. Honest, respectful, and appropriate communication should be your goal. As siblings and their parents grow older, necessary discussions tend to grow increasingly difficult.

Part II

THE EFFECTS OF THE
PAST ON THE PRESENT

Chapter Five

Sibling Rivalry in Adulthood

Bitter Rivals or Peaceable Companions?

The desire to be your parents' favorite can persist for decades. Alex, a twenty-two-year-old graduate student, shared that whenever he and his older sister were alone long enough for something more than just super-ficial chats, she always found a way to accuse him of being the favorite child, but she assured him that it wasn't his fault. It was because he was the youngest, and everyone knows that the baby of the family is the fa-vorite. Alex related that he had not figured out the best response yet. Al-though he was a little embarrassed to admit it, he shared that he actually hoped this was true, because, really, who *wouldn't* want to be the favor-ite? Alex did not perceive any real rivalry between him and his siblings because they all had followed very different paths into adulthood and had become successful in their own ways. Unfortunately, not all adult siblings feel the same level of equanimity as Alex.

SIBLING CONFLICT IS ONLY NATURAL

While most parents would prefer that everyone in the family get along, it turns out that some amount of sibling conflict is not only normal but also healthy. Sibling relationships provide our first entry into the realm of af-filiation, negotiation, persuasion, influence, and, for some, domination.[1] We know that we cannot escape our siblings, so some of us are more will-ing to work harder to get the upper hand—or control of the remote. It's probably not surprising that researchers found that sibling disagreements produced repercussions unlike those that arise from arguments between friends. When you go too far in an argument with a friend, the damage may be irreparable, at worst, or may place a damper on the friendship for a while until apologies are offered or the incident forgotten. With siblings, it is a different set of circumstances. No matter how ugly the disagreements might be, siblings still have face each other across the dinner table and, if they share a room, see each other first thing every morning. In fact, compared to disagreements with friends, it turns out that young adolescents may show little regret or experience any significant personal consequences after a fight with a sibling that would end a relationship with a friend. The stakes are much lower in terms of ultimate outcome in sibling squabbles, which is why, ironically, they can be so passionately fought.

SIBLING CONFLICT HAS PURPOSE

Your sister or brother provided you with your first opportunity to learn the skills of negotiation, whether you wanted to or not. For the oldest child, who has enjoyed the luxury of having no competition for family resources, the arrival of a younger sibling can be a reason for celebration or resignation. When asking study participants about the earliest memory they can recall of time spent with a sibling, the oldest child usually recalls the moment they first met their new sib. Some recall the memory with delight, as did one woman who shared, *"I was at my grandmother's house, playing on the floor. When my parents came in the door, I remember running past my father to get to my mother so I could see my new baby brother."* A young woman who was born into her family as the first and only sibling to her then eight-year-old brother had a very heartwarming story of her own arrival in the sibling set, *"My mom says when I was born that my brother was happy and excited and loved helping take care of me and never exhibited any signs of jealousy."* She and her family attribute this to the eight-year age difference—and the gender difference may have been a positive circumstance, as well.

Another woman related a different attitude toward her own brand-new sibling: *"I remember my baby brother in his crib, crying at night, and wanting him to stop!"* Regardless of how the first few months of the sibling relationship begins, learning to get along in close quarters with others is a valuable experience with lifelong benefits. Some of the other benefits that can be accrued to sibling rivalry include personal development, a better understanding of the social world and productive engagements, as well as improved sibling relationships in adulthood.[2]

Self-Development

Many individuals who seek counseling often present goals that describe how they do not want to be rather than clear descriptions of how they would like to be. A client might affirm that he doesn't want to be like his father; another client might not want to be as quick to anger as he usually tends to be. Growing up, siblings can fill the role of a "person of reference" for one another as they work to develop skill sets or strengths that allow them to compete—directly or indirectly—with their siblings. As one interviewee shared, *"I wouldn't consider us as having sibling rivalry due to the fact that we were involved in very different things and had interest in different activities. We both had things we were great at that the other was not and did not really use those to 'one up' each other."* By developing skills and strengths that are unlike those of a brother or sister, as this interviewee described, the desire to stand out or be seen as an individual can be more easily met than by trying to outshine a sibling.

Social Understanding

Social skills are best learned through direct practice, and the presence of siblings provides children with ample opportunity to learn how to negotiate from a young age. Unfortunately, research suggests that age and size are likely the most potent advantages in conflict resolution. In one study of siblings in early and middle childhood, Abuhatoum and Howe found that older siblings rely on coercion with their younger siblings, while the younger sibs try to use legitimate power and self-assertion to get their way.[3] Some adults don't remember things quite that way. More than one of the individuals interviewed for this project believed that their younger siblings were more likely to use their youth, not earned power, as a means of getting their own way or prevailing in conflicts. One "baby" of the family shared, *"[My siblings] used to call me Queenie because my parents were more affectionate with me."* Queenie didn't deny that she used her place in the birth order to gain an unfair advantage over her siblings, and most "babies" in the family feel justified to use whatever power they can to get the upper hand on older sibs. Another woman shared that her *"younger sister was the nark. If you used words that were not allowed in the house, she would bull horn it to mom."*

Working It Out for Optimal Self-Esteem?

A person's level of self-esteem is a good estimation of a person's measure of personal power.[4] Not only that, but a person's self-esteem is also predictive of her own relationship satisfaction in an adult relationship, as well as that of her partner.[5] Although most people want to believe that other people can change and develop over time, some qualities related to temperament and personality do not change much unless people work at it. If you are able to develop a positive relationship with your siblings as children, the benefits will include better friendships and higher self-esteem down the road.[6]

Parenting Skills

Indeed, it is also possible to benefit from conflict-filled sibling relationships by building enhanced parenting skills. If you have learned the hard way how to handle sibling drama as a child, you are much more likely to be an effective parent in terms of keeping the peace and avoiding authoritarian parenting. Parents with sibling drama histories are also less likely to show favoritism between their own offspring and are more likely to work hard to manage family conflicts in order to minimize the negative fallout these conflicts might have on their children. It's often a case of using what was done poorly in your family-of-origin as a model of what *not* to do in the new family you are creating.[7, 8]

MOTHERS AND FATHERS:
WHOSE LOVE IS MORE SOUGHT AFTER?

In analyzing data from all of the respondents to the survey questions for this book project, it became clear that children prefer the parent who is either more like them or appears to have their best interest closest to heart. Some siblings "divide and conquer" when it comes to parent dyads; the younger ones or the girls or some other grouping might prefer mom, while the other subset prefers dad. One participant shared that in his family, he had "*a dad and two moms*," as his mother and father divorced and his mother began a long-term same-sex relationship with another woman. The twenty-something young man joked, "*In our family of three kids, we had a one-to-one parent-child ratio. No one ever felt left out growing up.*" As adults, he shared that each child still connected especially well with one of the three "*primary parents*," which they all appreciated as adult siblings.

Being the "favorite" can be a highly sought after honor for many. Being the "not so favorite" may even be blamed for personal and professional failure—and success—deep into adulthood. Competition for parental approval or the recognition this approval offers can be a bitter and unsatisfying quest for some. Siblings may carry a sense of shame or poor self-worth if their parental behavior drummed up doubts about their value to the family. While some might think that sisters might be less prone to rivalry than their brothers, researchers have found that the presence of an older sister correlated with less competitive younger brothers, but an increased likelihood of competitiveness in younger sisters.[9] Throughout the plant and animal kingdom, and regardless of gender, sibling rivalry for survival resources exists. Following is a closer look at some of the ways that it can unfold between contemporary siblings.

WHAT IS THE SUBSTANCE OF SIBLING RIVALRY?

Sibling rivalry can take on many forms during childhood, and it can trigger everything from good-natured teasing to the infliction of intentional harm. Although not every set of siblings will experience any palpable rivalry, over half of the participants in the current study acknowledged it had been present in their families to some degree. Fortunately, not as many believed it was still ongoing, but its early presence left lasting effects for some. One participant shared the wake-up call she received about her older sister's own take on their shared history:

I always knew, from my earliest memories, that something was very wrong between my sister and myself, but I did not know what. When we were adults, and both in therapy [separately], [one day] my sister suddenly said, "Well, of course, as I discussed with my therapist, sibling rivalry is what has made our relationship difficult." I never considered the possibility of sibling rivalry, as odd as that may sound—especially as ever since the end of adolescence I have felt myself to be so very different from my sister. We are not interested in the same things, we are not interested in the same men . . . so what is there to have a rivalry about?

Who's the Favorite?

In some families, there is a clearly identified favorite, and this can stir up feelings of intense rivalry for parental love. One woman recalled, *"Wow! [The rivalry] was crazy and still is. My mom and dad had favorites and it has taken me a lifetime to understand the impact of so many things. I think that is why we still struggle with our relationships."* Another woman, Karen, shared that her mother pitted Karen's youngest sister against Karen as often as possible. She went on to note that her mother would believe her sister's false accusations against her and punish Karen for transgressions that she had not committed. For many older children, this can be a familiar story. The "baby" of the family often experiences the family from a sanctified position, of sorts. Sharing her experiences of being the youngest for the first decade of her life, Kim shared the following narrative: *"My eldest brother hated my guts with the fire of a thousand suns! Mum told me that when I was young, I would cry and say he'd hit me to get him in trouble . . . I think my eldest brother still has some issues with me. He's called me a 'spoilt little bitch' a few times in recent years."*

Researchers Megan Gilligan, J. Jill Suitor, and Sangbo Nam have explored family closeness and family favoritism using a large longitudinal data set.[10] Their goal was to explore how a childhood tie to one's mother affected later-life sibling closeness. Looking at over two thousand sibling dyads, they found that adult siblings who did not make the list of "Mom's favorites" tended to report closeness to their brothers or sisters who *were* their mother's favorite. Further, individuals who believed they had escaped Mom's "naughty list" exhibited little closeness with the siblings who did make that list. Ideally, children mature and grow out of their negative behavior patterns, but it appears that the need to align with the team that is led by Mom endures throughout the lifespan.

In another family, the "golden child" of the family reflected a more literal interpretation of this nickname. Imelda, a woman in her mid-fifties, shared that the hard facts of favoritism were circumscribed by a boundary based on birth order, appearance, and ethnic identity. When asked if birth order had played a role in her own family, she responded,

Huge. One word description. My mother says that she was the baby and that's why she favors my youngest sister (because they are alike, she had elaborated). Also, my mother is half Native American and half white. [Her heritage] wasn't something to be proud of when she was young. My white grandfather showed unbelievable favoritism towards the two daughters who looked whiter [than his other children]. My youngest sister has colored her dark hair blonde for years and had more "white" attributes. Although my mother spoke harshly about the unfair favoritism her father showed, she continues to repeat the pattern—even into adulthood with her own grown children.

Assumptions about rivalry being a "race to be the best" were totally upended in some families. Nell, a young woman in her twenties, shared that while she had always been her mother's favorite, her sister was the one that her mother would go out of her way to spoil and for whom her mother had higher expectations. Asked whether this rivalry had continued into adulthood, she responded, "*I think [my sister] has always been frustrated by how accepting my mom is of my failures, accomplishments, or life choices, whereas my mom is very opinionated and emotional about my sister's choices. I think she feels pressure to be successful with her career, but not so much in comparison with me.*"

The acceptance of Nell's failures by a mother who expected more from Nell's older sister created a unique dynamic in which one sister's achievements were never enough and the younger sister's failures were never an issue. When mired in a contest of wills or skills with an adult sibling, it can be helpful to step back and figure out exactly what the "prize" will be for the "winner," as well as determining if a winner can even be declared or if the battle is worth pursuing. For instance, if you resent a sibling for doing little in life and avoiding any emotional consequences from your parent, you might need to ask yourself if "doing little" is a goal to which you would really want to ever aspire to. Sometimes it is important to recognize that one person's achievements cannot necessarily be measured against those of another. If the envisioned prize is approval from your parent, it might be help-ful to honestly assess whether parental approval is even possible, knowing your parents as you do. Competing for attention as an adult suggests there are some areas for personal growth that might be explored: You may need to ask yourself if you are seeing yourself through your parents' eyes or if you can view yourself more objectively and recognize that you can function as an autonomous adult. The development of healthy family relationships may be an aspirational goal, but acceptance of the limits of your family members may be a much more realistic and achievable goal. When you are able to walk away from the race for the prize and focus on self-satisfaction and self-respect, you've already earned something even more valuable.

A similar point of contention can arise when parents continue finan-cially supporting adult siblings who refuse to fend for themselves. In a later chapter addressing addiction issues, further attention will be given to the ways in which parental support of addicted siblings can generate resentment and complicated relationships throughout the family system.

When Remarriage and New Siblings Are Added to the Mix

Wanting to win approval from a parent while vanquishing the competition may be the goal of rivalry, but when the family constellation grows in-creasingly complex, the goal may be much more difficult to attain. Termed *nontraditional* siblings, the presence of half- and stepsiblings in the family may negatively affect children's academic performance as well as the fam-ily environment.[11] It has been suggested that individuals who grow up in blended families experience more than their fair share of stress, relational complexity, uncertainty, and ambiguity regarding the family constellation. According to results from Kathryn Tillman's study, it seems that youth don't just "get used to" new family structures over time; the adverse ef-fects of family blending can endure. Fortunately, there are cases in which parents "lay down the law" early in the blended relationships and put forth expectations about mutual respect and fair treatment of new sibs.

More than a few interviewees in this current study noted that "losing" a parent to a new spouse is not easy, but "losing" a parent to new step- or half-siblings was much more painful. It can be devastating to children when they lose their unique place in the family-of-origin's original con-stellation through divorce and the subsequent appearance of stepsiblings or half-siblings. Felicia, a young woman with a variety of sibling types, recounted the rivalry for her father's affection that arose when he began a new family: "*I met [my father's new] kids during a play date. He informed me they were my brother and sister months later. He made us fight for his love; he played favorites. He took stuff that belonged to us and either gave or forced you to give it to someone else. There were days in which one kid would bear all the faultfinding or be the star of the week.*" Felicia went on to share, "*My dad repeated the 'Hey, that kid you just played with is your sibling by the way' twice again. My sister was very hurt and insecure because she had been his baby. It destroyed her. My brother and I were livid but okay with it. We pulled together to share our outrage.*" As can happen in many families, strong alliances can form between family members who identity a shared adversary or form an adversarial alliance. When there is a common enemy, so to speak, siblings often band together tightly to protect their stake in the family or the situational outcome. While this may provide a sense of belonging, it may also create rifts in the family system that grow deeper and wider over time.

Another woman, Emily, who is around forty, shared that the arrival of a stepfather eventually brought two new half-siblings into the family. When responding to a question about rivalry, she responded, "*There wasn't really sibling rivalry, but there was always a feeling that my little sister and brother (my mom and stepdad's two kids) were favored over me and my other brother since we had a different father. This was not how my mom made us feel, but how my stepdad did by his actions.*" Unfortunately, research indicates that the shared biological children of a couple are often favored over any stepchildren in the home.[12] The lack of a biological tie and the requirement that family resources be shared with non-related children are examples of the conceivable reasons for the relationship shortcomings. Emily's continued narrative provides support for this: "*My stepdad came into my life when I was seven, and until I [was around] twenty-two, it was very difficult because he hated the fact that he had to support my brother and me all those years.*"

Dealing with Long-Term Step- or Half-Sibling Stand-Offs

Research indicates that the relationship between stepparents and their stepchildren can grow closer over time, depending on their mutual interest in building a better relationship.[13] As Emily wrapped up, *"Once I moved out, he and I had a really good relationship until he passed away four months ago. He still was somewhat miserable to my brother . . . but I had a good relationship with him."* Relationships between stepsiblings, though, may be more challenging in adulthood than they were during childhood. Some of the most frequently voiced stepsibling complaints in adulthood address inheritances, equal attention and visits to adult children's homes, and end-of-life issues. These are the same issues that any set of siblings must negotiate, but the territorial ownership of a particular tangible or intangible commodity can grow much trickier over time. (Step)sibling rivalry can intensify as the stakes grow higher. Compared to full siblings, step- and half-siblings are much less likely to offer emotional support to one another.[14] Stepsiblings are not keen on offering assurance or helping out with needed tasks for one another even in adulthood, when some would hope that the more intense rivalry had burned out. If stepparent favoritism had been in play during childhood and adolescence, it is likely that the damage done during those years will have repercussions throughout adulthood.

Tips for Dealing with Step-Rivalries

Sometimes the best way to handle a conflict that really cannot be easily and fully resolved is to rethink how you believe a resolution should look. As a counselor, I know that many people would like to be able to simply undo the hurts—real *and* imagined—that they suffered growing up. While that is an unrealistic goal, there are ways to explore what it would mean to you today if the unpleasant experiences could be undone. Implementing the concepts found in solution-focused brief therapy[15] may shake up your current mind-set and help you begin to see your future as something that does not have to be constrained by your past.

- First, ask yourself, "How would I be different right now if my past hadn't been like it was?"
- Make a list of all the ways in which you believe you would be different, in terms of feelings. More hopeful? Less disappointed? Happier? Less controlled by resentment about past wrongs? Less preoccupied with negative thoughts?

- Starting at the top of your list, reflect on what you would be *doing* differently if you *felt* differently in each way that you described.
- For instance, if you noted that you would be "more confident about myself," how would you approach life differently? How would other people know you were more confident—what would be different about you?
- Now that you've fully explored the *doing* that you think the *feeling* differences would allow, challenge yourself to do life differently, as if you were free from the weight of the negative feelings that are keeping you down.

One woman shared her reflections on childhood hurts and feelings of inequity, noting that now that she was an adult, there was no reason to hold onto resentments that only provided excuses for her to be unhappy.

Sure, I hated my stepbrother and stepsister and frequently wished my mother hadn't married their dad. They tried to make me miserable throughout high school and complained to their dad that he shouldn't help pay for my college. Now I'm independent, my mother's gone, and [I realize] I've been letting my anger keep me down too long. I wish that I hadn't "punished" my mother by not being willing to visit her when his kids were around. I lost out on my relationship with her and I want to blame my stepsiblings, but I was the one who made the decision to stay away. I gave away a lot of power that I shouldn't have when I was younger. Now, though, I'm letting go of the negativity and making decisions now that I should have been making a long time ago.

RIVALRY INTO ADULTHOOD: WHAT ARE THE STAKES?

One young adult woman was able to sum up succinctly the evolution of the rivalry in her family in just a few words: *"Childhood—possessions. Teenage years—lifestyle choices. Adults—we give each other space now."* In some families, evolution doesn't happen quite as quickly, and the desire to best a brother or sister can get the best of many siblings. Following are some examples of especially sensitive and potentially rivalrous situations.

Holiday Time

Most married couples realize the challenges that traditional holiday celebrations can bring to their own nuclear family. Choosing whether to spend the eve of a celebration with one set of in-laws or the other and trying to balance out the feelings of everyone regarding their decision on where to spend the "big day," whatever holiday this might mean, is not simple. Regrettably, some parents create a sense of rivalry between their children when trying to persuade them to spend an important holiday at their home. One man shared, *"Around late September, my mom will start hinting that she wants my family to spend Thanksgiving Day with her and Dad. She goes about it all the wrong way—she reminds me that my younger brother and his live-in girlfriend have already bought plane tickets or started planning the menu or something. It's like the son who spends the most holidays with her and Dad wins the biggest chunk of her love. Man, I hate the rivalry she tries to keep going between us."*

There are few situations where the family stakes are as high as they seem to be at holiday time. Once a child has moved out—or even earlier, if she's involved in a significant relationship with someone—some parents may keep tabs on which child celebrates which holiday at whose home and may engage in active *guilting* of their offspring, if simple invitations don't work. Guilting can focus on such things as the frequency of a child's presence at holiday celebrations, the desire to spend time with grandchildren if the family lives far away, or a comparison between one sibling and another. If you feel you are being unfairly compared to your siblings, let your parents know that you appreciate their eagerness to have you home. Let them know that you wish you could be there as often as your brothers/sisters are, but that you and your sibs are adults now and should no longer be compared to one another.

Gift Giving

Whether the gift is just a set of china gathering dust in the china hutch or a down payment for a new home, if one adult child seems to be getting more than her brothers or sisters from their parents, it is doubtful it will go unnoticed or unremarked upon. One woman, Janie, shared that her sister would total up the value and number of gifts they received from their parents growing up and still had a tendency to ask about the cost of the gifts Janie and her children received from their parents even today. Worries that they may be "left out of the will" can plague some rivalrous siblings. One woman shared that her own mother had found a unique solution to this area of potential rivalry down the road. Kaycee was given a significant monetary gift to open her own hair salon, and her brother and sister were going to receive the exact same amount separately through her mother's will, but the three of them would equally share in the remaining estate. Kaycee shared that her brother was competitive, but not really rivalrous anymore, and they all appreciated their mom's forethought.

More than one respondent thought that sibling rivalry would dissipate more quickly if parents did not continue to encourage it through their own behaviors. Depending on the family, sometimes the "winner" of the rivalry is the sibling that gives their parents the first grandchild. Actually, though, it seems that parents become rivals with in-laws in some families—especially when grandchildren and occasions for gift-giving arrive. One participant in the study shared, *"Ever since my son was born, it seems that each set of grandparents tries to outdo the other in bigger and more extravagant gifts! One set is all about designer clothing and the other is all about technology. My kid is only four, but they give him more than a fourteen-year-old would even dream of asking for. When I ask them to back down a little, they seem to take that as a challenge to do more."*

IF CHILDHOOD FEELINGS LINGER

There's a common plea that many older siblings make to their family followers: "Why can't you just grow up?" Although it may take more time than preferred, most children do grow up and learn how to get along with others. Sometimes, of course, feelings of resentment or envy between siblings persist far longer than they should. When one young woman, Kerry, was invited to describe any sibling rivalry from childhood, she knew exactly who her childhood rival had been: *"My younger brother. He remains the family's favorite. I am jealous of all the love he receives and the appreciation. On the other hand, I feel I am always ignored. Being his elder sister, I do care about him and try my best not to lose my temper, but he is a [jerk] and rude. So, I guess you can say that he is the reason for my unhappiness sometimes."*

While the tone of this individual's response might suggest you were hearing from a frustrated child, when your earliest memories are being called back to consciousness, you may feel like you have traveled back in time to a place where childhood feelings still burn white hot.

Kerry's vehement comment about her brother's status as "favorite" reflects what is likely the most enduring resentment between siblings—who got the most growing up. Although the intensity of childhood jealousy may evaporate over time, when individuals express negative feelings about sibs in adulthood, comments such as "she was always the favorite" or "he always gets what he wants from the parents" often bubble up. When these comments begin to pepper family get-togethers, perhaps it is time to address the negative attitudes directly. As an interesting counterpoint to the resentment of the family favorite, some sibs report that they disliked being the favored child—it had placed too much pressure on them to succeed in life, and they felt they were always the "stick" for their siblings and not the "carrot."

BURNING BRIDGES

Siblings may reach the point at which they believe there is no longer hope for enhanced sibling relationships. In some circumstances, the decision to cut ties or cut back on time together may be the best option. When sibling rivalry from childhood transforms into detrimental animosity in adulthood, decreasing the contact you have with antagonistic siblings is encouraged. Many individuals, oftentimes sisters, overestimate their ability to heal old wounds or to establish healthier relationships with those who have hurt them in the past. Acknowledging relational limits helps you establish a healthier relationship with yourself as well as allow your own old wounds to heal unimpeded. As an example, Terrie, a respondent in her fifties, shared that her commitment to improving the relationship with her brother dragged on much too long: "*My second oldest brother has a partner who I struggled with. Finally, about fifteen years ago, I let the relationship slip away . . . now I do not see them except at big family events like weddings and funerals. It was a relief when he was no longer a part of my life, and I now realize that he was a bully.*" It is not unusual for individuals to only recognize the dysfunctional aspects of a relationship when they are *outside* of the skewed system.

RE-SETTING THE FAMILY SYSTEM

It is easier for some people than others to recognize that letting go of the past can be the most expedient path for facilitating more rewarding sibling relationships in the present. Trying to "fix" a family problem by trying to "fix" a family member is seldom successful. Family roles are the product of years of practice. While the saying goes that it only takes twenty-one days to break a bad habit, role-based behaviors can be much more intractable given that most siblings would rather deny having problem behaviors than acquiesce to a sib's suggestion that they change. The most effective way to break the cycle of relentless rivalry might be to re-set the system. As family therapists acknowledge, the quickest way to enact change in a family system is for one member to change her own behavior. When the old pattern is interrupted by the switch-up in another member's response pattern, the entire system must shift in response to the change. Following are a few suggestions for re-setting your own family system:

- Bear in mind that every sibling has a different relationship with their parents; not only that, but your parents were different people every time a new sibling joined the family constellation.
- Siblings who always want to "one up" you even after reaching adulthood clearly have a limited repertoire of engagement strategies. Recognize that a little bit of tempering of your own interactions may nudge them out of the competitive rut they are stuck in.
- Acknowledge that competition is driven by childhood feelings of insecurity and a reaction to perceived scarcity. Some siblings will continue to keep the rivalry fueled well into adulthood. If your sibling tries this, keep the conversation moving forward and do not let yourself be antagonized into responding.
- If your sibling simply cannot move past the past, perhaps you should have a face-to-face, heart-to-heart discussion with her. Perhaps you could share your own perspectives on how you felt inferior to her growing up or ways in which you perceived her as getting more than her fair share when you were younger. Do this only to broaden her perspective, however, not to intensify the competition.
- It is said that adulthood turns rivalry into envy; if someone is envious of what you have accomplished, that speaks volumes about his own self-

esteem and satisfaction with his accomplishments in life. If a sib tries to denigrate your accomplishments as being less than his own, perhaps you can defuse the building tension by agreeing that you haven't accomplished all that your sib has in his life. Capitulating to his need to be validated can sometimes be the most expedient path.

- If all else fails, limit time with your rivalrous sibling and, if you must be in her company, just imagine her disparaging comments floating by like clouds in the sky.
- The best way to end a fight is to refuse to engage in one in the first place. Parents often tell their children, "It takes two to start a fight"; if you've had all the sibling squabbling you can handle for a lifetime, simply stand your ground and refuse to take a sibling's bait—no matter how tempting it might be to bite.

FINAL TAKEAWAY: Sibling rivalry is generally the most natural reaction to limited resources in childhood, but learning to collaborate for shared gains may be the most effective way to leverage siblings' power and position—as children and adults.

Chapter Six

Family Roles

Did you and your siblings grow up in an atmosphere of harmony and peace or did you grow up wishing that you were the "one and only" and the center of your family's attention? Were you "all for one and one for all" or were you always scheming to get the extra cookie, the last can of soda, or the biggest slice of pizza? Research suggests that how adults remember their childhood relationships with siblings influences the quality of their adult sibling relationships.[1]

Rivalry between siblings, as described in the previous chapter, arises quite naturally as a response to limited resources. Sibling rivalry has been defined as "competition between siblings for the love, affection, and attention of one or both parents or for other recognition or gain."[2] Unfortunately, some parents who should know better actually contribute to the competitive environment by pitting their children against one another—some surreptitiously and some more openly. When parents demonstrate outright favoritism of one child over another in childhood, the less favored child can be negatively affected by this differential treatment into adulthood.[3]

DO LABELS STICK?

Did your parents put a label on you or your siblings growing up? Did you get a nickname that reflected a particular attribute? In some families, the early descriptors can stick around for a sibling's lifetime. Some of the unique monikers shared by participants in this study included "the bully," "the quiet one," "the feisty one," "Tiger," and "the crybaby."

Although comparing children to one another is assumed to generate rivalry, unique labels may actually serve as a form of protection for
children's egos.[4] Rivalry arises when children first realize that siblings
exist who can lay claim on parental attention and support that they once
believed belonged solely to themselves. This understanding is a jolt of
reality that provides unwanted proof positive that a child is not unique to
the family. To handle the inner conflict that accompanies this unhappy
recognition, Freud proposed that children experience an identification
process with their siblings to take the rivalrous feelings down a notch.
By aligning with their siblings, children are able to somewhat resolve
the love-hate relationship that exists between them. When it's "two kids
against two parents," the odds have just increased significantly in terms
of kids getting what they want from their parents.

The process of differentiation, or dis-identification, has also been suggested as a process that children use to de-escalate rivalry. When parents
label one child "the smart one" or another "the athletic one," some might
judge the practice as harmful and limiting. However, a different perspective recognizes the value of differentiation that can generate unique
identities that allow children to blossom in the way that best suits their
temperaments and skill sets. If one child is considered to be "the athlete"
of the family and her sibling is considered "the artistic one," both children
might revel in the absence of pressure to compete against one another
and appreciate having their own uniqueness and specialness reaffirmed
by their parents. A twenty-something interviewee from China shared the
following reminiscence about family labels in childhood: "*My older sister
was described as hardheaded and talkative (Personality Spice); I was
described as a mediator and smart (Smarty Spice); and my younger sister
as athletic and beautiful (Sporty Spice).*" She confirmed that even during
recent challenging family times, she still considers her relationships with
her siblings as friendships in adulthood. The unique family identities still
play out, in some degree, in adulthood, as well.

The downside of parental labels is easily apparent if the labels are
used to denigrate a child. There is a big difference between being called
"the beauty" of the family and being called "the crybaby" of the group.
When asked about childhood labels in his family, a twenty-three-year-old
man had no trouble reeling them off. "*My older brother was always the
argumentative one. My sister was the one that always complained about*

things. Me? I was the favorite," he shared with a smile. He was also the youngest, which is often the child awarded the "favorite" status in many families. He went on to note that the family roles still seemed to be in play and that his brother had gone into law, which the interviewee felt had been a great choice to match his brother's continued passion for argument. The interviewee himself chose psychology—he said he wanted to understand why people behave the way they do. While no lasting damage was done by the less than positive labels his parents used, the descriptors created grooves into which the young adults still find themselves most comfortable in terms of family interactions.

DOES EVERY FAMILY HAVE A BLACK SHEEP?

When asked about childhood and adolescent roles or labels that were assigned to sibling sets, one of the most frequently noted labels shared by the interviewees for this book was the "black sheep of the family." It can be difficult to grow out of this wayward role, even if children succeed in growing out of the behaviors that originally led them to be placed in that role. Janice, now fifty-seven, described the persistent efforts of her sister to break free of the negative expectations held of her by their family:

My older sister was the black sheep of the family. Although she had substance abuse issues in her life and I didn't, we were always compared to each other. When my sister achieved sobriety, I think that as a family, we tended to keep her in a box, expecting that at every turn or blink that she would revert back. I think she was completely aware of it and that it made her struggles even harder. I've often felt that our family has always had to have someone to "kick around." My sister smoked and died from lung cancer at forty-seven. It was a secondary cancer and we never knew where it originated. I always felt that it must have been her heart because it hurt her so trying to prove to everyone that she could change when no one really believed it. Everyone talked about how we were all becoming closer during her short illness from diagnosis to death. In actuality, we have become so distant. And I now fill her shoes [in the family]—not because of any addiction issues, but because I think differently [than the rest of my siblings]; I'm the less successful in their eyes and the "artsy one."

CLASSIC DYSFUNCTIONAL FAMILY ROLES

In dysfunctional families, there are fairly well-defined roles that children grow to fit that serve to maintain the shape and functioning of the family's dysfunction. In fact, Virginia Satir developed comprehensive "cast lists" of the players in a dysfunctional family,[5, 6] which were later refined and outlined by Wegscheider.[7]

The roles that are typically exhibited by siblings within a dysfunctional family include the Hero, the Mascot, the Lost Child, and the Scapegoat.[8] These roles are taken on by the siblings as a way to keep the system afloat, and once accepted, it can be difficult for siblings to divest themselves of the associated traits and expectations. While each of the roles is an integral part of the unhealthy system, the Hero and the Mascot are sometimes considered positive roles and the Lost Child and Scapegoat are considered negative roles, in terms of the way each role contributes to the overall functioning of the family.[9]

As the roles are described below, mention is made of the place in the family birth order that is typically associated with a particular role. One young woman shared the following rundown on the roles that she and her siblings had taken on in their own dysfunctional childhood home: "*I was described as the outgoing one, or the black sheep, since I was often breaking the rules. My older brother was described as the perfect child since he was firstborn and also very successful. My younger brother was described at the jokester and the sensitive one, and the baby of the family.*" In the descriptions below, the connection between these organically assumed roles and the sibling personalities described in Satir's and Wegscheider's work can be seen. However, depending on the idiosyncratic functioning of a family, the roles may be divided across siblings in ways that have nothing to do with birth order.

The Hero

Just as every novel or movie needs a hero, so, too, do families in distress. Heroes are hardworking and responsible, and they take life very seriously. In television or pop literature—or even mythology—heroes are expected to carry the good guys or the underdogs to victory. Every team needs a hero, and dysfunctional families need heroes more than most.

The family Hero is often the oldest child, and it is on his shoulders that the family's success rests. Heroes work hard to provide the family some sense of stability and point of pride. Whether the Hero dedicates himself to academic achievement, athletic success, or a wage-earning role, he is committed to carrying the weight of the family alone. In some cases, the Hero also becomes something of an enabler, as his efforts may be strong enough to allow the IP (identified patient) to avoid getting well, as long as the family keeps bumping along. Heroes seldom engage in leisure activities or traditional age-appropriate activities. Heroes believe that their sacrifice, obedience, and responsibility will somehow generate a force that changes the family's prognosis and progress for good.[10]

Life is serious business for the family Heroes, and they typically turn into adults long before their eighteenth birthday. In adulthood, Heroes may be surprised to uncover their own festering resentment of their less productive siblings, although Heroes make it their mission to allow "children to be children." Heroes work hard to ensure siblings experience childhood as unaffected by family dysfunction as possible. Heroes tend to be limited in their emotional responses, as they equate emotionality with weakness and typically choose anger as their go-to emotional response. Perfectionism, rigidity, and difficulty compromising often mark the adult traits of the embattled Hero.[11] Heroes may carry lifelong guilt for being unable to save the family from its problems and often distance themselves from their families over time.

The Mascot

The babies of the family are the most likely ones to fill the role of the Mascot. This is the sibling who relies on humor and clowning around as a way to battle the family's stress-filled state. Family Mascots actively work to keep the family distracted from the serious issues at hand. Mascots may also play this role in other settings such as at school or on the job. Perceived as more vulnerable or less intellectually sophisticated than their siblings, Mascots may not be exposed to the true depth of the family's chaos. This veiling of the harsh truth is also due, in part, to the Mascot's typical place as the youngest of the family. Older siblings are in position to protect the Mascot from the family's dysfunction. Families may overtly or covertly collude to keep the Mascot from learning the family secrets or the story behind the current family (dys)functioning.

Confusion and chaos, however, seem to be the buzzwords to describe the life journey of Mascots. They are often driven by a fear of the unknown, anxiety, and insecurity. While the Hero of the family is quick to anger, the Mascot responds to stressful situations with humor or entertaining behaviors. While this response may be perceived as immature or out of touch, it is the only response that the family allows the Mascot to own, and it is actually an insightful response to a challenging problem.

As Mascots move into adulthood, they may have a difficult time letting go of a tendency to overuse humor as a primary coping mechanism. In adult relationships, they may receive criticism for their tendency to make a joke out of everything or their refusal to take life challenges as seriously as significant others would like. While the Hero never learns how to laugh at himself, the Mascot grows skillful at laughing at everything. The person behind the mask of the clown is often hiding his true feelings and vulnerabilities underneath. Unable to react to tragedy in an authentic manner, Mascots lack practice in acknowledging or expressing their true feelings in a manner congruent with the gravity of a situation.

The Scapegoat

As the name implies, a family scapegoat is the person to whom all the blame for all the trauma is typically shifted. The Scapegoat, often considered the "black sheep of the family," is expected to be as troublesome as the Hero is expected to be heroic. Blaming the Scapegoat (often the second-born child in larger families) for the dysfunction in the family allows the true cause of the problem to go disregarded and ignored. Families believe that if the Scapegoat is acting out and bringing shame to the family, the parents cannot be at fault.

Dysfunctional families need to find a safe target for blame, and Scapegoated children are lightning rods for negative attention. If the Scapegoat shaped up, family members might say, the whole family would be in much better shape. Unfortunately, the Scapegoat's misbehavior is an integral component of keeping the true source of dysfunction from being revealed. On the other hand, the Scapegoat's behavior might actually be the impetus that forces the family into counseling. If clinicians are skillful, they can recognize the twisted family dynamics and bring the deeper dysfunction into focus. Only then can real change to the system, called second-order change, begin. For example, let's assume that a Scapegoat's problem behavior is smoking in the school restroom. If the counselor is able to get the Scapegoat to stop smoking in the school restroom, a first-order change has occurred. The problem behavior stops and the Scapegoat gets in less trouble at school, but the still dysfunctional larger family system does not change at all. If the counselor is able to skillfully expose and address the dysfunction of the parents or the family system, and the problems are addressed by the family, a second-order change has occurred, and it is likely to be more lasting and effective in helping the overall system than simply changing the behavior of a single family member would be.[12] If the Scapegoat's misbehavior served to get the family into therapy, then the Scapegoat's problematic behavior was worth the trouble it created for him.

Over the years, Scapegoats may become family pariahs, regardless of the value they provide to the family. They often feel that their families never cared for them or about them as much as they cared for the other, less difficult children. Scapegoats hide their feelings, just as the Hero and Mascot do, to protect themselves. When being "bad" is the role that serves the "good" of the family, significant conflicts result, as well as enduring feelings of anger or rage toward the family and others. Right and wrong can get mixed up for Scapegoats, and they may have difficulty comprehending the difference. They are unable to recognize the impact of their poor choices even when academic, professional, and legal troubles are the result.

The Lost Child

Often the middle child, the Lost Child is consistently overlooked by everyone else in the family.[13] They do not draw attention to themselves and seldom feel moved to provide feedback to others. Lost Children may build their entire identities beyond their family systems. Virtual escape mechanisms that these sibs employ were once limited to television and books, but today's Lost Children may spend hours engaged in video games or other online pursuits.

The family takes little notice of the Lost Child's presence or absence. Depending on individual personality, the Lost Child might flourish beyond the home and develop an unexpectedly successful social persona and identity far different from what siblings or parents might see. Other Lost Children might be so negatively affected by their feelings of disconnection that they experience chronic loneliness or sadness that renders them unable to function in normal social settings due to the damage that results from a feeling of perpetual invisibility in the home.

Lost Children tend to have low expectations of others in terms of emotional investment in their well-being due to the lack of notice that is taken of them at home. They may also have a chronic hunger for authentic relationships but lack the skills necessary to pursue these. They may be frustrated extroverts who feel pressured to throttle their desire for social engagement in childhood but feel hopeless and confused as they try to build relationships in adulthood. While the metaphorical "cloak of invisibility" is an asset to them in their family-of-origin, some Lost Children may have insufficient confidence to remove the cloak in adulthood.

CAUTION: NOT EVERY FAMILY PRODUCES THE "CLASSIC FOUR"

Much rarer now than when this theory was developed is the family with three or more children, so not all of the "classic four" dysfunctional family roles are filled. The Hero, however, is one role that seems to be fairly consistent even in families with just two children. The oldest child seems to find himself naturally in the role of protector of the younger sibling. Depending on the relationship between siblings, the perfect foil for the Hero might be the Scapegoat or the Mascot. Siblings unconsciously take on the role that is most likely to keep the focus away from the problem-saturated parental unit. Discussing her childhood, the older of two sisters shared that her biggest regret about their childhood relationship was that "*[our] upbringing was awful, and I wish I could have protected her more.*" The role of protector was highlighted as she described the childhood sobriquets given the two sisters: "*I was the 'white sheep' of the family and 'Miss Perfect.' My sister was referred to as funny and mischievous.*" Figuring out the role you played in the family drama growing up can help you recognize the role you play in your adult relationships, as well.

HOW DO SIBLING RELATIONSHIPS AND ROLES CHANGE OVER THE YEARS?

During adulthood, significant transitions occur at a pace that is generally a little less rapid than during the first eighteen years of life. Geographical relocation, education, significant romantic relationships, childbirth, career developments, and parental or grandparental loss are examples of the types of events that shape and change individuals' lives and familial relationships through adulthood. There is a predictable pattern to the rise and fall of the closeness between siblings as adulthood is entered.

Sibling Relationships in Emerging Adulthood

As siblings enter adolescence and young adulthood, it is normal to turn toward one's peers for a sense of belonging instead of the family.[14] Having strong same-gender friendships, in fact, is more predictive of an emerging adult's psychological well-being than warm sibling relationships.[15] The same study revealed that strong sibling relationships do not necessarily compensate for a lack of close friendships. Clearly, the need for young adults to distance themselves from their families is a normal and expected development, although it may be challenging for younger sibs to accept the changes willingly.

During the emerging adult years, individuals undergo a great deal of transition interpersonally and intrapersonally, as well as in their educational and professional journeys and their physical and psychological location in their environments.[16] Only twenty-seven years old, a respondent named Walt was already able to recount the way in which normative transitions had influenced his own relationships with his brothers and sister, whose ages spanned a little more than a decade. Walt shared:

> *My younger-by-a-year brother moved to the other side of the country and I haven't seen him in four years. We used to fight a lot, but we also used to keep each other sane. We developed our own crazy sense of humor and together we were kind of a duo of loud, light-hearted fun and nonsense. I always thought he was going through something and would return, but it's been six years since he left and [he] has no interest in keeping up with me. That's pretty painful for me, because he was a big part of my life and who I am today.*
>
> *My sister became less involved with the family as she got into serious relationships. She became absorbed with whoever she was dating. Now she's married and has a kid on the way and has no interest in hanging out with me. She mostly just spends time with my mom and nobody else in the family.*
>
> *My youngest brother has changed from being the baby to being a high schooler. He looks up to me now and listens to my advice. It's more of a mentor relationship than anything else. Like a half-parent/half-brother sort*

*of thing, but it's also very rewarding to have someone to look up to me and
ask me for advice, which I'm not used to.*

Walt was able to succinctly, and unknowingly, highlight the typical ups-
and-downs and ins-and-outs of relatively healthy sibling relationships.

In a qualitative study of the sibling relationships during this developmental stage, Milevsky and Heerwagen noted that it is marked by
significant diversity across sibling sets, and its transitory nature is due to
the multiple influences of extra-familial and non-sibling-related events.[17]
During the first couple decades of life, an individual's family shapes her
experiences, opportunities, family allegiance, and loyalty. As the end of
the teenage years approaches and the striving for independence grows
much more compelling and achievable, siblings are able to use their own
attitudes and experiences about their brothers and sisters as a governor on
the amount of time and energy they choose to devote to these relationships. For example, when the relationship between siblings is saturated
with negative interactions that produce fear or dismissal of the sibling,
there is a lack of contact or cooperation between the dyad[18] that reflects a
lower investment of energy or time. Sibling relationship maintenance is
now a choice for young adults, no longer a compulsory requirement.

When asked about any regrets concerning their relationships with siblings, emerging adults often focused on the increasing distance between
them and their siblings. The search for autonomy and independence from
the nuclear family is necessarily accomplished independently. Some
brothers and sisters, though, long for a deeper sibling connection than
they now have. A philosophical and insightful Millennial revealed the
greatest conflict between her and her siblings, which reflected this growing maturity: *"Transitioning from a child's to an adult relationship, and
siblings accepting individual choices and lifestyles when growing up and
becoming less of a family unit. This can be the source of instability (the
old relationship patterns and personalities shift as one becomes an adult)
and conflict when the whole family meets up."* Another woman noted, *"I
wish we all lived closer so that we could have closer relationships. We
often go weeks to months without talking, and I think it would be easier
to work past that if we lived closer to each other."* She summed up the regrets that emerging adults might experience from the intertwined actions
of growing apart while growing up.

Sibling Relationships in Full-On Adulthood

In the middle adult years, siblings are much more focused on the activities and developments of their partners and children than on the lives of their siblings. One of the themes that appeared in regrets surrounding sibling relationships for individuals in their late twenties and thirties was a wish that they could be more involved in the lives of their siblings but that geographical distance was too much of an obstacle. Adults in their forties and fifties often wished for the same thing. While individuals' lives are certainly full during these years, many adults look back to childhood and acknowledge that their most significant sibling regret is that their youthful treatment of siblings left a lot to be desired. Harshness, bullying, disrespect, and shutting out siblings were frequently reported as behaviors that they now regretted and that they felt incapable of undoing in the present.

Mattie is the older of two sisters, and she greatly appreciates the friendship she and her sister enjoy. Describing changes over time in their relationship, Mattie offered, *"We fought often when we were younger. We became closer friends as young adults and have grown closer over the years into middle adulthood. My sister and I having so many shared memories and shared understanding of how we were raised has been special. We are able to understand each other in a way that no one else does. We also have enjoyed being a sounding board for one another when we face challenges in our marriages, friendships, and in difficulties with our children."* For Mattie, sisterhood is one of the most important roles she holds, and this relationship has become a significant social and emotional resource for her. Research suggests that sisters typically engage in more advice-giving and personal interaction than brothers or brother-sister dyads do. Women also report feeling closer to their siblings than their brothers do.[19] Mattie and her sister prioritized their relationship during adulthood, and this will be especially beneficial to them as they enter older adulthood.

Both sisters *and* brothers can be motivated to maintain lasting friendships. Bettina, who is in late middle adulthood, shared her own sibling success story of how she and her siblings continued to carve out time for one another through the years: *"The four of us as adults continued our relationships . . . getting together often. We raised our children to know each other even though I was living three hours away from our family home. I came home for birthday parties, baptisms, holidays . . . you name it! My siblings came to visit my family in the country. We loved spending time together. Lots of laughter!"* One of the middle children in a group of six siblings, Vivian also shared how her sibling relationships provided a strong sense of structure and connection for her deep into adulthood. As she confirmed, *"We mostly live near each other and have celebrated many birthdays, family events, and so on [over the years]. Recognizing that our family ties had limits but generally persisted feels reassuring. The existence of my siblings provides a sense of history and a base of support . . . There is an exception though . . . the friendship with my older sister is profound and the most important relationship in my life."*

Sibling Relationships in Older Adulthood

In older adulthood, the status of the sibling relationship can reflect a number of different circumstances; one factor is the early familial experiences of the siblings. For instance, if more than a decade separates the ages of two siblings, their relationship may have been more distant or apathetic from the start. Sibling relationships, like any relationship, tend to change over time just as the people within the relationship must change. However, the need for support increases over time, but the number of individuals around to provide emotional or instrumental support typically does not. As people age, their social circles tend to diminish in size.[20] Mortality and mobility are two significant factors that affect social support networks, and often it is sibling relationships that grow more precious as friendships and acquaintanceships move into the background of an older adult's social landscape.[21] This leads to an exploration of ways in which the sibling relationship might change in shape or purpose in late adulthood.

As siblings mature, the differences or distance can sometimes be bridged if the value of family grows in importance. Becky considers herself in older adulthood and is the youngest child in a very large family. She shared, *"I did not know my older siblings very well because being the youngest of eleven they had already left home when I was born. As I grew older I made a conscious effort to call them and drop in to visit, and we got to know each other better. I can call them anytime I need someone to talk to, and they listen and do not judge me."* The unconditional positive regard that is offered to her by her siblings is an example of the increased appreciation for family that can develop. Another woman expanded on the softening that occurs with time. As she summed up the changes she had experienced with her siblings as they have moved into their sixties and beyond: *"We have grown less judgmental and more understanding. Able to overlook differences and embrace family. More empathetic. Less need to be right."*

As touched on in the opening paragraph of this chapter, our earliest memories of our siblings and family life play a long-term role in our well-being. Positive childhood memories actually were found to decrease the feelings of loneliness that widowed older adults might experience.[22] When older adult participants in the study were asked to share their earliest memory of their siblings, the majority centered on a moment of casual play if they were the younger sibling and a time of teaching or caregiving if they were older. This suggests that positive memories, even if the contemporary relationship is not quite as satisfying as it might be, may provide a unique form of social support. Thus, encouraging siblings or older adult acquaintances to focus on the positive memories that they have of their early years can actually be health promoting.

CONCLUSION

Just as the parent-child relationship differs between each parent and child dyad in a family, sibling relationships can be just as variable. Gender can play a role in the depth or closeness of a relationship, as evidenced by the frequency of women respondents who expressed a longing for a sister when relationships with their brothers did not offer the closeness they felt that a same-gender sibling would offer. Age differences also play a role in the amount of shared time and shared interests that siblings enjoy. No family is ever completely predictable or an epitome of the ideal, but the positive qualities of warmth, support, and connection are commonly considered the gold standard of a healthy family and, fortunately, are achievable outcomes for many once they reach adulthood.

FINAL TAKEAWAY: Every role played within the family system has a purpose, but every sibling has the opportunity to ditch the typecasting in adulthood. Falling back into the "kid brother" role might happen when you and your adult sibs get together, but don't let a childhood role keep you from becoming top dog somewhere else.

Chapter Seven

Family Secrets

Almost every "normal" family has a secret or two that family members are expected to keep hidden away from public view. Secrets can span the range from the superficial to the truly traumatic. In an academic exploration of the construct of family secrets, it was suggested that the development of secrets happens at three separate levels: the *macro-level of culture*, the *meso-level of an individual family's dynamics*, and the *micro-level of the individual*.[1] Cultural assumptions and presumptions typically determine the content a family keeps hidden, and every family system develops its own unique culture that gives rise to the shape and strength of family boundaries. The way an individual responds to tacit or overt requests for secrecy determines what information is kept covert and what information is shared. In this chapter, we will focus on the specific topics of abuse, mental illness, addictions, and parental divorce. Suggestions for dealing with the family secret fallout are also provided. Remember that most families have a few secrets, but you and your siblings do not need to carry into adulthood any of the shame originally attached to the secret.

Some families have tacit rules in place regarding what can and cannot be shared with others. Some families speak openly about their secrets behind closed doors but forbid siblings to speak about these issues outside the home. Rare are the families that keep nothing hidden or suppressed. However, responding to the invitation to share her experiences with family secrets, Betty, a woman in her sixties, provided a refreshing response when she noted with relief, *"No [family secrets] for us; our family just let everything all hang out and we didn't care who know what about any of us."* While some secrets are relatively benign, some siblings grow up sharing secrets that are considered detrimental and distressing.

Miki, a sixty-four-year-old year old woman, responded to a question about family secrets with a response that likely echoes the sentiments of many: "*[There were] so many family secrets . . . it was the norm in the 1950s and 60s not to talk about such things—'don't air your dirty laundry in public!' Alcohol abuse, infidelity, and sexual abuse . . . I thought there was something wrong with me, because my family sure didn't look like others I saw . . . not knowing that what I saw was just the public face and not the reality that went on behind closed doors.*"

Once siblings have grown up and left the family home, they may finally feel able to safely broach the subjects that were forbidden in the home. Lin, who is now forty-eight, described her experience with opening up about family secrets from childhood: "*We had a lot of family secrets, dysfunction, abuse, and racism. We kept our family stories so wrapped tight that some of the neighbors I've been in contact with as an adult have been shocked. We do not talk about the past. We don't talk about my brother going to jail. We do not talk about the past at all. It is taboo. If I bring up anything, I am immediately [asked], 'Why do you keep hanging onto the past?'*" The loosening of the rules can bring a sense of relief but also open up discussions that are fertile ground for deep-seated and long unspoken resentment to take root and bear bitter fruit.

WHEN IT WAS NOT EXACTLY HOW
YOUR SIBLING REMEMBERS IT

If you and your sibling reflect on the most unsettling memories from your childhood, would your descriptions of the same event or period in time align completely? As children, we tend to function from a uniquely narrow and self-centered perception. When events occur within the family system, each person develops their own personal interpretation of what is happening. This may serve as a safety measure in some instances or simply reflect the limited lens through which a younger person can peer. As Jane, who is now sixty-one, disclosed about her own limited childhood perspective, "*I thought we had a* Leave It to Beaver *kind of life where we all had fun and got along. But the family was split by age into two basic sections and I was part of the younger. There was always some resentment on the part of the older children toward the younger of us, but I did not know . . . then.*"

In the counseling setting, one of the most valuable services that counselors provide is the validation of a client's story and experiences.[2] A counselor may be the first person to accept a client's version of his life as a truth. Counselors working with families and couples learn that it is rare for family members to share a single, uniform memory of a shared experience. Every family member will have their own version of the shared story, and a family therapist must use all of the stories shared to construct a multidimensional and multi-perspective understanding of the incident. Just as Fritz Perls, founder of Gestalt therapy, emphasized, the whole is more than the sum of its parts.[3] To fully appreciate just how different family accounts can be, counselors-in-training are encouraged to suspend their disbelief and simply allow the stories being recounted to meld together to form a unified, though not necessarily congruent, explanation of an event. Therapists and family members alike should use the medley of memories as the lens through which the family relationships are observed.

When a family is in therapy, however, there is the hope that a shared comprehension or acceptance of diverse perspectives is possible. For siblings who are struggling on their own to make sense of the past as well as to obtain validation of their experiences, they may be surprised that their brothers and sisters may not be in a position to contribute to this undertaking. One forty-five-year-old woman, Rose, expressed her disappointment in her siblings' diverging memories regarding the past and their family's secrets. In her response to a question about conflict between her and her siblings, she said, "*Disagreement between our childhood memories and how we are able to articulate these today. Some believe what happened should be buried in the past. Some argue it never happened, but without strong conviction.*" Rose summed up, "*There are some family secrets, but only secrets for some, not to all.*"

It can be difficult for the siblings who recall the trauma and distress from childhood to reconcile adult relationships with siblings who have intentionally forgotten or subconsciously blocked painful memories. While much controversy surrounds the issue of repressed memories of abuse, adults do show evidence of highly selective memories. Some siblings may possess highly specific memories of early family trauma whereas others in the same family may have effectively blocked the memory or unconsciously reframed, revised, or softened the memory to make it more tolerable. One woman angrily related, *"We suffered years of emotional, psychological, and physical abuse from my parents; [one of my two brothers] has wiped it from his memory and claims I am 'making trouble.'"* However, getting stuck in the past is not the same as making sense of the past. In some families, it can be beneficial to engage in co-construction of the family narrative in such a way that multiple viewpoints are honored, strengths are celebrated, and a positive outcome is sought or described. This type of co-created story is a central aspect of narrative therapy.[4]

More often than counselors might like, clients blame their current circumstances on poor parenting received as children and refuse to take responsibility for the present. While circumstances during their early years may have been less than optimal, and memories of trauma or poor treatment may be present, each client has the opportunity to reconstruct their childhood narrative into a success story of overcoming obstacles in their paths and re-creating healthier relationships and family boundaries.

If adult siblings can acknowledge that they share a painful family history that keeps them from fully engaging in the present, they can work together to create a new family narrative. Co-constructed family stories can facilitate healing from trauma and distress.[5] In the 1960s, the Milan school of family therapy was founded, and at its core was the goal of exposing the flawed functioning of family systems and helping members develop new ways of interacting with one another.[6] [7] It is only through the open acknowledgement of family conflicts or hidden agendas that new ways of relating can be developed. Through the sharing of each different player's experiences—behaviors, thoughts, and feelings—a more complete understanding, meaning-making, and sense-making of the past can be developed. As each sibling contributes to the narrative of the past event, the most salient aspects can be gathered into the meaning-making, while less central or extraneous aspects can be filtered out. While the goal of this type of experience is to move beyond feeling stuck in the past, validating the shared trauma or the singularly unique traumatic experiences of siblings can provide the impetus to move into the present. Being heard and being believed are often what clients seek most ardently from their clinicians. Hearing words along the lines of "No, you're not crazy" is a shared need among individuals who are wrestling with psychological, physical, or emotional distress.

Narrative Therapy: Writing a New Story for the Future

Returning to Rose and her experiences, she found that not every sibling can accept the truth of other siblings' memories, which forestalled authentic communication. Bridging this gap in perspectives is challenging. However, building new, future-oriented narratives on multiple perspectives of the past can be healing. An essential component of narrative therapy is the externalization of the presenting problem so that the client and her family can stop trying to figure out who to blame for the problem. Rose could develop a narrative in which she recognizes the unique positive qualities she possesses that gave her the power to survive the childhood trauma as well as she did, acknowledge that siblings may have used forgetting in order to survive, and use this fresh multidimensional perspective to take control of her own feelings and accept that other family members utilize different strengths to succeed in their own lives. Getting past shared trauma requires siblings to focus on the present and the future, not allow the weight of the past to continue to drag them back to a place where they had little control and little choice.

CHILDHOOD ABUSE—AN ALL OR NONE PROPOSITION?

Is there a predictability to the choice of a victim of child abuse within a family system? While it has been hypothesized that the child who has become the family "scapegoat" exhibits certain characteristics leading her to be singled out for abuse, research suggests otherwise.[8] However, it does appear that older children are more likely to be singled out for sexual or physical abuse. It also appears that the domestic abuse of children is an all or nothing proposition. In Hamilton-Giachritsis and Browne's analysis of four hundred families, it turned out that it was more likely that a single scapegoat or all of the children in the family was victimized; seldom were there cases of only a subset of children being victimized.[9] The dynamics of every family may be different, but the damage done by maltreatment has a remarkably singular power to affect adult relationships for these children.

The effects of growing up in an abusive home can be long lasting, as one woman shared, *"There was abuse in our family. Fear and shame has caused a rift between myself and my siblings. Although my eldest sister cared for me when I was younger, she then abandoned me when I was nine. We were able to grow close again, but her husband and I do not see eye to eye now and I feel estranged from my sister. Later in life, [my brother and I] tried to reconnect; however, a deep sense of brokenness between all of our family members has kept a wedge between us. A high level of mistrust is also present."*

The high level of mistrust described by this individual precludes the straightforward development of healthier relationships in adulthood. Letting go of early learning and being courageous enough to break with past patterns of engagement are formidable goals for some. In one study, it was reported that childhood abuse or trauma predicts later adult victimization.[10] In fact, according to Cloitre and colleagues,[11] the majority of women who report that they have experienced prior abuse as a child or in adulthood have experienced both forms of abuse. If you are fortunate to have never experienced childhood trauma, bear in mind that if you are baffled by a friend or sibling who consistently makes poor relationship choices, it may be that he or she was subjected to abuse growing up and these choices may reflect familiarity with the dynamics of relationship abuse, not necessarily a conscious or intentional choice for self-sabotage.

Siblings as Fellow Victims, Abusers, or Both?

Children learn by example, and when parents model the targeting of a specific child as a scapegoat, siblings may follow suit. Sadly, being victimized by parents or siblings has been found as a predictor of violence in later relationships, including romantic relationships.[12] When there is parental violence in a family, there is also more likely to be sibling abuse.[13] One woman, Cindy, shared the following narrative in which she describes the challenge of coming to terms with the realization that her fellow victim was also one of her own tormentors:

[My sister and I] have both been abused in our childhoods. Not sexually; mostly, and thoroughly, emotionally and also to a much lesser extent physically. I have always seen the both of us as victims, and of course we both are. But it is now, when I am fifty-one years old, that I am beginning to realize that my sister has actually been one of my abusers. This is hard for me to accept. And of course "the world" is not very open to that; it is hard to explain that you feel a victim of abuse not by your mother or father, but your sister.

The stories shared by interviewees who suffered significant abuse at the hands of their parents provide evidence that compromised mental health plays a role in abuse. In addition to the toll that mental illness and its expressions take on families, when it includes child abuse, increased opportunities for sibling conflict exist, as well. In one family, adult siblings still disagree regarding whether mental illness justified what Manda described as criminal behavior:

> *[My older sister] believes mom was mentally ill to treat us so bad. I can believe that, but still mom's acts were criminal and no child deserves that and people have dark and light sides; whether or not she was mentally ill, what she did to us was wrong. My sister does not want to go beyond her mental illness comment because that would mean she would have to show her wounds and she does not want to acknowledge she has them. So our current relationship is on the superficial level. My sisters and I fought a lot as children. I think the lack of parental love and parental negligence caused chaos. I am not sure if this would be considered rivalry as much as "monkey see, monkey do" reality. Mom beat us senseless and we beat each other the same.*

Many of us grow up fearful of emulating the behaviors of our parents—as teenagers and young adults, most cringe if they hear the words, "You're just like your father" or "You're just like your mother." When parental behaviors are symptoms of mental illness, those words are even more unwelcome. For some people, growing up with siblings in the home can provide an intimate and much-needed support group, of sorts. Manda's story illustrated the disappointing way in which she and her sisters tried to make sense of their shared upbringing. For Manda, her sisters had joined her mother as benchmarks for how she did not want to be perceived. Mental illness can compromise parents' abilities to parent their offspring, and their deficits can continue to influence future generations.

A PARENT'S MENTAL ILLNESS

Some people may jokingly proclaim, *"Here at our house, we don't hide our crazy—we sit it out on the front porch and offer it a sweet tea."* In many families, however, people work hard to cover up and cover for members who are mentally ill. There is a pervasive fear that a single family member's weakness will affect how all members of a family are perceived by outsiders. Unfortunately, this fear does not necessarily qualify as an irrational fear.[14] There is a saying that is often found on the walls of pediatrician's offices and day-care centers that reminds parents that "a child learns what he lives." Dysfunctional family members have the power to affect the family system in such a way that dysfunction becomes the new normal, and relationships and behaviors reflect the skewed functioning.

When asking research participants about family secrets, responses provided strong evidence that the stigma associated with mental illness is still deeply embedded in our culture. Not only does the stigma lead to too many family secrets,[15] but it also results in too few people seeking and receiving mental health care. This is especially true in such groups as military families,[16] minority communities,[17] and other disadvantaged groups.[18] When a parent suffers from mental illness, children have a limited number of potential pathways for coping with the situation.

Some children grow up believing that the symptoms of mental illness that are evidenced in erratic and irrational parental behavior are "normal," if they have no easily accessible external reference points. Other children, who are able to spend time in homes in which parents function well and the family hierarchy is in place in a typical structure, may recognize that their family is not as "normal" as other families and may seek out ways to spend time at the homes of their friends. Some children may take on the behaviors and beliefs of their psychologically distressed parents and act out the symptoms themselves. In families where the parents' symptoms are the glue that holds the family together, children will enable the mentally ill parent and do what is necessary to keep the flawed system staggering forward. Leaving home as soon as possible is a goal that some children work hard to achieve—they can see what "normal" is and what it is not, and they are desperate to escape the unhealthy, unbalanced family system in which they feel trapped.

Even in adulthood, discussing mental illness in the family can be difficult. Some siblings would prefer to remain quiet about a loved one's diagnosis, while others may feel the need to share their experiences with one another and finally talk openly about a forbidden topic. Suggestions for addressing this topic include:

- Invite your siblings to share their own childhood autobiography and share your own.
- Talking about your own perspective, and listening to another's, may allow siblings to piece together the family story more clearly.
- Sharing with one another may help each sibling make sense of the overall "whole" of the person who was suffering from mental illness.
- Research the relevant diagnoses and share your knowledge with your siblings. Being able to provide a fact-based explanation for the distressing behaviors may allow you to forgive your parent if you are still "blaming the patient" for the symptoms of the diagnosis.
- Opening up your relationship with siblings to allow open discussion of mental illness may provide the supportive environment for discussing any fears you and your siblings might have of developing the same diagnosis yourselves or any fears related to the genetic transmission of the illness.
- If your parent is still alive and still suffering from the same or a related illness, sharing knowledge with your siblings may help each of you establish a more satisfying relationship with that parent.
- Remind yourself that the stigma of mental illness is only reinforced if you and others choose to avoid discussion of this form of illness. By giving others permission to discuss the incidence and influence of mental illness in families, you are helping yourself and others to find new strategies for coping with the past and preparing, potentially, for the future.
- Trying to pretend a parent's mental illness does not exist or did not affect your childhood, when you bear the psychological and emotional scars yourself and in relationships, will not take away the power of the past to negatively affect your future.

Narcissistic Parents: A Special Side Note

While any form of untreated mental illness can permanently alter the functional dynamics of a family, perhaps having parents who are suffering from narcissism may create one of the most intractable and unhealthy forms of engagement. This is related to the symptoms of narcissism and the need of narcissists to view children as extensions of themselves,[19] in the worst way. While most parents take pride in their children's accomplishments and live a little vicariously through their children, narcissists basically feed on their children's successes. They identify so strongly with their children that they cannot tolerate any show of failure or weakness in their children, as this would be perceived as a personal failing of the parent, a situation that narcissists cannot tolerate emotionally. Children are not allowed to develop their own identity beyond being an extension of their controlling narcissistic parents. Narcissistic parents punish their children for asserting independence and use shame and humiliation as tools to control them. The resulting trauma can disrupt an individual's relational skill set well into adulthood.[20]

If you and your siblings were raised by a narcissistic parent, there is a laundry list of possible types of damage done.[21] The list includes such seemingly paradoxical traits of feeling hatred toward the narcissistic parent while parroting the parent's words and views. Parents keep children from individuating, forcing children to wrestle against their own deep desire to form an independent identity. As an adult, you may experience diminished self-esteem and a pervasive, but unfounded, sense of shame.[22] One woman, Susan, who was interviewed for this book shared that she and her sister have "split the load" in terms of how they played into their mother's narcissistic personality, and this is responsible for the most significant conflict between the two of them: *"Arguing over our narcissistic mother [is the greatest challenge], as I choose to cut Mother from my life completely and my sister feels guilted into continuing to care for her."* This is one example of what is a seemingly abnormal response to a parent, but a normal development within narcissist-parented families, as narcissists seek to ensure that siblings are triangulated into unhealthy alliances with the parent. There is generally the Perfect Child, such as Susan's sister described above, and the Scapegoat, who is the child who can do nothing right in the parent's eyes and who likely alienates herself from the narcissist in adulthood. At face value, alienation of a parent who is suffering from a mental illness may seem unnecessarily harsh; however, adult children who do not end the narcissistic cycle through direct action are the ones most likely to perpetuate the detrimental patterns in their own adult relationships.

If you and your siblings believe that your parent was clinically narcissistic, and you feel ready to let go of the undeserved emotional burden that you carry from your childhood, here are a few suggestions for putting the past behind you:

- A good first step is acknowledging the loss you experienced through the absence of what should have been a caring and supportive parent. Parental loss is difficult at any age, but when the loss occurs early in life, it can be especially heart wrenching to process.
- Allow yourself and your siblings a mourning period.
- You and your siblings should remind one another that none of you were to blame for the problem. Young children often volunteer to carry the blame for a family's dysfunction. As an adult, it is time to let go of any falsely placed guilt.
- Acknowledge the intrinsic strength and good of one another.
- Use the positive developments within the sibling relationship as a way to receive the empathy and unconditional regard that your parent was unable to offer to you as children.

Anecdotes of emotional fragility or mental illness in the family also included reports of unacknowledged or untreated depression, anxiety, bipolar disorder, paranoia, schizophrenia, and one of the most prevalent disorders, substance abuse. In the following section, the focus shifts specifically to addiction.

PARENTS' ADDICTIONS

According to the National Association for Adult Children of Alcoholics (NAACOA), there are twenty-eight million individuals in the United States who are children of alcoholics and seventeen million of those are adult children of alcoholics (ACOAs). Unfortunately, alcohol and drug abuse are fraught with stigma, and families may go to great lengths to avoid openly admitting that a parent is suffering from addiction. As forty-seven-year-old Melanie shared, *"Our family secret is that Mom and Dad used drugs . . . they would use in front of us kids and told us repeatedly not to tell anyone."* Double standards tend to exist between siblings based on age, gender, maturity level, and so on; privileges also differ for parents and children. However, when parents openly engage in illegal or socially unaccepted activities, it can throw an entire family and a child's sense of right and wrong out of balance.

When addiction takes hold of a family, it is almost impossible for children in the family to grow up feeling normal and unscathed. The feeling of being different arises early for children and, if not challenged, can cast its shadow for years. The alcoholism-related themes that surfaced for interviewees for this study included the parentification of children, as they must take on age-inappropriate caretaking responsibilities; isolation, as families with alcoholics are reticent to allow others into the residence or family network; reactive behaviors, as children grow up in a home in which there is a blurring between right and wrong; and, frequently, abusive parenting practices, whether abuse was verbal, emotional, physical, sexual, or took any other form.

Addiction fallout knows no borders and leaves no demographic group untouched.[23] In one qualitative study, four basic themes were found to describe the experience: 1) losing family, 2) life with holding a bomb, 3) my life ruined, and 4) being bound. Each theme captures the power that a parent's addiction holds on the *entire* family, not just the active addict.

Gaye, a fifty-three-year-old woman who was the oldest of eight siblings, all girls, shared her story of how parental alcoholism negatively affected the entire family system—especially Gaye herself. She began by sharing that the biggest family secrets in her large family were "*alcoholism and physical abuse*." She went on to explain that not even all of her sisters were aware of the secrets: "*My younger sisters have no recollection, the first four children remember, the second four did not have that same experience and do not believe the first four.*" The lack of a shared family narrative can generate cognitive dissonance for those who know the truth but are not believed.

Continuing to share the damage done by the family secrets, Gaye noted, "*I was physically abusive to my younger siblings . . . I have had absolutely no contact with any of my siblings except my older sister since 2010.*" Not only were her parents' addictions and abuse a concern to her well-being, but Gaye admitted that she also participated in these behaviors. Gaye summed up, "*The outcome [of the family's dysfunction] for me, through twenty years of therapy, is to know to stay away from them. The truth will never be known or accepted because each of us experienced the abuse differently—no one trusts or believes each other.*"

There are many books, websites, and open online forums for individuals who grew up in alcoholic households. The website for the Adult Children of Alcoholics World Service Organization (www.adultchildren.org) provides multiple resources and suggested sites for individuals struggling with the residual effects of growing up in this type of dysfunctional household. Support group meeting information is also available online. Much like Al-Anon and Alcoholics Anonymous, ACOA offers lists of Twelve Steps, Twelve Beliefs, and Twelve Concepts. Over a dozen characteristics are typically included in the list to describe the now-adult children who grew up with alcoholic or addicted parents. Included in the popular literature are traits such as a strong need for approval, being fearful of others' anger or criticism, significantly low self-esteem, and feeling driven by the need for chaos to feel comfortable.[24]

The presence of these and other associated traits can influence the sibling relationship into adulthood. In a meta-analysis of the literature exploring the effects of growing up with addicted parents, evidence does suggest that there are several specific negative outcomes that can be attributed to this type of upbringing.[25] These include substance abuse, antisocial behavior or under-controlled behavior, depression, anxiety, low self-esteem, family relationship difficulties, and distress or maladjustment in general. It has been suggested that these negative outcomes may well be a product of an interrupted or foreshortened development of stress management skills.[26]

There is evidence of several protective factors that might mitigate the damage of growing up with alcoholic caregivers.[27] Having a positive relationship with the non-using parent, if available, has a protective effect, as do high levels of academic and cognitive development. Resilience, too, is associated with avoiding some of the grimmer outcomes, and it is also associated with higher levels of self-esteem. If you and your siblings are ACOAs, working to enhance one another's self-esteem may help all of you develop resilience that may have not been nurtured as you grew up.

PARENTAL DIVORCE

Although contemporary statistics suggest that divorce is no longer an unexpected or uncommon family turning point, the acknowledged dissolution of a marriage may have packed a powerful punch during your childhood years. Mary, who is now thirty-nine, recounted just how confidential she and her siblings had to keep the state of their parents' marriage. She shared, *"[Our parents] usually didn't like us kids to say things related with life at home to anyone outside. Seems reasonable at certain points of my life, but today I think that [my parents] were afraid that people knew they weren't a perfect couple. They still cannot deal with that. They have lived for years in the same house but separate rooms and almost no talk, besides some hard discussions sometimes, but never really [admitted] their separation."*

Siblings may be drawn closer together when parents separate or divorce, and some sibs can be great supports for one another.[28] In one study, young adult sisters described an increased closeness with their brothers and sisters that they attributed to their parents' divorce.[29] In other families, the divorce may negatively affect sibling relationships in enduring ways. Cathy, now fifty-one, described the most significant event that she and her siblings faced: *"The divorce of my parents when we were nine, eleven, and thirteen. It caused each of us to live separately on an emotional level after that. We were no longer a cohesive unit. This has affected our relationship to one another to this day. The death of our mother when we were in our twenties exacerbated the situation."*

The dynamics of the family system can shift after a divorce. Enmity between parents may disrupt the parental hierarchy, and children may gain an inappropriate amount of power in the family structure. Research has indicated that the more conflict there is between parents, the greater the amount of conflict there will be between siblings, even into adulthood.[30] If conflict ravaged your family-of-origin, recognizing that the conflict modeled for you and your siblings as children is not the only option for relational engagement can help you and your siblings build a healthier adult relationship with one another. Finding a new way to relate to siblings with whom you have difficult relationships can provide you with a larger network of support, which is something that only increases in value over time. Being patient and empathetic and offering unconditional positive regard can lay the foundation for enhanced sibling relationships.

AND STILL OTHER SECRETS?

Other secrets that may be hidden in a family's legacy include the existence of half-siblings, parental infidelities, abortions, sexual orientation, adoption status of a child, legal wrongdoings, and incarceration, to name a few. Oftentimes it is not the nature of the secret, but the mere presence of a secret, that continues to have a hold on the family. Whispers or meaningful side glances at family gatherings between adult siblings might be first timid steps toward demystification and resolution of the family secret. Open discussions and honesty among the family members who are ready can do a lot to begin the healing process. Sometimes, simply the disclosure of secrets from the past can contribute to the resolution of the distress or disquiet they gave rise to.

CONCLUSION

This chapter opened with Betty's story of her "open book" family juxtaposed against Miki's litany of secrets that she and her family were required to keep hidden. As an adult, Miki now recognized that secrets were burdens that served no useful purpose and, instead, could cause significant distress. Being required to keep so many family secrets throughout her early years influenced Miki to break a pattern of secret-keeping that only served to do more harm than good. *"Today I refuse to keep secrets ever, and freely share my childhood history. No one should ever feel or believe that abuse only happened to them."* Her conclusion is right on target. If you have been carrying a secret that has become too heavy to carry alone, share with those who support you and have concern for your well-being. Siblings who wear the same shackles are an excellent choice—childhood secrets should be stripped of their power to cause harm for adults. If your siblings are not ready to bring shared secrets into the present, trusted friends and professional counselors are excellent places to turn.

FINAL TAKEAWAY: Family secrets that continue to weigh you down in adulthood are probably secrets not worth keeping. If you don't feel comfortable sharing with another family member, partner, or close friend, consider speaking with a counselor or writing it down and letting it go.

Chapter Eight

Taboo Topics

Growing up, children learn how to approach conversational topics based on modeling by their parents. Unfortunately for some children, parents' refusal to openly speak about some topics leaves them unable to ask questions about important issues. In other families, parents' perspectives about some topics may be the only perspective accepted, so children grow up believing that there is only one way to address a particular topic. This chapter's title refers to a few specific topics that many people have a hard time learning how to discuss openly or intelligently with others due to the secrecy or, potentially, deceit that surrounds them.

The topics described in this chapter can set off metaphorical fireworks and drive wedges between people who hold differing opinions. The four broad categories are sex, politics, religion, and money. Within this chapter, the majority of the focus will be on the challenges related to issues surrounding sex, including sibling incest trauma. The chapter opens, however, with discussion of politics, religion, and money. While many children are trained not to talk about these in public, even conversations between adult siblings are not always easy, productive, or possible.

POLITICS

Political beliefs are a flash-point topic for some families, and there can be a "political ideology lineage" that is expected to be accepted by each successive generation. Political party membership is actually expected to be transmitted from one generation to another.[1] From as far back as the 1960s, researchers have explored the family transmission of political allegiance between generations.[2] Breaking with family political tradition can create deep divides between parents and children; recently, however, the willingness to break free from the past has strengthened.

As the United States has grown more deeply entrenched in a system in which political parties diverge so widely, individuals' party affiliation and political leanings have become a stronger aspect of personal and social identity for many.[3] In terms of political affiliation, the Millennial generation is the largest group of Democratic-leaning individuals that the United States has ever seen.[4] Increasingly, political outcomes affect personal lives in intimately intricate ways that stretch from personal choices about our romantic or sexual partners to decisions regarding where we choose to live or work.[5] With the move toward socializing young adults to "Rock the Vote"—the MTV-sponsored grassroots movement to encourage young adults to register and to vote—it appears that political socialization is no longer confined to the private household, and efforts to increase trust in young voters are expanding.[6]

RELIGION

Family faith traditions are a rich part of many people's lives and can be one of the pillars of a family's strength and support. Conversely, depending on the family and the faith tradition, religion can be the chasm over which no sibling is safely able to step. Even though the country appears to be decreasingly engaged in religious activities, faith differences can shake a family's foundation to the core.[7] Recounting the ways in which diverse religious beliefs and practices had negatively influenced her family, one woman, Bari, shared, *"Our maladjusted childhood caused alienation between family members. The Jehovah's Witnesses religion had an even more divisive affect between us, and our mother's passing brought irreparable damage due to conflicts."* Bari went on to note that the most enduring conflicts between her and her siblings were rooted in these faith-based differences: *"Estrangement due to different approaches, life decisions, and values [continue to cause conflict]. One sister regularly reaches out and shows kindness to everyone but won't eat a meal with us due to her being a Jehovah's Witness. I am very discriminating in choosing my close circle of friends. My friends are my family, and I choose those who offer uncon-*

ditional love and support, are open minded and nonjudgmental, positive,
live life to the fullest, display honesty and integrity, have a purpose and a
solid work ethic, and place value on people over tangible things."

Bari had learned early that how people live, not the beliefs they es-
pouse, is what matters most to her for long-term healthy relationships.
Other siblings may have less of a global perspective on values but learn
to accept one another's faith-based differences in adulthood, as well.
People may change over time, but sibling relationships endure; it's important to make the allowances and choices that will serve the relationship over the long term.

MONEY MAKES AND BREAKS FAMILIES

Traditionally, parents carry hopes that their children will fare better finan-
cially than they have in life, although children often are not fully aware of
how well or how poorly their parents have done.[8] Regardless of the vague
hopes for their children that parents hold, the discussion of financial sol-
vency and financial circumstances within the family remain a taboo topic
for most.[9] However, money as a metaphor within a family can speak volumes about power and control, which may reflect the historically situated
gender roles in U.S. culture.[10] In many traditional families, the father or
other male head-of-household is expected to hold the power and position
as head-of-household. As the colloquially termed "breadwinner" of the
family, it is assumed that he will hold the power to manage the finances
and dole out funds to family members as he sees fit. This can create a
sense of ambiguity for his partner and children, as income and available
financial resources also contribute to personal identity.[11]

Some families keep the conversation regarding financial means and any
related stressors so covert that children may be completely unaware of the
family's financial status.[12] Some parents believe that avoiding the topic of
money may spare children worry if parental anxiety surrounds financial
means. Other families may use financial control as a means of power-
broking beyond what an individual family role would inherently allow.
Hidden assets may also serve as tools of covert power. One respondent,
Rita, shared that her now sixty-year-old brother continues to struggle as
he tries to manage his finances, but her father surreptitiously bails him

out as needed—to keep her brother from reflecting poorly on his father. The siblings' father was "old world" in his ways, and money was a taboo subject that the son never learned how to address directly or handle well. For both the father and son, money was a tool used to keep them "*looking successful*," according to Rita.

If a sibling from an average family "makes it big," this can provoke surprisingly diverse sibling reactions. Responses may include outright jealousy, genuine happiness, or anything in between. Feelings about others' financial status may be held tightly in check when families raise children to believe that money and income should not be openly discussed. For the more successful sibling, there may be delight in her own financial well-being, but she may also harbor fear that members of their family-of-origin might express a desire for sharing her wealth or ask for loans that are unlikely to be repaid. The successful sibling might also experience a sense of guilt at how well she has done if the rest of the family is still living at a socioeconomic level well below what she has achieved.

In some families, money is viewed as a measure of self-worth, and the sibling with the heftiest bank account might also be the one with the heftiest ego. Fairly, a woman in her forties, shared an anecdote about an exchange between her and her brother decades ago. As a new mother who had decided to resign from her job to raise her daughter, Fairly was remonstrated for the decision by Tom, her older brother. Tom counseled his sister, "*Remember, Fairly, a measure of a man's worth is his paycheck.*" Fairly was unable to articulate a calm, cool, or collected response and, instead, angrily defended her decision to her brother. Tom just smiled and let his little sister roll through her diatribe. Fairly, however, enjoyed a little "turnabout as fair play" some years later when her brother's employer gave him the choice of relocating to Spain or being let go. Tom chose to remain in the United States and seek a new position. Fairly made sure she got in the dig: "*Well, Tom, if the measure of your worth is your paycheck, it looks like your stock has fallen considerably.*"

SEX AND SEXUALITY

For parents, it can be difficult as they witness their children grow into sexually mature adolescents and young adults. The siblings of sexually active teens may also experience a tightening of their own freedom as parents attempt to hold back the maturation of their younger children. A woman in her late thirties, Amina, shared that her family's silence on sexuality and all related topics created unexpected difficulties. She related that the fallout from her older sister's teenage pregnancy had surprisingly intense negative repercussions for her: *"I was four years younger than my sister, who became pregnant at the age of seventeen. That, alone, taught me about teen pregnancy, birth control, divorce, and tragedy. My father assigned the shame of my sister's pregnancy, to me . . . along with many other people in this small town. Actually, I was a virgin until quite late in my life. Guess they were wrong. How does a thirteen-year-old girl cope with this? It was awful. Judgment, without facts, should be a crime. I married twice, both to abusive men."* Amina considered her own faulty judgment to be a result of her parents' treatment of her as teen.

Diverse Sexual Orientations

In some families, there are still strong expectations that children will grow up to be monogamous heterosexuals who keep bedroom conversations hidden behind closed bedroom doors. In the "coming out" stories of adult lesbians and gay men, they often share that their families recognized their sexual orientation before they, themselves, recognized they were gay. Today, most emerging adults are accepting of non-heterosexual identities. A recent Pew Research poll indicated that overall acceptance of gay marriage had increased over the last fifteen years.[13] In 2001, 57 percent of respondents reported being against gay marriage and 35 percent were in favor of it. In spring of 2016, the pendulum had swung significantly—55 percent of respondents were now in favor of gay marriage and 37 percent were against it. Unfortunately, there are still families in which minority sexual identities must be kept hidden from others. One respondent shared that she was still trying to figure out how to effectively communicate with her sister who is involved in a lesbian relationship regarding her sister's identity and romantic relationships. Never being able to see difficult conversations modeled as a child results in long-term barriers to these types of conversations with family members later on. Even when the conversation is difficult to manage, it is important to offer support to siblings and to seek support from siblings when broaching topics that were once cloaked in secrecy.

When Prior Sexual Abuse Is Revealed

Secrecy surrounds sibling sexual abuse, and perpetrator threats to the victim and the inherent shame associated with abuse, especially sexual, can keep the secret hidden for decades. In spite of the devastating consequences of silence, many victims fail to acknowledge their abuse and may feel that they were complicit in their victimization.[14] Research also indicates that the quality of the response of the family or other trusted persons to a victim's disclosure has a strong influence on the overall effect of the victimization on the discloser; in fact, the severity and duration of the abuse can be less of a factor in predicting psychological and emotional fallout than the response of those to whom the victim discloses.[15] Thus, if a sibling trusts you with the details of prior abuse, the tone and content of your response matter greatly—even if the abuse occurred decades ago. The weight of such a secret can be burdensome for the victim, and when a decision is made to disclose, your support can be a significant component of the victim's healing process.

In psychotherapy settings, clients may begin their stories with disclaimers, such as *"It wasn't really a big deal, but . . ."* Or *"It was so long ago that I know it doesn't matter now, but . . ."* A victim's self-blame and feelings of complicity and mutuality often shape an individual's perspective of the past abuse. Making the decision to acknowledge the suffering experienced at the hands of another takes courage and a willingness to risk not being believed by others. It is a risk worth taking. Secrets carry hefty emotional and psychological weight, and by opening up to a caring helping professional, supportive friends, or supportive family members, the weight of the secret loses some of its power to hold you down. While some people relate that their experience "could have been worse" or "only happened once," the fact that abuse occurred and the incident still causes distress for the victim gives evidence that "just once" is once too many. For some victims, validation by others is what is most needed to begin the process of moving through the hurt. Although the scope of this book does not permit a deeper look at treating the residual effects of sexual abuse, the following books are a small sampling of many on the market that may be helpful in this journey:

- *The Sexual Health Journey: A Guide for Survivors of Sexual Abuse* (3rd ed.), by Wendy Maltz

- *The Courage to Heal: A Guide for Women Survivors of Child Sexual Abuse,* by Ellen Bass and Laura Davis
- *Victims No Longer: The Classic Guide for Men Recovering from Sexual Child Abuse,* by Mike Lew

Tips on Responding to a Sibling's Disclosure of Past Abuse

The interviewees who had experienced abuse as children shared that the pain was multiplied in adulthood when their disclosure of past abuse was disbelieved, trivialized, or minimized. When a sibling is placing trust in you to share what may be a decades-old secret, it is important to listen to her story with empathy and nonjudgment. As noted earlier, child victims of sibling sexual abuse may hold themselves to blame for the abuse regardless of how powerless they were to stop it from happening or to reveal it to adults. Willingness to open up about the past should be acknowledged for the courage that it shows. Shame keeps many people from speaking out about abuse, and victims who were coerced into silence through the threat of harm may still carry a fear of retaliation even as adults. If a sibling is ready to speak about an incidence of abuse, offer the following to your sib to help support the healing process:

- Remain open to a sibling's personal perspective and experience. Just because your own early interactions with the perpetrator of your sibling's abuse were not similar does not mean that the abuse of your sibling did not happen as he remembers it.
- Validate your sibling's story by confirming that you believe her account of what happened. If she's not yet ready or able to seek professional counseling, a sibling's validation of her story can be of great value in the present.
- Be supportive and, if appropriate, offer to help your sibling to locate community resources such as counseling or support groups for survivors of sexual abuse.
- Remind your sibling that the abuse was not his fault; children who are abused are targeted for their vulnerability, and it is the fault of the abuser, not the child, regardless of what the perpetrator tried to convince the victim to believe.

- Recognize that no one's reaction or response to abuse and trauma is the same as another's. If you and your sibling were both victims, don't expect her experiences of distress or healing to mirror your own.

Several books are available for partners of sexual abuse survivors that are useful resources for increasing understanding and support between members of a couple. These include *Allies in Healing: When the Person You Love was Sexually Abused as a Child*, by Laura Davis, and *When a Man You Love Was Abused: A Woman's Guide to Helping Him Overcome Childhood Sexual Molestation*, by Cecil Murphey.

Statistics indicate that sibling sexual abuse is more common than parental incest or sexual assault, yet Morrill noted that it receives much less attention than these other forms of abuse.[16] Individuals who suffered at the hands of their siblings typically had smaller social support networks during their childhood[17] and may be reticent to seek out support or assistance as adults. Some adults choose to end their relationships with formerly abusive siblings, while others continue to stay connected for the sake of the larger family system. Each individual must make the choice that works best for him. Early sibling experiences can significantly shape the ways in which we relate to others throughout our lifetime. Each sibship is unique—even within a single family with multiple children. Seek professional assistance if past abuse of any type is keeping you from making the choices that you would like to make or leading the life you would like to lead.

CONCLUSION

Regardless of the taboos that did or did not exist within your family-of-origin, adulthood provides you with the option to openly address difficult topics that were buried in secrecy in your youth. The norms you learned as a child regarding acceptable topics can follow you into later relationships.[18] Shedding light on the role that early beliefs play in your subsequent relationships can provide the opportunity for more open and honest adult relationships with family, friends, and romantic partners.

FINAL TAKEAWAY: Learning how to discuss typically taboo topics without shame or judgment may provide avenues to highly productive opportunities for communication that has long needed to take place. Just say it.

Part III

FOCUS ON THE PRESENT

Chapter Nine

Values Conflicts between Siblings

If you know what a person values, you know a lot about that person's true identity. Our values provide the structure and guidelines for how we select our short-term and long-term goals and the ways in which we feel comfortable working toward these.[1, 2] Values are being set in place early in life. In fact, elementary-aged siblings already understand the value of compromise through the sharing of one another's goals and desires.[3] The ability to understand the needs of a sibling was identified as the key to young children successfully working out difficult decisions together. As children grow older, however, the desire to individuate from their families-of-origin may lead to stronger reliance on peers as reference groups, regardless of the conflicting needs or purposes of family members. As adolescents mature, their need for nurturance by others decreases,[4] which suggests that their need to please their caregivers declines and room for independent views and beliefs grow. In this chapter, we focus on values related to behavior and attitudes.

WHEN AND WHERE DO WE FORM OUR VALUES?

Children learn about family values through immersion in their family systems. Values learned from parents often shape behavior from youth into older adulthood.[5] The most enduring values across generations tend to be the ones that address the preservation and protection of family connections and family collaboration. Expectations about right and wrong are also often made crystal clear when a child crosses the line between acceptable and unacceptable behaviors. As one woman recalled, *"As a kid, my*

mom's word and opinions were 'God's words,' but as I grew older, I real-
ized she is just a human who has a higher than average tendency to have
flawed opinions and poor decision-making skills." Sometimes it is late
adolescence or adulthood before children recognize the perceived and actual shortcomings of their parents, while others take notice in adolescence.

Pushing limits in adolescence reflects behavior that is both expected
and age appropriate. However, once past adolescence, siblings may follow a different trajectory and develop new lasting values as they break
free of traditional family values. They may come back around to their
parents' perspective, but they may also continue to follow their own path.
When value formation paths diverge significantly, conflict between adult
siblings can negatively affect their relationships. Sometimes the conflict
is specific, as explored further in the next sections, or more global. As
one twenty-something sister in a family of five siblings stated succinctly,
"*[Our most] significant conflicts revolve around siblings wanting to*
change one another for the better."

WHO'S MORE LIKELY TO EXPERIENCE CONFLICTS?

When you think of sibling conflict that reaches into adulthood, which sibling dyad do you believe experiences the most conflict? Brothers? Sisters?
Brother-sister pairs? It appears that sisters experience the most conflict.[6]
Their conflict can run the gamut from typical superficial squabbling to
weighty values differences. When asked about the most significant conflicts she has experienced with her sister, Tammy, the middle sister of
three girls, had no trouble pinpointing a values issue that was close to her
heart. Her role as a parent was the landscape of their most urgent disagreement: "*I have children and she does not. She tells me marijuana should*
be legal and my response is: 'If you are watching my kids, you are not,
under any circumstances, to smoke pot during the time you are watching
them.' She says I'm raising my kids in a bubble." She went on to add that
her professional role as a nurse created a sticking point between her and
her sister: "*[We] also [disagree about] anything medical. I'm an RN and*
she has no college education. She tries all kids of alternative stuff. Some
of it is crazy and she doesn't like my advice."

The inclination for sisters to disagree is likely a natural result of their tendency toward more verbal engagement than a pair of brothers might exhibit. In fact, young girls generally learn to talk sooner than their male age mates;[7] they are able to use longer phrases and sentences to get their points across; they pick up on grammar rules more quickly than boys;[8] and they typically have larger vocabularies.[9] Perhaps sisters also more enthusiastically argue their points due to the fact that women use both sides of the brain for language functions, but men generally use only the left.[10] Sisters disagree more, but they also can enjoy enduring and increasingly close sibling friendships throughout adulthood.

WHERE DO CONFLICTS ARISE?

In many families, as described in chapter 5, conflicts may develop between siblings who are seeking to stand out from one another or trying to vie for the limited resource of parental attention. Shared values and values conflicts have been found to be important markers of romantic relationship success.[11, 12] Recently, a research study has revealed that the *nature* of values conflicts between siblings is somewhat related to sibling relationship quality.[13] Two types of values were considered in that study: extrinsic and intrinsic values. The extrinsic values included power, achievement, and materialism, and the intrinsic values included benevolence and universalism. It turns out that siblings don't necessarily develop the same values even though they grow up in the same household. However, competitiveness between siblings was found to predict lower salience of intrinsic values among sibs, but higher salience of extrinsic values. This makes sense because extrinsic values reflect a desire to have a larger share of finite resources, such as power and success. When two sibs vie for the same end goal, rivalry can erupt between them. If siblings hold a higher appreciation of intrinsic goals such as benevolence and inner peace, there is less likelihood of competition—there is no limit to how much kindness one person can offer to others. Following are descriptions of a few of the frequently acknowledged flash points for values conflicts between siblings.

OPENNESS TO DIVERSITY OF ANY TYPE

Do you and your siblings share similar beliefs regarding attitudes and moral dilemmas? In a meta-analysis of studies investigating the role of parent training on children's biases or prejudices, it was noted that while the details of the actual transmission method were not yet clear, a significant parent-child influence on attitudes does exist.[14] This suggests that siblings are raised to hold congruent attitudes toward diverse individuals in childhood, but a divide between beliefs among siblings grows wider over time. Some children grow up with the Golden Rule emphasized at home and away, but there are loopholes in the rule for some siblings that only materialize or take on significance with the passage of time. Conservativism and biases seem to be the make or break issues between many siblings. "*I used to think that my brother and I were very similar. He and I were always alike in terms of temperament. As we've gotten older, we differ significantly on issues of politics and values. We've never had a blow-up argument or fight because I don't think it's really in either of us to do that (at least not me). But the things that bother me most [include] his conservative family values and derogatory language (in contrast to my liberal values and desire for inclusivity).*"

A woman of color shared that she and her sister had grown increasingly divergent in their beliefs over time. While she firmly expressed her commitment to diversity and tolerance, she acknowledged that she had little tolerance for her sister's narrower views. Following is her response to a question about conflicts she and her sibling have had in adulthood:

Wow, that is a good question! The conflicts we have as adults are mainly with our very opposite views of right/wrong, her inability or unwillingness to stand up to her husband, who is . . . racist and quite uneducated. He is a white police man-turned detective. She and he are quite conservative and Republican. I am the opposite . . . I just wish her values and morals were more in line with mine. I have become far bolder and more outspoken the older I get. I say what I think needs to be said and I don't hide truths.

The hesitation to embrace people who are different from themselves can be the point at which some adult sibling relationships dissolve. As Kim, a woman with five siblings and the youngest in the family, recounted with disappointment, "*I'm atheist; they are Catholics. I'm progressive; they are conservative. I'm childless by choice. They think these things are charac-ter flaws or misguided, in part because anyone who doesn't think just like them has to be wrong."* Michaela, the twenty-six-year-old youngest of four siblings, shared a similar disappointment. When asked what she wished that her siblings could understand about her, she replied, *"That I am an atheist. I can't even say that. . . . If they ask me about religion I just say I don't know. Because* not knowing *is better than* not believing *to them."*

Kim had noted that her own upbringing was somewhat different than her siblings, as her father was no longer traveling for his job once she was born. She continued her narrative to note that this disparity had created significant distance between her and her siblings:

> *I have gotten fed up with them always acting as though my opinions, ideas, and feelings not only don't matter, but that they are flat-out wrong. [This is] because I don't share theirs and because I suspect that on some level, they are afraid I am right. I regret not only that they treat me as a scapegoat, but also that they are just not very nice people [in general]. They have shown explicit bigotry towards persons of color, homosexuals, and women. You can't have a discussion with them—at least I can't—only a fight, unless you agree with them or keep your mouth shut.*

AND EVERYTHING IN BETWEEN

For many siblings, the greatest value divergence is located in political and social views, in general. One young woman shared that the greatest conflicts between her and her older brother tended to surround social is-sues such as *"views on vaccinations, breastfeeding, and liberal politics."* Another woman shared that moral and ethical decision-making differ-ences had driven her and her sibling apart in adulthood. When a person holds strongly to a belief, it can turn into the line in the sand between even formerly close families.

FAMILY VALUES

Just as individuation takes us all down a path to independent thought, autonomy, and a stronger sense of self, it may also lead us back toward similarity to our early role models. As a woman around forty affirmed, *"I am closer to my mom, because I am a mom [now, too,]. I now realize that everything she had told me when I was growing up—every single thing—is true when it comes to values and morals in life."* Coming full circle may reflect the propensity to "become more like ourselves as we get older," and becoming a reflection of our parents' early value modeling may be where we end up as adults.

The role of family, respect for elders, and the preservation of the family are aspects of *familismo* in Latinx culture; this construct is similar to the filial piety prioritized in Asian cultures. While this valuing of family plays a strong role intergenerationally over time, it may be more supportive of closer sister-to-sister bonds than predictive of brothers' bonds or brothers' bonds with sisters.[15] Collectivist cultures value the good of the group over that of the individual; in one study, the perceived success of their parents' parenting practices were found to predict the adolescents' collectivist values.[16] This suggests that in healthy families, such as those in which parents are accepted and respected as the heads of the family hierarchy, siblings generally develop strong loyalty to the family.

Unfortunately, not every family provides a strong foundation for positive and shared values development. For some, a stormy childhood can leave relationships in chaos, and some siblings are never able to begin again or let go of the past in their adult sibling relationships. In these cases, family values can fall to the wayside as siblings struggle with their own demons in life.

For some of us, there is comfort in being around the people we have known the longest—and once knew best. Shared histories connect siblings in ways that can transcend time. One fifty-nine-year-old woman highlighted the intersection of shared genes, values, and history by noting, *"I don't choose to be around my siblings very often, but when I do I usually enjoy it very much. There is something about the familiarity of our senses of humor, about politics and about values, that strikes an inner chord that is quite pleasant."* Even when a sibling isn't the one you most want to see, a shared past can keep the connection strong.

SEXIST ATTITUDES

For some siblings, sexist attitudes became the line in the sand between them. Aisling, a woman from Ireland, shared her regret that she and her brother were not as close as they might be: *"My younger brother and I have rarely had confrontations. However, we have a much more distant relationship than I would like. I feel I have lost both of [my brothers, as one died early]. My younger brother doesn't like it when I talk about women's rights because he has internalized the attitudes of older role models from the generation above us, which I find extremely challenging."*

Rita, a woman around thirty with four younger siblings, shared, *"[The biggest conflicts we face as adults] are differences in perceptions and opinions. Like my brother, who is the middle child and a chauvinist. And that bothers me immensely."* Rita noted that she felt a great deal of pride in being the oldest, and when describing what she wished she could get her siblings to understand, she said that *"making them realize that one shouldn't be judgmental"* was her hope. She further lamented, *"We live in a very prejudice-driven society, so it's hard to make them open up their minds and be more loving and accepting."*

PERSONAL CHOICES: ISSUES OF SEXUAL IDENTITY

Growing up, siblings are often present to witness and comment on each other's experiences and decisions. Some siblings can be more understanding of your personal development than others. A shared bond creates a uniquely supportive relationship. As siblings move into adulthood, intimacy and closeness may be harder to attain. In some cases, opening up about one's personal life can add to, not minimize, the distance between siblings.

Kris, who identifies as trans*, shared that in high school, they had been their brother's protector, but that the relationship had changed significantly as they entered adulthood. *"I wish we didn't grow apart in high school. Our relationship really never recovered after that."* Kris went on to relate that the most difficult sibling discussion to date focused on *"my gender identity. I discussed that I was trans*. My brother didn't say much, but that is how he is . . . little communication. I have to contact my brother if I want a relationship with him. He will not be the first to reach out. When we are together, he doesn't talk much and gets annoyed when asked questions."* Although Kris does not directly attribute the gulf between the siblings to gender identity, Kris did admit that the relationship with their mother had been affected by Kris's transition: *"We can talk about a lot of things [now], even though we did not talk for two years after I came out."*

In some instances, all the members of a family reach a tacit agreement to not discuss minority sexual identities if a child comes out as gay, lesbian, or bisexual.[17] While this may allow siblings to avoid difficult discussions, it also makes invisible a very real aspect of a sib's identity. Rather than ignore the metaphorical elephant in the family, it is more productive to learn how to have these difficult discussions. It is not uncommon for individuals who are coming out to their families to hear a sibling respond, "Yeah, I figured you were gay" or some variation of these words. For sibs who always knew a sibling was gay or lesbian, maintaining a stance of acceptance and support will ensure that the sibling relationship isn't sacrificed.

Researchers have begun to study the ways in which siblings can be accepting and supportive of their brothers or sisters who come out as non-heterosexual. One of the factors that were found to enhance the coming-out process for sibs was a preexisting positive sibling relationship, which probably is no surprise. Other factors, however, included the heterosexual sibling having prior contact with lesbian or gay individuals, expressed support for the civil rights of lesbian and gay individuals, and frequency of attendance at religious services, with lower attendance being predictive of higher acceptance.[18]

While coming out as trans*, lesbian, gay, or bisexual can present a challenge to sibling relationships, other values related to sexuality also can cause rifts to develop. Depending on the family's beliefs about morality, heterosexuality can also create conflicts between siblings. Candace, the middle sister of two brothers, shared that the most significant conflict she's had with her siblings involved her moral beliefs: "*Living with my partner out of wedlock [caused conflict]. My brothers go to church, but I don't anymore. So they had a disapproving view of my partner and me living together. The outcome was that I told them I respected their wishes when they chose to marry and they should respect my wishes to live with my partner before marriage.*" Luckily, this morality-based conflict was resolved, and Candace reported that the most meaningful experience for her and her brothers in adulthood occurred when she was a bridesmaid at each brother's wedding and then when they served as groomsmen at her own. When the foundation between siblings is strong, values conflicts can be put into perspective and kept from permanently compromising a healthy relationship.

Not only does a sibling's sex life raise concerns and potential value conflicts between sibs, but in some families, it is the *absence* of sexual activity that can give rise to a breach. Asexuality is considered to be the absence of sexual attraction toward anyone of any gender and is projected to be found in at least 1 percent of the population.[19] In addition to the construct of asexuality, or lack of sexual attraction, there is also the construct of aromantic, which refers to a lack of romantic attraction to others. Respondents in this study provided evidence that a lack of erotic engagement with others, versus erotic engagement at the wrong time or with the "wrong" gender, can also disrupt sibling relationships.

CAUTION: YOUR CHILDHOOD EXPERIENCES ARE NOT THE SAME AS YOUR SIBLINGS

In many families, children choose what to selectively "forget" as they move into adulthood. In some cases, memories are just too painful to carry across the lifespan.[20] Others may hold tight to the memories of the trauma experienced, and trauma may become both a defining component of their self-perceptions as well as a gulf between the memory keepers and the memory releasers. Not all children in a single family will have the same relationship with their parents, for instance. Sharing the reality of her siblings' varied experiences and divergent relationships with their parents, a woman noted the difficulties she had experienced recently with her siblings as they gathered for their father's funeral: *"[A significant challenge for us has been] being able to reminisce over childhood memories and feel okay doing that. This was both challenging and rewarding. The most challenging was at our father's funeral. We all had different types of relationships with him, which sometimes caused friction in the conversation."* The value placed on the father-child relationship varied greatly among the siblings.

CONCLUSION

It is essential that adults acknowledge and accept that not everyone with whom they come in contact is going to see the world through the same lens that they do. A person's perspectives and beliefs are uniquely shaped by their individual life experiences. Even if raised in the same household, siblings may follow disparate developmental paths. Siblings mature and develop at their own pace. Some are naturally more open to diverse people, experiences, and beliefs, while others are limited in their behaviors and attitudes and see the world from a narrower perspective. Some siblings have no hesitation in condemning the behaviors and beliefs of those who are different from them, and other siblings seek out new people and experiences from which to learn. Moral and ethical perspectives may also differ dramatically between siblings.

In terms of addressing values conflicts, it is important to determine for yourself and your sibling where the real conflict exists. Is it a question of morality? Ethical behavior? Attitude? Bias? Once you get a handle on what is bugging you, you may benefit from figuring out exactly what value of your own is being compromised by your sib's behavior. Knowing this will help you know yourself better. This knowledge can prepare you for future situations when you feel the same frustration or anger building. It can also help you to know how to defuse that anger if expressing it is unlikely to bring about change or anything positive in a relationship or setting.

If your sibling has little interest in listening to your perspective or accepting your views, it may be best to "agree to disagree" in some cases. This is a component of healthy boundary setting, a practice that provides the safety of knowing that you can protect yourself from the unwanted encroachment of others into your personal psychological space, as well as relieve you of the burden of feeling that it is your job to "fix" someone else.

Some families enjoy a lively debate—or even a boisterous argument—from time to time, while others choose to remain silent and allow disagreements to fester below the surface. If avoidance is the tactic your family uses in response to diverse perspectives and your prior attempts to open discussions about sensitive topics have been unsuccessful, remind yourself that no one can choose their siblings or their families, and it is not your job to change family members for the better. Offer your opinion if asked, volunteer it respectfully if you feel you cannot keep quiet, but remind yourself that you cannot change the minds of others if they are not ready to admit it needs changing.

FINAL TAKEAWAY: If you know what your adult sibling values, you know who your sibling has become; unfortunately, we don't always like the person our sibling turns out to be. Sibling bonds can weather a surprising level of adversity and many siblings find themselves balancing family loyalty against personal preference. Make the decisions that you feel are necessary for your long-term well-being.

Chapter Ten

Dealing with Sibling Shortcomings

Most families have a few secrets hidden away concerning the vices of a family member or two. Whether the secret is addiction, legal trouble, abuse, or other unsavory behavior, adulthood provides an opportunity for siblings to break away from the family saga and problem-saturated family system to create an independent life story of their own. While moving out and moving on might be priorities for young adults, the influence of family history can be difficult to shake.

In the popular media, movies such as *Our Idiot Brother* and television shows like *The Waltons, Parenthood,* and *Modern Family* depict the value of caring for and about your siblings. Some circumstances make it more difficult than others when it comes to helping out siblings. In addition, some sibling shortcomings are easier to accept than others. Scholars have explored the influence of negative life events, such as illness, divorce, addictions, legal issues, or financial problems, on the sibling relationship.[1] In the following sections, a closer look at the potential impact of some of these negative life events on these relationships, specifically addictions, legal issues, and financial difficulties, are addressed.

ADDICTIONS

Fortunately, adolescent use of illegal substances and cigarette smoking have been on the decrease, according to recent reports from the Centers for Disease Control.[2] While this may be a positive harbinger for future adult sibling relationships in the grand scheme of things, it does not alleviate the challenges faced by families wrestling with substance abuse today.

Not only does the presence of an addicted sibling create difficulties for the family, but it also suggests that other family members are likely dealing with the same beast. Unfortunately, if you have a sibling with a drinking problem, you are extremely likely to be at risk for a similar problem or equally likely to have a propensity to engage in other risky behaviors.[3]

Explorations into the physiological predisposition for addictive behaviors continue to support the presence of a genetic link among family members. It is important to note, though, that it is the environment, not nature, that predicts alcohol use in adolescents and young adults.[4] If you and your siblings grew up with an alcoholic parent, surviving that experience can increase your awareness of the power that substance abuse holds in disrupting what should be normal family interactions. This may lead you to completely avoid substance use—or it may normalize the pattern of use and abuse of substances and leave you wrestling with the same tragic behaviors that your parents may have modeled.

When Adult Family Members Drink Too Much

While media advertisements for legally purchased intoxicating substances encourage everyone to think that a bottle of beer means good times or your choice of liquor speaks volumes about your personal power, the dark side of inebriation is experienced all too intensely in all too many families. According to statistics provided by the National Council for Alcoholism and Drug Dependence, in fact, a family history of problem drinking or alcoholism is present for over 50 percent of adults. Almost eighteen million people are actively suffering from alcohol abuse or dependence. The result of all of this drug-induced good cheer and intoxication can be families that are ripped apart and adult siblings who no longer interact or, in some cases, even acknowledge one another's existence. One woman, Maria, shared that alcohol had cost her family dearly: "*I have not spoken to [my] middle sister in years. Her alcoholism has damaged all of us and our relationship to her. It is a book [in itself].*" Another interviewee shared about her current relationships with her own adult siblings. The most difficult conflicts they experience, she shared, are "*trust and selfishness. All three siblings are alcoholics at various stages of the disease. We struggle with so many issues.*" Yet another woman described the damage done by her sister's alcoholism with these words: "*My regrets about our relationship are too painful to describe. I feel like we were a three-legged stool and we have been missing one of the legs and . . . navigating life unbalanced for almost fifteen years."* Her greatest hopes for her relationship with the alcoholic sister are forgiveness and reconciliation, which are fairly common aspirations and are as ideal an outcome as can be hoped.

Forgiveness is indeed good for the forgiver; it has a salubrious effect on mental *and* physical well-being.[5] Choosing to forgive frees the offended individual from carrying bitterness toward the offender. Luckily, it is only Maia's sister who is addicted to alcohol; researchers have found that growing up in an alcoholic household and the presence of an alcoholic sister increase the likelihood that a sibling will develop an alcohol problem, as well.[6]

Addicts may battle an all-consuming obsession with their next drink or fix; this leaves them incapable of being fully present in any personal relationship. When it comes to adult sibling relationships, the shared history and lifetime connections run deep enough that they may assume that no matter how bad things get or how deep into addiction they may be, they will always be accepted and supported by their siblings. This expectation can weigh heavily on their brothers and sisters, especially if the addict is out of options and desperate for assistance.

As discussed in an earlier chapter, growing up in an alcoholic household negatively affects children's developmental paths. When adult children are brought back into the diseased family system—through caretaking responsibilities for addicted parents or dealing with now-addicted siblings—it can stir up a lifetime of buried feelings and resentments. While there are no simple solutions for handling siblings who are actively engaged in substance abuse, following are suggestions and perspectives that may help family members cope.

It's Not Your Problem . . . Unless You Make It Your Problem

Recognizing that no one can force another person to make the decision to stop making poor choices is the first step in helping family members gain a sense of direction in dealing with addicted family members. Many individuals mistakenly believe that through their own force of will, they will successfully convince a sibling to end their substance use or abuse. Letting go of unrealistic expectations can free a person to let go of the need to "fix" others. If you grew up in a dysfunctional family and had taken on the role of the responsible sibling, it can be disheartening to realize in adulthood that your role of "fixer" is no longer appropriate or effective with your siblings.

An interviewee shared that she was the only sober member of her family-of-origin and this caused friction between her and her siblings: *"My family [is] still drinking [and] not liking the fact I'm in recovery. My sister is very miserable around me. They are all getting sicker and I'm very alone in this with my daughter. [It is] frightening and sad to see how this family disease is getting worse."* She went on to confirm that her encouragement to her family to seek help falls on deaf ears. The abject misery of the contagion of what she considers the family disease is hardest for her to bear as she watches her daughter being overtaken by addiction: *"My twenty-year-old daughter is a heroin addict, too. She turned to drugs after a rape. [Dealing with her addiction and the rape] make this . . . the hardest time of my life."* Being in recovery herself, Janet shared that her hope for her relationships with her siblings stretched beyond those relationships: *"[I hope] that I may be a light for all of my family, for the sake of my daughter . . . and I have hope she will want a better life, [just as I do] for my parents and sister."*

Recognizing that you may be the one who is standing alone on the side of sobriety while watching your adult siblings sink deeper into addiction can be an extremely isolating situation. As noted earlier, some families never speak of addiction problems. You may undertake your own "search and recovery" mission to assist substance-using siblings, but there is little likelihood that efforts will be effective unless your sibling is ready to climb out of the pit of addiction. In addition, sibling addictions should not be used as excuses for your own poor choices or abandoned dreams once you become an independent adult. In childhood, your siblings' problems may have created troubles for the whole family in ways that should not be replicated in adulthood. Knowing what you will and will not tolerate is essential to freeing yourself from a sibling's problem.

You Do Not Have to Be Your Brother's (or Sister's) Keeper

Most children growing up in alcoholic households develop highly sophisticated skills for tracking a parent's drinking. They are hypervigilant and can assess just how drunk a parent might be by the time of day, the parent's gait, or the extent of the slurring of a parent's speech. Depending on the family and the circumstances, some children try to intervene to break the drinking cycle. Some children pour out a parent's alcohol and others hide the car keys. Other kids may take on the role of "family problem" (or, conversely, "family hero") themselves to shift the focus from dealing with the addict to managing the new problem family member. Some kids begin getting into trouble at school while others seek attention in more positive ways—academics, sports, and so on—in an effort to be "good enough" that a parent feels less driven to drink. When a child leaves home, the futility of their intervention and prevention efforts usually becomes crystal clear once an external perspective on their childhood can be established.

When growing up with siblings who were drinkers or illegal drug users, children may be explicitly or tacitly asked to cover up for the addict. Whether you were asked to lie about the time a sibling came home or keep the secret when a sibling would sneak out at night, your sibling was unfairly placing you into the role of an enabler. You may have been asked to pick up a drunk or high brother or sister if they were unable to safely make it back on their own. You may have agreed to complete chores that were the responsibility of your hungover sibling. In many families, the more successfully you concealed a brother or sister's substance abuse, the less stress and less turmoil the family experienced. Pulling together to hide the problem, whether it is a parent or sibling problem, is one of the strategies employed to keep the family looking decent and respectable from the outside, regardless of the chaos and shame on the inside. There is typically a strong sense of shame among family members of substance abusers, and a cultural stigma that attaches itself to the addict and to members of the addict's family.[7] Perhaps not surprisingly, the stigma associated with drug abuse is stronger than the stigma associated with mental illness. The drug abuse–related stigma will stick to the family, regardless of the family's efforts to get the sibling into treatment, unfortunately.

Family Games

While some "family games" can be fun for all, there are some clinically identified family "mind games" that perpetuate unhealthy patterns within a family.[8, 9] The following section addresses the danger of two specific "games"—Don't Tell and the Blame Game—and provides a reminder that adults have the power to choose whether or not to play.

Some families choose to play the game of Don't Tell regarding addictions in the family. Although family members may openly speak about the problem with other members of the household, everyone observes a simple, single rule regarding outsiders: "Don't tell." This creates an invisible boundary that not only has the strength to keep others out of family business, but it can also isolate family members from the community and from friends. This particularly twisted dynamic can have a devastating impact on the development of children's social skills. Guarding secrets, hiding the truth, and other forms of deception become the expected pattern of behavior.

Another game that families play is the Blame Game. If one sibling is dealing with substance abuse, parents might blame each other for the drug use. If a parent is battling addiction, siblings may blame one another for exacerbating the drinking or drug use. Blaming anyone but the addict allows the problem to go unmentioned, but untreated, as well. One woman, Elizabeth, now in her mid-fifties, related that when she was in high school and her brother was away at college, it was only on the weekends that he came home that her mother went *"seriously overboard"* on the drinking. Elizabeth remembered the painful moment when she told her brother just how she felt and how she blamed him for their mother's problem. Elizabeth admitted, *"I damaged our relationship that night and totally overlooked how hard he had worked to protect me from mom's drinking when he had lived at home. After that night, he and I never talked about mom's drinking again. She's been gone ten years now, and we still don't mention that part of our childhood."* Not only does the Blame Game take the focus off the addict, it also creates unnecessary conflict instead of productive alliances between other family members.

Establishing House Rules Is Your Right

Most children have probably created a list of things that they will do differently from their parents when they become adults. Whether it is eating cereal for dinner or having indoor pets or playing music or video games as loud or as long as they want, one change they might not think about is their right to establish boundaries between themselves and adult siblings whose behavior is not acceptable.

Don't Waste Time . . . Don't Condemn, Don't Condone, and Don't Conspire

Sadly, addicts seldom respond well to external directives or encouragement from family members to change their ways. The etiology and prognosis of addictive behaviors cannot be explored in any real depth in this volume, but it is important to acknowledge that addictive behaviors are not as easy to turn on and off as siblings might like.

Al-Anon May Have "Gotten It Right"

Many people believe that once they move away from their families, they will be free from all the drama and unpleasantness that their siblings created. It is not always easy to break free from family influences, though, no matter how earnestly siblings might try. As one interviewee shared, the most tragic moment in his relationship with his brother was

> *having my brother arrested this February, four days after our dad passed away. We had to leave him in jail and refuse to bail him out to save his life. He refused rehab for his heroin addiction. He is still there. I'm hoping my brother not only cleans up from heroin, pills, and drinking, but hope he actually gets therapy and help so he can stop being so angry with me and our family. It would make life so much nicer to be around him. He doesn't feel good enough in life, so he makes the rest of us feel terrible around him so he can feel better about himself. It's horrible.*

Rose, who was first introduced in chapter 7, shared her regrets regarding her alcoholic brother: "*I wish my brother told me how unhappy he was and what was bothering him. We only talked about childhood in passing. His alcoholism was a factor that kept us from talking much.*"

For families of addicts, meetings sponsored by Al-Anon may provide a sense of solace and normalization of the trauma and distress they have experienced. While not everyone feels comfortable with the strong spiritual foundation of the twelve-step programs sponsored by Alcoholics Anonymous (AA), there are multiple other organizations that provide support for the addict and support for the families of addicts that do not incorporate an expressed belief in a higher power. The first step in the AA guidelines, however, is for addicts to admit they lack control over the substance abuse.

It is not only important for addicted persons to admit their powerlessness, but it may be especially important for family members to acknowledge the limits of their own power to keep a sibling from using.

For the Parents and Siblings of Adults Wrestling with Addictions

Children growing up in dysfunctional households are often overly familiar with the signs of substance abuse and are quick to recognize this ineffective coping method in their own family members. Unfortunately, parents are about as powerless at helping their children end their addictions as children are at getting their parents to end theirs. If you are a parent, or a sibling, of someone who is suffering from addiction, the following seven points may help place personal power in a more realistic perspective:

1. Remind your child or sibling that it was his choices that placed him in the circumstances that currently surround him. Emphasize that it is *his own decisions,* not just happenstance or bad luck, that led him to this place. Interventions may be effective when you let your child or sibling know that his poor behavior affects everyone in the family and in his social and professional constellations, as well. One of the most important aspects of an intervention is that it is one of the family's steps toward health—it is a sign that a family is moving into the recovery process.

2. Offer assistance and support only to the degree that you are financially able to do so, and invest only in expenses that will move your child or sibling toward a better life. Don't give money that you know will take her further down the path of the addiction. Some people suggest that financial assistance be tied to a child or sibling's good faith efforts to improve her situation. However, if you feel guilty for not giving your child or sibling money for food because you are fearful it would only be spent for illegal drugs, buy her a bag of groceries instead of giving her cash.

3. Offer to help your child or sibling find support services, but don't blame yourself if he refuses to use them. You cannot help someone who does not want to help himself. Honestly, you cannot, as much as you would like to be able to do so. It simply does not work that way.

4. Love your child or sibling. But remember that loving someone does not mean enabling her. It means holding her accountable for her behavior and refusing to allow her the power to dismantle the family.
5. Do not assume that you can rescue your adult child or sibling—that is simply not possible—and attempts to do so are definitely not the way to encourage autonomy and responsibility in any adult.
6. Protect yourself and the rest of your family. Not every adult child or sibling has to hit "rock bottom" before turning around his life, so do not allow your child or sibling to bring you or the family to rock bottom, either! No longer is rock bottom seen as a necessary starting point for changing an addict's life; your family does not need to hit rock bottom before getting stronger, either.
7. Love yourself. Family members do the best they can, so they should not hold themselves accountable for the poor choices of adults. For parents, their role has no end point. However, the responsibilities of that role definitely shift over time as a child matures. They lessen, not expand. Loving yourself and accepting your limits will keep you from spiraling down as a result of a child or sibling's choices.

People—Even Siblings—Can Change

Watching a family member sink into an addiction and beyond the reach of lifelines can wrench apart a family. Fortunately, humans are always capable of effecting change in their lives when relevant motivation presents itself. One woman shared the following "happy ending" anecdote:

I think that the most difficult issue my siblings and I have discussed was our older brother's addiction. We saw that it was something serious. In this experience, we saw that he had an inability to hold employment, inability to focus and handle responsibilities, difficulties of handling financial obligations to family and children and bills, became homeless and going from home to home. We as his siblings knew what was best; however, we had to wait for him to realize that he needed help and needed to do something different. We expressed our concerns and encouraged our older brother to make positive changes, but our dad actually stepped in and assisted. Ultimately, our older brother realized that he hit rock bottom and needed help, so we assisted him in getting into a rehabilitation program. He has completed treatment, has a full-time job, goes to church and is involved, has a fiancé, and interacts with his children. He has been sober for three years.

Not all substance abusers will be able to find a reason to fight their addictions. If your sibling refuses to address her problem, perhaps it is best if you focus on the changes that you, yourself, can enact.

LEGAL ISSUES

If a sibling faces a legal or judicial issue, will it affect your relationship with that sibling? Research indicates that it very well might. When a brother or sister experiences an unpleasant legal tangle, the sibling relationship was likely to grow less engaged; less support is likely to be shared; and the relationship grows more strained.[10] The reasons behind this are multifaceted and similar to the reasons some siblings provide regarding their distancing of themselves from a sibling dealing with mental illness, and include stigma, fear of the "contagion" of legal problems, or simply not knowing how to maintain the relationship in the face of divisive differences in personal outlook or perspectives.

One woman shared the following summary of how legal problems had harmed her relationship with her brother: *"We grew farther apart as I became independent and brother became dependent. My brother had legal issues, which created a huge vulnerability, and mother swooped in and destroyed any chance of him progressing into any real independence."* A woman in her fifties shared a similar narrative: *"My brother is a criminal, alcoholic, and crack addict. He is a despicable human being. My mom continues to help him kill himself by financing and letting him loaf around."* Looking for someone to blame when a sibling is engaging in unacceptable or criminal behavior is not an unusual response to the situation. The blame might fall on any family member, depending on the person who is seeking a place to situate it.

Parents often take the blame for the problems their children create for themselves, as parents may believe that inadequate parenting or some other personal failure led a child to make poor adult choices. In another family, a young man whose brother had ended up in jail reported, *"My parents, I think, blame me for my brother's bad behavior, somehow . . . so*

I have not been able to see my baby brother since he went to prison for two years. He has been out for over a year now and my mother moved him out of state as soon as he was released."

Laying blame is just one of the many ways in which legal problems develop into family relationship problems. There are also numerous ways that a sibling's legal troubles become family issues—or family issues become legal troubles. Siblings might support a sister or brother by offering to testify on the sib's behalf in court—whether as an alibi, a character witness, or another purpose. If the sibling backs out or the court decision does not go the way the defendant had hoped, blame may be placed on the sibling who showed up in support. Co-signing a loan for a sibling may lead to trouble for both sibs if the loan goes into default. The fallout for the co-signing sibling may be materially detrimental to her own financial situation or lead to legal action and related expenses.

Both shame and blame are frequently attached to legal problems, and sibling loyalty does not always counterbalance these two typical reactions. Sometimes the shame experienced by the person in trouble, however, can actually provide a path to support, as a twenty-seven-year-old man discovered with his own family when he "came clean" about the desire to "come clean." He acknowledged,

I've had to discuss my getting in trouble with alcohol, drugs, and into associated legal trouble. I was incredibly ashamed about what I'd done once I knew they knew. Especially with my youngest brother. I've found ways to talk to him about my experiences by making generalized statements about what happens when people "party a lot, drink, do drugs, smoke cigarettes, and stuff like that" and how it's important that he chooses his friends wisely. He's been very receptive to that. My sister and I had a similar discussion in which she was crying about how bad things had become with my addictions, and that was probably one of the single most difficult conversations I've had, but it caused me to get help.

MONEY

There is a saying that no one should ever give money to a family member unless they consider it a gift, not a loan. While this perspective seems to reflect a pessimistic attitude, it has the potential to protect siblings from unnecessary anguish later on. When a sibling asks for financial assistance, you need to be thoughtful and careful in your answer. Some brothers and sisters believe their offers of assistance represent a concrete commitment of caring to their siblings. However, if the loss of the money you are considering giving to a sibling would create a personal hardship or lingering ill will if not repaid, it may be best to turn down the request.

If a sibling agrees to loan money to a brother or sister, the receipt of money can create an uncomfortable sense of obligation that alters the relationship. As one generous older sister shared, *"My younger sister was my best friend for a long time, but we have recently grown apart. I used money from a redundancy package to help her buy her flat, and it has changed the dynamic of our relationship."* The deterioration of their friendship saddened the benevolent sister, and she was not sure that the relationship would ever regain its former warmth and closeness. Another sister shared that her biggest regrets with her siblings had been loaning money to siblings who had not truly appreciated the sacrifice she had made to do so. On the other hand, the refusal of one sibling to loan another sibling money may cause the rejected sibling to feel resentment, as well. As a woman in her sixties recalled, *"[Years ago], before he left for Australia, my brother asked to rent a room in my flat in San Francisco. While he lived there, I once asked him to loan me twenty dollars . . . he turned me down, saying something like 'I don't know if I'll ever get it back.' I was humiliated. It still hurts today."*

Being able to provide assistance when your sibling most urgently needs it can generate very positive feelings for you as the benefactor. The ideal relationship is one in which the "ask" and the "response" are not used as weapons against one other. Following is a positive anecdote shared by a young woman who deeply appreciated her siblings. In answer to a question about the most difficult discussion she and her brother had faced, she responded, *"[It was] about money. When I was in my first year in university, my brother needed money and he asked me to help him by giving him money from my student loan program, but I could not. At that time, I felt guilty because I could not help him. He understood and told me it was okay."*

While legal issues, addiction, and financial woes can all cause conflicts for brothers and sisters, they all carry different repercussions for families. In a study comparing the effect of apologies in situations of addiction versus money problems, it was revealed that individuals felt they would be more likely to maintain trust and communicate directly with family members who had money disputes than those with drug issues.[11]

CONCLUSION

In considering all the ways that siblings can disappoint one another, it is clear this chapter could cover many more pages. The three presented here, however, are the ones that were most frequently shared as significant concerns among interviewees for this book. If you have maintained open and honest communication and heartfelt support of your siblings over the years, even their shortcomings can be accepted and strong relationships maintained. Recognizing that your responsibility is to support, not enable, your sibling provides guidance for effectively responding to a sibling's shortcomings or requests for assistance. Understanding and honoring your own boundaries will contribute to more balanced and rewarding sibling relationships.

FINAL TAKEAWAY: Most of us figure out our siblings' weaknesses early in life. Recognizing the limits of siblings, though, does not necessarily influence a sibling's willingness to assist a sibling in need. Offer assistance when you can, but keep your expectations of appreciation or reciprocation realistic.

Chapter Eleven

Siblings and Their Partners

There are only a few people who will see you at your worst in life—usually these are your family, your partner, and perhaps one or two of your very best friends. For some individuals, it may seem a little ironic that your siblings' opinions of your love interest may be the very thing that drives them to exhibit some of their worst behavior. Gaining family approval of a partner can head the list of priorities in some families; unfortunately, not every sibling is going to welcome every girlfriend or boyfriend into the family circle with open arms. On the flip side, not every sibling's partner will *want* to feel like a member of his or her partner's families.

As one of three sisters shared, the only significant conflict they experience now surrounds their spouses: *"We don't voice it, but I think the only issue with my siblings comes down to the fact that we don't agree with each other's significant other's treatment towards us. For example, we all complain to each other that the other's spouse is in the wrong many times, but we never actually express that directly to the person we are referring to."*

PAVING THE WAY FOR A PARTNER

It can be difficult, in some families, to bring a partner into the family system. If a family operates as a closed system, their boundaries can be too tight to stretch. It can be useful to visualize family organization through the lens of a *structural family therapy*[1] therapist. Structural family therapy is a model that was developed around five decades ago through the work of Salvador Minuchin, Braulio Montalvo, and Jay Haley at the Philadelphia Child Guidance Clinic. This model presents the family as a unique, discrete system that owes its individual footprint to both idiosyncratic and universal factors. The universal aspects of family systems involve the existence of a power hierarchy and the mutual engagement of family members within their roles. For instance, the typical family structure places the parents at the top of the family hierarchy, and both parents are expected to work together as a leadership team. However, there is also the idiosyncratic aspect in which each family member's behavior and expectations influence the functioning of the system.

A family's structure is built on the interactions that occur between family members; examples include siblings being allowed to argue back with parents or parents giving over care of their younger children to their older children. Within a family system, there are also subsystems that develop—the parental subsystem and the sibling subsystem are a couple of common examples. It is within the respective subsystem that members learn the rules and roles they are expected to follow and fill. Depending on the family, the subsystems may look remarkably different from one another. Step- and half-sibling relationships may influence how subsystems develop, as do multiple marriages, the presence of multiple generations in a home, and so on. Any family member, too, can be a member of multiple subsystems—uncle, aunt, brother, sister, parent, child, and so on—depending on their particular family system. Some subsystems are openly acknowledged and openly active within the system, while others may be covert and reflect subversive and unhealthy alliances.

According to Salvador Minuchin, a family's structure can only be known through observation.[2] In most instances, family members have a difficult time visualizing the larger structure because they hold integral roles in the family system. Whether or not members are fully able to comprehend the system as a whole, most do recognize that their roles are vital to the functioning of the unit. Most also recognize that family systems tend to resist change from within or without. As you and your siblings have matured and grown into adults, you have probably gained a more sophisticated understanding of your own family's functioning, even if you are unable to change its shape. You may also be aware of the various boundaries that exist within the system; Minuchin described boundaries as the rules that govern participation. For instance, when you argued with a sibling as a child, were there rules about fair fighting? Or did your younger sibling's needs always come first when the two of you were arguing over a finite resource? These are examples of engagement rules that reflect specific family boundaries, which develop as a means of ensuring that all members of the system play their specific roles.

Boundaries

Family boundaries tend to vary between levels of fluidity and rigidity, and they serve to keep separation between the various subsystems within a family as well as to maintain the family's level of openness to others who may be potential participants in the family system. Minuchin[3] provided clear descriptions of the range of boundaries that might exist within family members and family subsystems; following are summaries of these boundary types along with examples of how these might show up within a family and how they might influence the response to a family member's efforts to "sponsor" the admission of her new partner.

Clear boundaries are self-explanatory and are the functional ideal for most families. While the boundaries are clear enough to indicate separation of a family subsystem, they are also open enough to allow reflexive contact with other individuals outside the subsystem. An example of this family system would be one in which the members exhibit respect, offer support, encourage the development of one another, and value positive and warm relationships. These ease the introduction of new significant others into the family. While there may be disagreements even in subsystems with clear boundaries, conflict is accepted and managed in a mature manner. Each subsystem's membership accepts its inherent limits and does not normally try to push against the tacit rules that govern its power or influence.

Rigid boundaries are the most confining form of separation. Rigid demarcations between subsystems and the family, in general, are overly restrictive and allow poor functioning to continue unchallenged and unchecked. Little contact with any external systems is allowed, and this can result in disengagement from other members, subsystems, or the greater environment. Rigid boundaries make it difficult for new members to be absorbed into a subsystem. In childhood, perhaps you had a parent remarry and stepchildren were brought into the mix. If a strong and rigid boundary already existed in your own sibling subsystem, you and your sibs may have actively lobbied to exclude the new stepsibs from the group. In adulthood, these types of boundaries may create resistance for a sib's potential partners to be accepted into the group. Rigid boundaries are like fences that cannot be scaled; unless one of the subsystem members chooses to open the gate, metaphorically, the boundary cannot be crossed. If disengagement from the family has already occurred, siblings may never introduce partners into the family systems.

Diffuse boundaries in subsystems have a different influence and hold the power to dissolve necessary boundaries between subsystems. While dysfunctional rigid boundaries are like concrete walls, dysfunctional diffuse boundaries between family members or subsystems can be virtually nonexistent. Diffusion leads to over-involvement in the experiences and lives of other subsystems or family members. At its extreme, it can lead siblings to be overly dependent on one another, which can inhibit the normal desire to explore and seek independence. Counselors use the word *enmeshment* to describe relationships in which family members are unable to function independently—socially, cognitively, affectively, and so on—without collaboration or consultation with their families. When something happens to one family member, the reverberations are felt throughout the family.

Overly enmeshed families may also manufacture reasons that a sibling's time should be spent on family tasks, or, alternately, family crises might be fabricated to keep the sibling's energy directed toward the family-of-origin instead of the potential new mate. Unfortunately, sometimes the members of an enmeshed family will actually seek a way to covertly sabotage her own budding relationship. There's a running joke about the wisdom of choosing not to date a thirty-something who still lives at home. While this may not be as concerning as it once was, if a potential partner cannot make a major or minor decision without running it by sibs or parents, you may want to do some testing of the boundaries within the family system before you are too far into the relationship to easily back off.

Honoring the Boundaries

Being able to edit the boundaries that exist between family members and the greater family structure takes a deft hand and willing family members. However, being able to place the needs of your siblings ahead of your own desires can pay off in positive relationships over the long run. Karen, the oldest of two siblings, shared the secret to her and her sister's continued close relationship: *"[We honor] boundaries when it comes to giving advice. [Our most significant discussions have centered on our personal] relationships; we understand not to impose our values on one another."* Karen and her sister have thus far successfully navigated their relationship from childhood into adulthood; it is not always that easy.

CHILDHOOD INTO ADULTHOOD

It is during childhood that people learn the family rules and their roles in the nuclear family system.[4] It's been noted that healthy families have problems just like unhealthy families do, but the difference between functional and dysfunctional families resides in the ability of the family to solve its problems. As children enter the family system, parents must flex and respond to ever-changing needs. As children accept new sibs into their subsystem, they must learn how to manage the shifting sibship membership and changing expectations as they grow. It is when a family fails to accommodate the changes and transitions of its members that difficulties arise.[5] One of the most potent transitions that young adults experience is the entry into a romantic relationship.

A BROTHER'S A BROTHER UNTIL HE TAKES A WIFE?

There's an old saying that "a daughter's a daughter for all her life; a son's a son until he takes a wife." This adage also raises the question of whether there is a corollary to a son's status—does a brother remain a brother after he's taken a partner? Based on the stories of women interviewed, the answer is in dispute.

Vacating One System to Join Another

As noted previously, a sibling's decision to walk away from the family-of-origin rather than bring a new partner into the family can reflect his need for more rigid boundaries between him and his family-of-origin. Sometimes, it is the family subsystem that works to exclude the potential new member.

Both of these transactions may occur within the same family, as illustrated by the experiences of Cora. Cora is a woman in her sixties who has been on both sides of the boundary fence with her two brothers. She summed up the influence of her brothers's wives on her relationships with them:

> *My second-oldest brother has a partner who I struggled with. Finally, about fifteen years ago, I let the relationship slip away so that now I do not see them except at big family events like weddings and funerals. It was a relief when [my brother] was no longer a part of my life, and I now realize that he was a bully. My younger brother was a playmate when we were young and close through young adulthood. When he married, however, he aligned with his wife's family, and although we were still friendly and lived in the same town, we were not close.*

Although Cora probably doesn't have a deep knowledge of family systems theory, by stepping back from her experiences through sharing the narrative, she can recognize that each subsystem—siblings, sibling and partner, family unit—works within a set of expectations and roles that alter the shape and form of the resulting system.

When a Brother Yields to a Partner's Power

When asked what was the most significant challenge she has faced with her siblings in adulthood, Sandy, a woman around forty, answered, *"Their partners have been overtly rude and disrespectful to me. This has challenged their loyalty to me."* This is a regrettably frequent experience. Loyalty to the family-of-origin must be balanced against loyalty to the newly formed romantic partnership.

Most individuals grow up with the saying "Blood is thicker than water" somewhere in the back of their minds. Of course, as our cultural mores and traditions have flexed, as demanded by modern society, there are often situations in which bonds beyond blood hold greater significance for family system members. Blood bonds may be overshadowed by fidelity to a partner. Bobby Jo, an interviewee three decades younger than Cora, also felt a sense of loss after her brother married: *"I wish I could tell my middle brother that allowing his wife to control his life has ruined our relationship. I wish I could tell my youngest brother that his happiness is just as important as his future wife's, and he needs to speak up and voice his opinions."*

For this sister, her role of caregiver or protector of her younger brother's well-being is deeply ingrained in her identity as a sister. When this woman was encouraged to share what she would like to communicate to her siblings or if she had any specific hopes for her relationships with them, Bobby Jo responded: *"I hope to continue to be friends with my middle brother and his wife—which is not easy for me. That means I have to work extra hard to reach out and connect with them because it's much easier to just cut communication and act like things are okay. I also hope to keep open communication with my youngest brother as he is getting married and beginning to make choices that don't seem congruent with the person I know. I'm hoping these deep conversations will enhance our friendship and not push it apart."*

A SISTER'S A SISTER FOR ALL HER LIFE?

When you think about traits that you would like to find in your own ideal partner and then think about the list you would make for your idea of the ideal partner for your sisters or brothers, are the two lists similar? Recent research suggests that the lists may actually be particularly unique.[6] For themselves, most women want a partner who embodies strong genetic fitness, but they were not so concerned about the same characteristics for their sisters. Women preferred that their sisters' partners exhibit qualities indicative of concern and caring for others, including extended family members. In a separate study mothers were found to want the same thing.[7]

The corollary of the "son's a son" axiom would be that a sister is a sister for the long haul, and it seems that many sisters agree that this is true—or they may just have a lot to say about their siblings' mates. They also may feel strongly about the reception that their own partners receive from their brothers and sisters. One young woman had only one current regret about her relationship with her brother: *"I wish I had been better about navigating the relationship between my partner and my brother. However,"* she continued, as the admittedly stubborn sister that she is, *"I would not change my ultimate decision to date my partner . . . I also hope my brother and I return to being best friends and that he appreciates my relationship with my partner.*" Not quite yet twenty-five, she believes that the relationships still have plenty of time to work out.

Sisters Weigh In on Brothers' Partners

Even as adult siblings create new families of their own, they may still long for closer relationships with their siblings. Cynthia, a woman who desires more closeness with her brother, realizes that some of her past mistakes coupled with high expectations may have done irreparable harm to their relationship. Just as every organization needs a leader or someone in charge to direct its activities, there is typically a sibling within the sibling subsystem who wants to govern the behaviors and choices of the others. In Cynthia's family, she believed that she had the power to direct the lives of her brothers, but this backfired on her, and she not only lost a potential friendship with a sister-in-law, but the relationship with her beloved brother, as well. "*I should not have been so hard on my younger brother's wife. It ruined our relationship,*" shared the young midlife woman. Her hope now is that she can be there for her siblings in a way that she wasn't before. Another woman shared that she wished she "*had not said mean things to or about [her] brother's girlfriend.*" She, too, hopes for reconciliation, but doesn't believe it will happen anytime soon.

Mazie, a woman who took pride in the strength of her relationship with her brother, her only sibling, revealed, "*I had a difficult conversation with my brother when he was getting married to a woman who I believed did not care for him. This discussion occurred at his destination wedding in another country. He explained that they already legally married a few days prior to the out-of-country wedding in a Justice of the Peace ceremony. They divorced six months later when he discovered she was having an affair.*"

When individuals are willing to be flexible about their boundaries, their subsystems, their in-groups, and their out-groups, reconciliation is indeed possible, but it doesn't always come easily, and it can rely on the attitude of the sib's partner more than the sibling. As Mazie continued, "*During my brother's first marriage, we did not see each other as often since his wife did not enjoy spending time with me or my family. However, since the divorce and his new marriage, we see each other more often again.*"

A LITTLE BIT OF DISTANCE KEEPS THE PARTNERS AND THE SIBLINGS ON GOOD TERMS?

Sometimes, geographical distance can be the most effective way of maintaining clear boundaries as well as avoiding unwanted interference between siblings and families. A woman who has spent a quarter of a century with her husband and family in a country not their homeland shared the positive and negative effects of geographic separation from her siblings over time: *"While I would not do anything differently for my own family in terms of the choice to work and raise our family overseas, I struggle with feelings of guilt and also genuine sadness over not being there for my siblings and parent. Our family's experience of twenty-five years raising our four kids overseas has been fantastic for them and us. My husband and I are by far the most stable in terms of marriage and finance, but we are separated by an ocean [from my siblings]."*

HERE'S TO ALL THE SINGLE SIBS OUT THERE

The increasing delay in the age of first marriage and the shrinking size of the nuclear family suggest that some sibs never encounter the need to adjust to a new member-in-law. Although the sibling subsystem may shift as adulthood is reached, some sibs may never need to pave the way for a partner to be assimilated in the family. They may need only to flex into new identities themselves. Becoming the "cool bro-in-law" or the "adventurous auntie" may be exactly the type of transformation they prefer. In fact, research shows that unmarried siblings tend to be more involved with their families-of-origin and their siblings than married sibs.[8] Even brothers who do not marry tend to be strongly integrated into family systems if they are still geographically local to the family home.

SEXUAL ORIENTATION/IDENTITY AND AUNTS AND UNCLES

Being the "maiden aunt" or "bachelor uncle" can be an uncomfortable situation, depending on your own family environment. Although these dated terms are seldom used to describe lesbian or gay siblings there are still siblings who are uncomfortable acknowledging or explaining their siblings' sexual orientations to their children. One young individual, who identifies as transgender and prefers the pronouns them, their, and theirs, shared the emotional challenges experienced on a recent trip back to their hometown to see their brother's newborn son:

> *I'm not "out" to my brother, which means that I edit my clothing, jewelry, and make-up when I'm there. It bugs me that he wouldn't be open to knowing me as I really am. I spend 90 percent of my life in an environment where I can use the pronouns I prefer, identify my gender as nonbinary, and dress however I like each morning. But I go home to the people who have known me the longest and have to wear "drag," which is what I consider my more masculine clothing. And be Uncle Jake, to keep up the charade for my brother and his wife and their newborn son.*

Many transgender individuals face the question, "Why can't you just be gay?" by their families—suggesting that divergent sexual orientation is less threatening than divergent gender identity to family members. As one gay man shared, *"Yep, as long as I present as a little more masculine than feminine—and my spouse does the same, we are 'no big deal' at family events. Making sure we don't crack the mold that my brother expects us to fill is worth keeping the peace right now. Maybe down the road, I'll feel freer, but for now, it works."* A lesbian shared that her sister-in-law had developed a secret language for instructing her on what to wear to family events. *"Dress like you would at church usually means come in more feminine clothes. We're having some friends over means just don't dress too butch. I can't believe it is 2015 and I'm expected to hide who I am. And they have made it kind of clear that I should watch how I look at my partner when people are around!"* Although the rules come across as old-fashioned, she loves her brother enough to follow them. Healthy sibling relationships, like friendships, require compromise on occasion.

SUGGESTIONS FOR DEALING WITH YOUR SIBLING'S PARTNER

While parents may resist the changes to their nuclear family's routine, siblings may also be ready to pounce when brothers or sisters introduce new people and associated changes into the family system. Some sibs feel jealousy when new partners "steal" brothers or sisters from the nuclear family. Holiday traditions may change—whether due to the absence of a familiar face or the presence of a new one. Family discussions may be different, as new partners may believe their voices and opinions carry equal weight to those of long-time family members. Tiptoeing around the "outsider" can be trying, as trust can be slow to develop when new faces are present at once-private moments. Differing temperaments, traditions, and experiences produce widely diverse responses to family concerns or family crises, and it may be necessary to learn to bite your tongue and just listen to what the in-laws, or "out-laws," as some families jokingly call them, want to contribute. Complaints to your sister about her "know-it-all boyfriend" won't make difficult situations any easier.

If it's a case of concern about your sibling's well-being that needs attention, addressing the issue directly, but supportively and empathetically, with your sibling is warranted. Remember that there's a significant difference between telling a sibling what to do and gently exploring a concern and potential options to resolve it. If it's a safety concern, put your sib's health and well-being first and let him know sooner rather than later—but be prepared for resistance to your efforts to discuss the situation.

SUGGESTIONS FOR MANAGING THE RELATIONSHIP BETWEEN YOUR SIBLINGS AND YOUR PARTNER

When your own family makes you cringe from their careless remarks, bigoted comments, emotional outbursts, or bad behavior, the thought of bringing home a partner can be highly anxiety-provoking for even the most placid of people. If you have family secrets that you would prefer to keep hidden, you may want to carefully plan out any introduction of your partner to the family. Although some family secrets may not be as upsetting to your partner as they might be for you, make sure you are emotionally prepared for the meeting. Preparing your siblings for the meeting might also be a priority. One young man shared a story of his dismay and discomfort the first time he met the fiancé of Cara, his older sister: "*No one had told me that Cara's fiancé was a different race than us. I don't care about that at all, but I think I would have handled the first meeting better if I'd been told. I mean, Alex is awesome and I'm glad he's my brother-in-law, but whoa! That first meeting.*" Some siblings might enjoy the shock value of surprising families with their romantic partner choices. If you're making long-term plans, however, you might want to make sure the introductions are done with the feelings of others—including your significant other—in mind.

Introducing a fiancé or live-in partner to your siblings can be significantly different from bringing a casual boyfriend to a Super Bowl party or to join the family for takeout pizza. When you are in a committed relationship that you expect to last long term, you may need to broach difficult subjects with your partner early on, as she may be called on to support you—or members of your family-of-origin—in difficult times. Letting a partner know about essential components of family history can help him be a better partner to you. Not everyone enjoys surprises, and even fewer enjoy surprises of the unpleasant kind. Share what you feel is necessary at the moment and at the level at which you feel comfortable. Partners worth keeping around usually care more about your well-being than they do about family foibles or prior mistakes. And if your partner is overwhelmed by your sibs, remind your partner that their presence in your life has likely shaped you into a more easygoing relationship partner overall. Research has shown that only children tend to believe that their partners are more demanding than those who grew up with siblings tend to do.[9] Sharing a home with siblings apparently shifts your perspective on just how demanding and difficult living with other people might be.

CONCLUSION

In some less functional families, adult siblings may simply prefer to keep any partner as far from the family as possible and create rigid boundaries around their marriage/relationship if they are required to interact with the family at all. The sibling may have a partner, but for all intents and purposes, she and the partner are an external unit that functions completely outside of her family-of-origin. When a sibling's partner—or your own partner—seems to be the tipping point for family relationships, it can be important to recognize the role that you play in family dynamics and take action, as appropriate.

A regret that was frequently noted by participants in this study was the lack of emotional closeness between siblings. Although you may not be as happy with your sibling's spouse as he would want you to be, don't punish a sibling for a romantic partner choice. Getting along for the sake of peace in the family can ensure that sibling relationships have an improved opportunity for growing deeper throughout adulthood. The sister of two brothers confirmed that their relationships had grown closer over time as they had settled down with their partners: *"As they have had families of their own, we socialize more than when we were single. When they married, my brothers' wives became the sisters I needed."*

FINAL TAKEAWAY: When siblings choose partners that you know are wrong for them, you may not hesitate to share your opinion with your sibs. Unfortunately, everyone has to make their own mistakes in relationships and partners usually outrank sibs in most matters. Be patient with sibs and be supportive where you can.

Chapter Twelve

Health and Well-being Concerns of Siblings

Just as every family has its own culture regarding secrets, celebrations, and family rules, families also exhibit specific patterns of response to illness or tragedy. Sometimes the only people left standing to support you are your siblings, and sometimes the only people you want around you are the ones who have already seen you at your worst. Siblings take a lot from one another, and sometimes family loyalty is all that keeps them coming back around for more. In other relationships, it is mutual affection and genuine warmth that bond siblings together for life through the good and the bad. Some might assume sisters are more likely to jump in and offer assistance to a sibling, but brothers are also ready to help when they can. One midlife woman, Maxine, shared, *"The most significant experiences I've had with my siblings as an adult were related to my grief process after my spouse died. My brothers were there for me and helped me as much as possible."* This was exactly what this grieving widow needed, and Maxine's brothers were eager to lend support.

CAREGIVING FOR SIBLINGS TAKES MANY SHAPES

After coming full circle through a lifetime of shared experiences, reaching the final arc of the lifeline can be lonely, as a person's network of support is diminished over the years. In some families, caregiving for older family members is a more challenging task than younger generations feel capable of attempting. Parents and parents-in-law are typically the relations that many first think of when they hear the word caregiving. Divorce and geographical mobility, though, may alter the generational landscape, and widows, widowers, divorcees, and so on may be seeking care from their sisters and brothers, if no one else is able to step in to help.

Giving up one's independence and moving into another's home—or allowing someone to move into your own—often takes great courage on the part of both parties. Siblings may have grown up together in the same household, but by the time older adulthood is reached, decades of independence from the family-of-origin may have yielded two very different lifestyles for siblings. Learning to give and take with someone who may seem more of a stranger than a familiar family member presents unique challenges. However, there is an encouraging research finding for individuals who look after their siblings: Caregiving siblings actually fared better in terms of well-being than caregiving spouses or parents.[1] Multigenerational families living under one roof are no longer as common as they once were. Without exposure to an early model to help shape a person's identity as a future caregiver, it can be difficult for individuals to adapt to this more than likely unexpected set of circumstances.

DEALING WITH PHYSICAL HEALTH OR DISABILITY CHALLENGES

Caring for a sibling diagnosed with a disability or debilitating illness can bring out the best and the worst in people. Family loyalty can be the pillar that keeps the family support network centered on the care of a sib. While it may seem natural to assume that it is affection or closeness that plays a role in sibling caregiving, other circumstances or constructs may be involved. In a recent study of adult siblings of individuals diagnosed with Down syndrome, Monica Cuskelly found that the quality or warmth of the sibling relationship played a role in the participants' intentions to care for their sibling in the future.[2] Obligation and loyalty may be the most likely predictors of our willingness to care for sibs in adulthood. In another study, it was found that individuals who anticipated having to care for an intellectually disabled sibling were most concerned about planning for the future, while siblings who actively cared for siblings with these types of disabilities were more realistically concerned with navigating social service systems.[3] The researchers also explored current and future caregivers' attitudes regarding the receipt of financial compensation for caregiving.

Future caregivers had much less interest in pay than current caregivers. What is *imagined* to be the experience of caregiving is uniquely different from what the *actual reality* of sibling caregiving entails.

RESPONDING TO AN URGENT MEDICAL CRISIS

Linda, a woman in her sixties, had experienced a health crisis with her older brother that had brought them closer together as a family. She shared, *"My brother and I live about six hours apart but do visit each other fairly frequently, talk multiple times per week, email multiple times per week . . . my husband and I went to stay with my brother and sister-in-law when my brother had to have cardiac bypass surgery . . . it was a very important time for all of us . . . we pulled together as a team throughout the experience."* Linda and her brother had always had an easygoing, positive relationship. She and her brother happily played the "big brother, kid sister" roles. When illness was added to their narrative, Linda was eager to jump in as the "helpful kid sister" and support her brother's health and recovery.

In the example above, Linda had a lifetime of experience and maturity to put her brother's immediate health needs in perspective. Violet, a woman in her late twenties, shared the negative impact her own illness had placed on her younger sister. Responding to a question about the most significant challenges in her sibling relationships, she answered, *"Definitely health-related issues, as my younger sister felt abandoned when I went through serious health issues in high school (multiple brain surgeries and weeks of physical therapy) and becomes vicious if I bring up my health."* Especially in childhood, siblings may resent the attention and care that debilitated siblings receive from other family members.

BEING THERE WITH SUPPORT

Our culture tends to place stronger expectations of caregiving on sisters than brothers, whether the person needing care is mother, father, grandparent, sister, or brother. With the expectations so gendered, one might wonder if siblings stick to these roles or take time to recognize the gift of the care they are given. A thirty-five-year-old man, Scott, shared his appreciation for his sister's willingness to be there for him at a time when he faced a potential health crisis as well as romantic relationship troubles: "*I had an STD scare she was there for, reading statistics and how to deal with the disease. Side note: I didn't actually have it, so YES! I had two chaotic breakups and rather than swim around in waves of chaos, she was a solid anchor to grab onto and provide clarity. You know who loves you when everything is terrible.*"

Scott was astute enough to know how fortunate he and his sister were to have such a warm and supportive bond. When prompted to share any challenges he and his sister had experienced, he responded, "*The only challenging experience was when she got breast cancer. I felt really powerless. I talked to her as much as I could and tried to be there, but ultimately it was up to Western medicine. Plus she was physically unable to be there for her kid that much, what with the chemo. Scary time, but she beat it. Life is fragile, it's really true.*" Scott was as present for his sister during her medical ordeal as she had been willing to be for him.

A sibling's commitment to another's well-being can take many forms. One woman, Marta, shared that her own sister went above and beyond expectations in her efforts to help Marta overcome a physical ailment. Marta was busy planning and preparing for her wedding, and the stress might have contributed to her illness. Marta recalled, "*Around that time, I was trying to resolve some health problems, and my sister created a special diet based on her belief model that was supposed to help. That was meaningful because it showed that she cared enough about my health to get involved, and even to cook for me every day.*" Although her sister's efforts were not enough to cure Marta, her sister's commitment to her well-being had done a great deal to improve Marta's spirts at that stressful time.

DEALING WITH MENTAL HEALTH CHALLENGES

When a woman in her eighties who smokekd practically all her life was asked her thoughts on how she had escaped any negative health consequences from smoking to date, she responded, "*Must be my good genes.*" Most people recognize that a predisposition to certain physical, mental, or emotional illnesses can be traced back through the family tree. Not only does your "nature" potentially predict compromised well-being, so, too, does the "nurture" that you experience.[4] Research has found a direct relationship between conflict with siblings in adulthood and mental well-being. Perhaps not surprisingly, it turns out that sibling conflict is a better predictor of mental health in adulthood than parental conflict in adulthood.

Over forty-three million adults in the United States suffer from some form of mental illness, according to the Substance Abuse and Mental Health Services Association.[5] This indicates that about one out of every five individuals has a diagnosable illness. When siblings suffer from mental illness, their brothers and sisters may be hesitant to take on a caregiving or visibly supportive role due to the stigma associated with mental illness.

Personal attitudes can play a significant role in an individual's willingness to care for a mentally ill sibling; in fact, one of the significant predictors of a sibling's willingness to take on the caregiver role of a sibling with schizophrenia included the sibling's beliefs regarding how well symptoms of mental illness could be controlled.[6] Research on relationships between siblings during early adulthood has shown that this type of diagnosis can drive a firm wedge into the sibship. When siblings received diagnoses of mental illness, there was a strong drive for healthy siblings to distance themselves from their less fortunate siblings.[7] Not every sibling, fortunately, responds by turning away from a brother or sister.

A woman around forty, Nancy, who is also the oldest of her siblings, shared the following path through which her sibling caregiving journey had evolved:

I am seven years older than both the half-sister I was raised with and the half-sister I wasn't. I've only met the one I wasn't raised with (different mothers) a couple of times. The relationship with the one I was raised with (same mother, her father is my stepfather) was more as a ward than sibling when growing up. In my adolescence we weren't particularly close because I was rebelling against my role as her caretaker, somewhat, and trying to distance myself. As adults we hadn't lived in the same city until the last year. She was recently diagnosed with a mental illness, so has moved in with me and I've become her caretaker, again. But we are friends, as well. We have many of the same interests and tastes.

When asked to share how this relationship has affected her other adult relationships, such as friendships, Nancy responded, *"I can say she's probably my only friend and certainly (besides my parents) one of the few constants . . . though she's not a terribly consistent person due to mental illness. My plans for the future are to keep on keeping on and hoping to keep us all afloat as long as I can.*" That's about all any of us can hope when it comes to caring for ourselves and caring for others.

SIBLINGS WITH DEBILITATING PHYSICAL ILLNESS

Most of us think of siblings as peers and assume that their physical health is as robust in adulthood as it was in our shared childhood. This is not always the case and caregiving for a sibling may be required long before caregiving for parents is needed. One of two sisters in her family of four siblings, Cat learned early that caring for a sibling could be as rewarding as it was taxing. Cat's brother suffers from myalgic encephalomyelitis (ME), which is a debilitating disease that affects multiple areas of the body including the heart, muscles, and brain. The severity of symptoms can wax and wane, and its unpredictability can add to the challenge of caring for an individual with ME.

Cat recounted her own personal development related to her caregiving experiences with her brother:

I'd say the most profound experience with a sibling was about six years ago. My brother who has ME was so chronically ill he was suicidal. We had all had a very emotionally traumatic childhood—I think the burden of our past took its toll, our dad in particular was very unkind to all of us throughout our adolescence. My brother was at rock bottom and had not wanted to contact me or our sister or eldest brother for couple of years. But he was now in a very dark place in his mind. So I went in and got him. I gave up my job to look after him—I was on-call 24/7. It's been hell. But worth it. He's gone from being very much shut down to being back in contact with friends he'd lost touch with for fifteen or twenty years. He goes for walks and bike rides and looks totally different now.

When I stepped in to help, his legs and glutes were so badly atrophied that he looked like an old man. He enjoys food again. His life is not perfect by any means—he's not well enough to work, still has days when he cannot walk far, doesn't want to eat, a list of symptoms as long as your arm—but he manages and copes with his symptoms so well. I'm so proud of him—I told him from the start, I can only hold out my hand, so the onus is down to him whether he chooses to take it. And he did. What a brave thing to do when you've lost trust, ergo faith, in everyone around you. It's meaningful to me because he chose to trust me, confide in me, and I think that was a massive leap of faith for him given his frame of mind back then.

Throwing herself into the care of her brother was more physically challenging than she had expected it to be:

It's been detrimental to my health being an on-call caregiver for six years—I'm bloody knackered and I'm in therapy. But I'm not needed as much these days, so I'm concentrating on getting myself back on track with a view to returning to work. When I decided to roll my sleeves up and get stuck in to help him, I had recently come out of hospital, had a near death experience. I'd returned to my job too soon afterwards—hadn't given myself enough time to recover as much as I should have, and I wasn't well enough to be working full time during the day and up all night with my brother. It's had quite a knock effect on my health. But I'm getting back on my feet gradually. As the song goes—"he ain't heavy, he's my brother" [she closed with a smile].

Cat's story is an example of the great lengths that siblings will go to for their siblings in distress. Not everyone can make the sacrifice necessary to allow sibling care to become their full-time occupation. At the other end of the spectrum, concern for siblings' welfare may be the most that circumstances allow. For instance, Nelda, who is in her sixties, has taken on something of a long-distance caregiving relationship with her own brothers. As she summed it up, *"I call my brothers regularly to see how they are doing. We are much older now, so there are health issues. They seem to appreciate my concern. If they have a problem of any kind, I am expected to advise them on how to handle it."*

CONCLUSION

Most siblings assume that any family-of-origin caregiving they do in adulthood would be caring for their parents. Providing care for siblings is often an unexpected development, and not all siblings are ready or able to provide the level of assistance desired or required. One of the themes found in the results of this current study was that the provision of support to siblings with whom even rocky relationships existed could be a rewarding and gratifying experience for everyone involved. Whether the assistance was emotional support, phone call check-ins, or showing up and moving in, both the cared for and the caregiving sibling were often pleasantly surprised at the emotional payoff that sibling support provided to them both.

FINAL TAKEAWAY: Caregiving for a sibling might be the last thing you ever thought you might have to do, but it is something less uncommon than it might seem to be. Sibling loyalty has the power to cut through many past hurts to bring sibs back together again when one is in need. Be willing to pitch in, as needed; be willing to know when enough is enough, as well.

Part IV

MAKING CHANGES
FOR THE FUTURE

Chapter Thirteen

Caring for Aging Parents

In the early years, sibling rivalry is about parental resources—sibs want to make sure that they get their fair share and more, if possible, of whatever resource is available. In adulthood, some siblings begin angling to be the child who is remembered most lucratively in their parents' estate-planning documents. Bitterness may develop if one sibling feels that they are being left out or passed over by their parents, and bitterness can also develop when one sibling feels that the care of their aging parents falls solely on their own shoulders.

DO DAUGHTERS AND SONS
PROVIDE EQUIVALENT CARE?

Studies suggest that as parents age, it is daughters, not sons, who step into the role of caregiver, often regardless of actual proximity or facilitative circumstances. In fact, mothers actually prefer their daughters over their sons when they seek closeness and support, according to one study.[1] Women are traditionally expected to be both nurturers of the next generation and caregivers of the prior generation. If mothers of girls do their job well, daughters will step into the caregiving role as their parents grow older. However, there are certainly some sons and sons-in-law who do take on the caregiving of older relatives within the family. Grace, the "big sister" to one sibling, a brother, related an encouraging story regarding how she and her brother had handled her mother's failing health and subsequent death. Grace affirmed, *"My brother was there for me during the difficult times in my life. He took care of our mother in later years be-*

cause I lived out of town." The loss of their mother was difficult for both Grace and her brother, but she shared that *"[any of our previous] sibling rivalry resolved when our mother died. After the death of my mother, the most meaningful experience was talking to my brother about what it was like growing up."* Grace's only regret about her sibling relationship was that she wished she and her brother had been born closer together, as she had perhaps lacked a little empathy toward him when they were younger.

Grace and her brother had no lingering conflicts about who did what and when for their mother during her final years. And while each sibling set would like for the investment in the care of their parents to be shared equitably or at least agreeably, minor squabbles can sometimes turn siblings into enemies depending on the stakes involved.

SUPPORTING AND SEEKING SUPPORT FROM AGING PARENTS

In a related research finding, it might be surprising to learn that when aging parents offer support to one of their children, they are likely to be providing support to their other offspring, as well.[2] The converse, however, was not found to be true—older parents who were on the receiving end of support from one of their children were less likely to be receiving support from their others. It appears that while parents want to be fair to all of their children, siblings are willing to let a brother or sister take on the majority of the caregiving for their aging parents. A child's resentment of a parent's financial support of a sibling can fester for years, even if the parent's decision makes good sense. As older adults grow less independent, adult children may grow surprisingly bold in their efforts to assist their parents with financial matters. Sometimes this can be for the good of their parents; sometimes it turns out to be for the direct benefit of the child.

DOES PARENT GENDER PLAY A ROLE IN THE CARE PARENTS RECEIVE?

Before further exploring the influence of gender on caregiving to parents, it is useful to explore the gender differences that are observed in the care that aging parents might request. Traditionally, women have stronger and more intimate social support networks than their male counterparts.[3] In fact, using data drawn from the Wisconsin Longitudinal Survey from 1993 and 2004, it was found that there were definite gender differences in support needed and received.[4] Women's frequency of social contact was higher than that of men, as were their expectations of social support. If men fell ill, they received less "talk" support than women as well as less support from non-related individuals. Although not specifically relevant to the caregiving children, this study did indicate that less educated individuals—regardless of gender—suffered from compromised social support. It is important for siblings to help their parents learn about available resources and help them access these resources, as well.

DOES GENDER PLAY A ROLE IN THE TYPE OF CARE PROVIDED?

Research shows that both men and women provide some form of care to their aging parents.[5] However, there is a traditional belief that the nature of the care provided falls out into a gender divide. Sons are more likely to assist with typically male chores, such as caring for the lawn, maintaining the car, and so on. Daughters are more likely inside the home providing personal direct care to their parents as well as offering emotional support and concern. Although there are cultures in which the eldest son is expected to provide care for his parents, it is generally his sisters or his wife who provide the necessary daily personal care.

In another study exploring the caregiving provided by sons and daughters, Cynthia Collins interviewed sixty widows who resided in independent living centers.[6] Her findings suggested that sons may be helping out their mothers at a higher rate, but the gender divide remains rigidly in place in some domains. Reports from the participants indicated that while sons provided assistance with technology issues (cellphones, computers, and so on), they also were doing more shopping for their mothers. Sons were also more likely to assist with transportation needs and financial management concerns. The areas in which daughters bested their brothers were, not unexpectedly, housekeeping and laundry tasks.

Does a gendered split in household chores influence sibling relationships over time? Perhaps. The division of household labor by gender in the family-of-origin was explored as a factor in predicting the quality of sibling relationships.[7] It was found that when parents had a more egalitarian division of chores, their children reported higher-quality relationships with their siblings. Perhaps it is never too early to model behaviors that break with traditional gender stereotypes. As parents age, the geographical availability of their children to provide instrumental support may be constrained. Through early efforts to model caregiving that crosses traditional gender lines, parents may enhance the odds that one of their children will be available and willing to provide needed assistance, whatever the task might be. Regardless of how care is addressed or responsibilities shared, research suggests that sibling relationships can be greatly strained when an inequity in the care burden is observed.

RESPONDING TO PARENTAL ILLNESS

Depending on the family's customs and expectations, a parent's illness may serve as a "call to arms" in which adult siblings drop what they are doing and rush to their parent's side—whether it's across the street or across the country. In other families, health issues may be held more privately and children not alerted until the crisis has passed or the prognosis has grown grave. Regardless of when medical news is shared, the geographically closest sibling typically steps into the role as primary caregiver.[8] While the taking of bereavement leave seldom creates issues in the workplace, arranging to be an on-site caregiver can be more challenging depending on a sibling's professional and geographical limitations.

Deciding whether or not you can provide a home to your parents as their health declines can also lead to animosity between siblings. One caregiving daughter, Wanda, who is now fifty-eight, shared the poignant story of how this choice placed a wedge between her brother, her sister, and her. She shared, *"I decided to take care of our mom until she died. My siblings wanted to put her in a home and I could not do that. I told them that it was on me because it was my decision and that they did not need to help me. If I had put her in an old age home I would not be able to sleep at night."*

Distance Caregivers

Siblings at any distance should be included in family discussions, given access to medical personnel, and have input in family decision-making. Considered *distance caregivers* (DCGs), they make up approximately 15 percent of all caregivers for older relatives.[9] It makes good sense for on-the-ground siblings to shoulder the primary responsibility of caregiving, but their far-off siblings can be excellent team members. *"My sister and I have become so very close over the last twenty years. We work in tandem to care for my parents. She lives forty-five minutes away and I live four hundred miles away,"* noted one DCG who is truly invested in her parents' well-being.

While these DCG siblings are spared the day-in-and-day-out caregiving stress, they may face an even more complex set of stressors. They can be every bit as emotionally invested in their parents' care and well-being as their on-site siblings, but they also may be wrestling with significant guilt, betrayal, and shame due to their inability to be physically present for their parents.[10] Depending on the distance they must travel, there may also be significant financial costs associated with their efforts to travel home as often as possible. Caregiving from a distance is seldom a lighter burden than on-site caregiving in terms of the emotional and psychological toll it takes on DCGs.

CAREGIVING AND LOSS AS
SIBLING BONDING OPPORTUNITIES

Growing up, many siblings look for ways to outdo or show up one another. Some may choose to be the athlete or the artist, the scholar or the popular kid, and so on. When a medical crisis hits home, however, siblings often release former grudges and antipathies to band together in their efforts to help their suffering family member. Whether it is existential anxiety related to the fear of death or the evolutionary need to seek social connection in time of distress, even highly dysfunctional families can often find ways to join together to care for a family member.

A young woman shared that she and her brother leaned heavily on one another when their father was fighting with cancer: *"When my dad was diagnosed with cancer, my brother and I were huge emotional supports for each other. It is rewarding that we are able to have intellectual conversations and be goofy and playfully make fun of our parents together."* The middle child of an admittedly "disconnected family," Kelly shared that the most meaningful experience she and her siblings shared was *"navigating my mom's cancer diagnosis and treatment together."* When siblings come together to confront a common enemy, the illness afflicting their families, it can open up new depths of communication between siblings.

Being able to share pain and fear with another person actually serves to lessen the stress associated with unpleasant news as well as to ease the burden. The benefits of talk therapy with professional helpers are often realized through the actual sharing of a client's story with a nonjudgmental, accepting, and supportive individual.[11] For many siblings, their ability to share their pain as well as fall back into the comforting and familiar patterns of interaction involving humor can mitigate distress.

The ways in which you and your siblings respond to family tragedy may vary considerably based on your own unique cultural identities. A woman in her thirties described the bonding that evolved as she and her sister faced the most significant challenge either had faced in adulthood. *"[It was] the death of our beloved grandmother. My sister and I were both heartbroken over the loss. We drew together in our grief. We got matching yellow rose (my grandma's favorite flower) tattoos."* At the present moment, the sisters are doing their best to cope with their mother's diagnosis of Alzheimer's disease. *"I have fought with my sister about not having help with caring for our sick mother. My sister and I can scream at each other, but we always make up. We have a deep affection for each other and enjoy each other's company . . . consider her a good friend."* Being able to express the best and the worst of your feelings with siblings is one of the perks of a strong sibling relationship.

If you and your siblings are providing, or preparing to provide, care for an aging parent, it is beneficial to discuss the expectations of everyone involved in the decision or the daily care. Until each sibling has been given space to share his thoughts, there will be more room later for complaints, resentment, and dissatisfaction with the arrangement or the care given. Gratitude for the direct caregiver as well as for the siblings that provide financial or other forms of support should be communicated openly. A recent qualitative research study was designed to allow caregivers to discuss the level of appreciation that they felt from their siblings.[12] Specific expressions of gratitude that make a difference to a caregiving sibling range from simply expressing appreciation with a "thank you," to taking time to commend the caregiver on all that he does, to offering a tangible expression of gratitude. Behaviors to avoid include making promises of respite care and canceling out at the last minute, offering to run errands if you know that you won't have time to follow through, and dismissing the efforts of your sibling in his caregiving duties.

MOURNING THE LOSS OF LIFE

The loss of a parent can alter the relationship between siblings as well as alter a person's sense of self. While parental loss is an expected transition in middle or older adulthood,[13] this loss can pack a significant punch at any life stage depending on the nature of the parent-child relationship. Hayslip, Pruett, and Caballero explored parental loss among both young and middle adults.[14] They determined that daughters had a much more difficult time dealing with parental loss than sons, although younger adults of both genders were more affected than midlife adults. Adult children who were single or separated from their partners also had a more difficult time coping with the loss than married offspring. Grief is a complex emotion, and the loss of a parent from whom a child is estranged can cause a significant grief response quite different from the normal sadness experienced during the mourning of a beloved parent.

COMMUNICATING ABOUT LOSS
FACILITATES HEALTHY MOURNING

While each person processes grief differently, there are frequently family rituals and expected reactions to loss. Mourning rituals may be connected to religious beliefs, cultural traditions, or family customs. In terms of family communication patterns, which were explored in chapter 4, it has been revealed that the greater the level of conversation prior to a loss, the more likely it is for mourners to experience a sense of personal growth from the grief process in addition to lessened feelings of detachment from one another.[15] Unexpected and untimely sibling loss was addressed in chapter 6, and the unexpected nature of early loss adds complexity to the mourning process. When older adults die, the timing might make more "theoretical sense," but family members may show great variation in their responses to the knowledge of the impending loss and the loss itself.

Caring for an older relative can be a uniquely rewarding experience when an effective support system is in place. Carly and her many siblings grew up in a multigenerational home, and now they are facing the death of their grandmother. Although the loss is expected, the immenseness of the situation affects them all. Carly shared,

> *My siblings and I were raised with our maternal grandparents. My maternal grandmother is currently on hospice and in the last couple months of her life. Her deterioration has been dramatic over the last year. Her deteriorating health and impending death has been hard on the entire family, especially my parents and I since we care for her in our homes. While there has been no outcome to this experience, discussing who will speak at her funeral, accepting her death, and discussing the process of getting her back to New Mexico for the wake and funeral has been a difficult topic for my siblings and I to discuss.*

This will be a multigenerational loss for Carly and her family, and the closeness and openness they share may allow the coming months to be less painful than other circumstances might have made them.

CAUTION: ALL SIBLINGS GRIEVE
IN THEIR OWN UNIQUE WAYS

One research team recently reported that sibling relationships tended to be affected by one of eight different response types.[16] These categories were identified as "even closer," "just us now," "new roles, responsibilities, and relationships," "unsettled estate," "never close," "from bad to worse," "back together, temporarily," and "no change." While sibling relationships are typically the product of years of routine engagement, some end in cold-shouldered standoffs, or even worse, there can often be surprise endings when the loss of a parent, especially the last parent, occurs.

A midlife adult woman with two sisters and one brother recounted their difficult childhood and its effect on their current relationships with one another: *"There was abuse in our family. . . . Fear and shame has caused a rift between us."* Asked about their relationships today, she shared, *"The most challenging and meaningful event [for us siblings] was at our father's funeral. We all had different types of relationships with him, which sometimes caused friction in the conversation."* Mortality comes into focus and the inescapable tenuousness of relationships becomes clear. Sometimes this realization galvanizes siblings into action to rekindle sibling relationships; for others, it is further impetus to leave the sibling relationships as they are and focus on other more rewarding relationships and activities. Following are examples of the ways in which a parent's death might affect brothers and sisters. We will begin with the less encouraging scenarios and end the chapter with expressions of hope for growth.

Filial Guilt Shared or Self-Owned

Depending on parents' ages or the presence of significant others, siblings may be asked to step up and make medical decisions for their parents that may have grave consequences and lasting influence. When siblings differ in their opinions about what is best for a parent, they may form alliances together to overrule a dissenting opinion.[17] The resulting disagreements can be challenging for healthcare workers to navigate, as well as for the sibling who holds the least power in the family.

In the case of one respondent, Judy, her mother's cognitive decline had placed Judy and her brothers into the position of healthcare decision-makers. Describing the most difficult conflict the siblings had faced, Judy recalled, *"My mother's care when she had dementia and decisions regarding her health. I made all of these decisions as she appointed me as her care provider. I wanted her to be fed at the end, but my brothers felt that it was more humane to allow her to die in hospice with feeding intervention. I finally gave in to my brothers but feel ashamed and hurt that she died that way."*

Jim, who is seventy-four and one of eight siblings, shared his own experiences with end-of-life decisions that he and his siblings were required to make. Jim noted that he and his siblings still feel heartache when they reflect on their mother's last years. When asked about the most difficult

issue he and his siblings had faced, Jim replied, *"The fact that Mom lin-
gered in a nursing home for many years before she died at age ninety-two
is the hardest thing for all of us to bear. Only the three youngest brothers
and their spouses lived close enough to visit her, and the rest of us were
spared that agony and I now feel that guilt. They say they understand
because of the distance, but I wonder."*

Children cannot always be where they would rather be when a parent is
ill; geographical distance and professional responsibilities can make it difficult for siblings to get together until life is nearly ended or as soon as a
death has occurred. One midlife woman, Ellen, shared that she was seven
hundred miles away from her parents' home during her mother's final days.
She grieved the distance and had visited often in the final six months of her
mother's life. Arriving home for the funeral, Ellen reported feeling like all
of the hometown family and community eyes looked at her in disapproval
for not being more present during her mother's illness. Two years have
passed since she and her brother lost their mother, but Ellen still feels that
her brother is more distant and less caring than he had been before their
mother died. *"I did the best I could, my brother knew that. He had retired
and lived across the road. My life didn't turn out the way that his did. I just
don't want to feel guilty the rest of my life,"* Ellen explained. It can be terribly difficult to lose a parent, and the guilt that one sibling may feel for not
doing all that other siblings may have been able to do can endure.

Greed Versus Equity

Too frequently, siblings allow formerly repressed feelings of inequity and
resentment to bubble over when a parent is at life's end. In some cases,
the desire for a "fair share" of a parent's estate can overshadow feelings
of grief and regret at the loss of a parent. Below are just a few examples
of conflicts and regrets expressed when sibling relationships are spoiled
by concerns about financial gain upon the loss of a parent.

Growing up in a home where siblings were allowed to engage in physical altercations with one another, Dyan, a forty-nine-year-old woman,
shared that when her father died, the attacks were no longer physical, but
rather emotional and financial attacks designed to steal Dyan's share of
the family inheritance. Her biggest conflicts with her siblings revolved

around "*inheritance and fairness. They became intensely angry that I wanted them to be fair and stop spending the money on themselves before it was divided up. The outcome was that they got worse with being unfair and refused to set up the trust as they had been instructed to do, and I had to hire an attorney. They still shorted me, cursed me out, and treated me horribly. I went 'no contact' with them.*"

Dyan's bitterness runs deep and has effectively ended all interactions between her and her siblings. When responding to a question about what she would most like her siblings to say to her today, she replied, "*Here is all the money we stole from you and we are very sorry for what we put you through. Please forgive us, we love you and what we did was wrong, and we want to make everything right again.*" Sadly, Dyan has little hope of this happening and no expectations about any future relationship rebuilding between the siblings.

Mark, who has three sisters and one brother, shared that his parents' estate has produced the greatest conflict between him and his siblings—while they were living and now that they have passed away: "*My parents let us know their wishes about the estate they left when they were alive, and they spent significantly on estate planning to control the estate upon both of their deaths. Regardless, the process was ruined and controlled by my brother and one of the co-trustees, who bullied the other two trustees (the oldest two siblings).*" Mark now has little contact with his siblings, but his biggest regret related to them is "*that I allowed myself to be bullied for fear of not getting inheritance.*"

In a society in which money is equated with power, affection, and self-worth, it is apparent how the final gift from a parent can have such tangible and intangible value to a child. Efforts to win the rivalry game once and for all will always produce at least one loser. Bridgette, a sixty-year-old with three sisters and two brothers, shared, "*After my parents' deaths, my siblings sued me to keep me from inheriting anything. They were unsuccessful. I was found to owe them nothing. Ironically, they ended up owing each other monies. [My siblings] stopped talking to me after the death of our parents. At the time, I wanted to have a relationship with them. Now I wish to be permanently estranged.*" While Bridgette was able to come out the winner in the legal arena, she had already lost her place in the sibling support network years earlier.

There is a special poignancy in the outcomes of some inheritance battles that cannot be avoided once the conflict starts rolling forward. A woman in her sixties who is one of four siblings noted that earlier in their adult years, "*[there had been] very little conflict [among us] until our parents' passed away and we had to 'save' their home and split the inheritance. My younger siblings had unexpressed feelings that came out with the pressure of dividing our inheritance. I had always heard about families fighting over money, but I never thought it would happen to mine!*" This set of siblings, though, is luckier than most, as they have continued to move forward in life. Their older sister affirmed, "*I plan on continuing to reach out to my siblings in positive ways . . . I will always love my siblings deeply. I am sure of that.*"

Headed Downhill

Sharing the history of parental losses she had experienced, a midlife woman, Karla, recounted the following: "*My dad was my 'rock' in our family. Mother had mental health issues and frequent migraine head-aches. She committed suicide when I was twenty-four years old. My Dad was there for all four girls (including myself). He died when I was thirty-three.*" Karla shared that her father's death created power struggles between her and another sister that have led to estrangement between them all: "*The serious relationship issues began at the time of my father's death. He left me as executor of a small insurance policy with directions to divide equally between the four siblings. One sister was bitter as she thought Dad would leave her in charge.*" Currently, she describes the relationship between herself and her sisters as: "*Simply stated, we are cut off from each other. Over time each sister has chosen to not speak to each other. My attempts have been futile. As the oldest sister my role as surrogate mother ceased.*" Although Karla was not an only child, she wondered if her current situation was similar. "*[I'm] not an only child, yet I think often, with sadness, the loss of three sisters must be similar. Maybe the exception is there were relationships; loss is like a death of my siblings.*" Returning to the topic of the loss of her father, to whom she was very close, she recognized that all parents have their faults, although some children tend to idealize them when they are young. She noted, "*My favorite quote about my father [is from Anne Sexton]: 'It doesn't matter who my father was; it matters who I remember he was.'*"

Granting Parents' Wishes for You and Your Sibling?

Sometimes it is a parent's wishes for their children that help shape adult sibling relationships. Sharing her frustration at feeling locked into a relationship with a disappointing sister, JoDonna, a woman in her mid-forties, related, *"Twenty-one years ago, I decided to sever the bond with the sister who disrespects me, since I would feel so depressed and bad about myself after I had spent time with her. However, my sister invoked the help of my father to 'guilt' me into staying connected. He said he 'could not die knowing his daughters did not get along.'"* She added ironically, *"He is still alive and well to this day."* Researchers Glenna D. Spitze and Katherine Trent noted that after a parent dies, there is a diminished level of support between siblings.[18] Whether the loss of a parent provides the freedom to break away from your family-of-origin or the beginning of a different obligation altogether, finding ways to leverage support—from friends, family, or clinical professionals—can help you handle the new circumstances in which you find yourself.

Growing Up

As noted earlier in this chapter, sudden and unexpected deaths can be harder to accept and emotionally process, although siblings are spared the anticipatory grieving, which can weigh heavily on a family. However, Winnie, in her sixties now, shared how devastated she had been when her mother died suddenly. Her two siblings, both brothers, lived far away from where she and her mother resided, and in her family, she had always been the reliable one. She found out exactly how reliable and strong she needed to be when faced with the loss: *"I was left to make funeral arrangements and pay for everything. I simply did what needed to be done as they could not get back home in time. After all, I am the 'responsible' one. It was one of the most difficult things in my life until then."* She took on a new level of maturity from this experience.

Continuing, Winnie shared that the strength she developed at the loss of her mother was practice for the challenges that were to come next in her life.

The most meaningful times that my brothers and I spend together include attending family marriages, births, and deaths. The death of our mother at sixty, death of my best friend at forty-six, and then the death of my husband at fifty . . . all gone too soon, leaving gaping wounds in my heart and soul.

The losses were hard on all of us, but I was the one to keep things together as grief hit us all. Others fall apart when crises hit. I can only fall apart inside because arrangements have to be made and no one steps up to take over. Yup, always the responsible one to the end . . . and I hate it at times. I love both of my brothers and will always be here for them. Hopefully my youngest brother's heart will open someday, and we can rebuild a friendship. I can only hope and keep love in my heart.

Becoming the Matriarch or Patriarch before You Are Ready

Morgan is the only sister to four brothers, and they have always looked up to her as the leader of the sibling set. She noted that she has varying degrees of closeness with her brothers, but overall she feels the relationships are good. When asked about the most difficult discussion that the five of them had endured, she responded,

Working with them to plan our mother's funeral was both challenging and rewarding. I got to see them function as adults for really the first time. We had to navigate our mom's illness and her death, in the midst of a larger family battle over our grandmother's estate. Seeing how my mother's siblings handled her mother's death helped us to be very diplomatic with our mom's estate and belongings. It went really well, for as miserable as it all was. Once mom passed, I became the new matriarch of the family. They trust me for advice and for help, and sometimes that's terrifying.

Morgan modeled a strength during the difficult period of loss, and being given the role of the new matriarch provided evidence of just how much her brothers valued her wisdom and experience.

Relationships Deepen and Connections Re-Form

When asked to share a particularly meaningful experience with her adult siblings, Birdie, a woman who has entered older adulthood, shared that any time she spent with her siblings felt meaningful to her. On reflection, though, Birdie was able to identify an experience that stood out especially strong in terms of a sense of connection and affection between the siblings. As she related, *"When my dad passed away and we all got together, we had a blast watching the old movies he took when we were kids and reminisced about the good old days. It was a bittersweet experience."* Even when the experience between grieving siblings is bittersweet, it creates a shared adult experience that can help cement the sibling bonds at a time when social support is growing in importance.

New Hopes for the Relationship

When adult sibling relationships have been less than satisfying, siblings may reconnect at their parent's death and openly acknowledge the need for closer relationships. They may vow to be better about keeping in touch and being supportive of one another in the future. Asked about sibling regrets, Mary, a woman in her mid-sixties with just one sibling, a younger brother, shared, "*I would like to have been closer. I understand some people have close and rewarding relationships with siblings. We are re-setting our relationship following the death of our mother. We are trying to plan a joint family trip, which may enhance ongoing relationships.*" Mary and her brother recognized the value of their remaining family connections.

CONCLUSION

Regrettably, caregiving for aging parents often takes place in residential treatment centers or in the home by paid healthcare workers. Distance and professional responsibilities are common barriers faced by siblings who are trying to devise workable caregiving arrangements for parents. Being able to be there for your parent—and your siblings—can make a significant difference to their peace of mind and your own over the years. Further, it is important to encourage older adults to engage in estate planning to limit potential conflicts that might arise if parents' wishes are not clear. Some older adults are reluctant to approach the topic of end-of-life planning due to a desire to avoid potentially depressing topics or, in some cases, to maintain power over others. Some adult children are also reluctant to engage in end-of-life conversations with their parents. Regardless of the resistance present on either side of the conversation, the topic should be addressed in a rational manner early, before circumstances lead to ill-advised choices or before adult children must make decisions that parents would have prevented had they outlined their wishes prior to a medical emergency. While parents do not need to lay bare the final details of their wills prior to their deaths, adult children need to know where to find the will and any other documents that will be needed when the time comes.

FINAL TAKEAWAY: Regardless of your shared history and gene pool, when a parent falls ill or dies, sibs will respond in their own individual manner. Don't hold a sibling to your own personal yardstick. Each family may have an accepted practice related to caregiving or mourning, but each sibling's response reflects her own individual makeup and experiences that other siblings do not share. Practice tolerance for behaviors you don't understand.

Chapter Fourteen

Deconstructing Unproductive Communication Patterns

Trying to undo a lifetime of ineffective behavior patterns is not an easy task. Humans crave the comfort of the familiar, and successfully encouraging people to change their behavior is a daunting task for even trained professional clinicians. As family therapists know, however, it only takes one member of a family system to shift his behavior and the entire system must shift in response. In chapter 6, the influence of Satir's typology of dysfunctional family roles was briefly addressed. In this chapter, discussion of Satir's typology of family communicators will be presented as well as examples of new response behaviors that can short-circuit some of the more unproductive communication exchanges between siblings. Keep in mind that the definition of a healthy family is not the *absence* of conflict, but the ability to successfully address conflict.

FAMILY COMMUNICATION PATTERNS DEMYSTIFIED: FOUR SURVIVAL STANCES PLUS ONE

Just as birth order can be a determinant of the respect and responsibility you carry within the family and with your siblings throughout adulthood, the communication style we rely on with siblings can affect these factors, as well. We fill particular communication roles depending on what our family system supports. In her seminal book, *Peoplemaking*, Satir provided an in-depth look at four survival stances/communication styles that thrive in many families.[1, 2]

Satir recognized that family members choose unhealthy behavior response patterns to moderate low self-esteem and assuage their fear of being unlovable.[3] She described four communication roles that support family functioning, no matter how dysfunctional it might be. Unfortunately, the patterns that begin in childhood can become an integral aspect of adult behavior. These types are the blamer, the placater, the computer, and the distracter. There is a fifth communication standpoint, one that is signified by congruence and the ability to remain level and balanced in discussions. It has been termed the *leveller* by some, and it is the one from which the most effective communicators respond.

The Blamer

The *blamer* is the sibling who is always ready to find someone else to blame for anything that goes wrong or creates difficulty for her or the family. Her first response to a problem is to look for someone or something external to herself to blame. The blamer's first thought when faced with a conflict is *"Who did this to me?"* External events and others' behavior are personalized. Blamers are driven to find a perpetrator to blame and to punish.

The Placater

Placaters are the family members who will do whatever it takes to avoid conflict between siblings. The need for harmony can even lead the placater to take responsibility for events that are not his fault. The placater's first thought when faced with a conflict is *"What did I do and how can I fix it?"* Placaters minimize external events and others' behaviors. Their goal is to find the quickest method of defusing a conflict.

The Computer

Just as the nickname suggests, the *computer* will focus on data and information and refrain from displaying any emotion, taking little notice or consideration of others' emotional states. This sibling is usually very reasonable and will cut through the "fluff" of charged emotions to focus on the incontrovertible facts of a situation. The computer's first thought when faced with conflict is *"What events are in play and what is a logical response?"* External events and cause and effect are valued, while feelings are forbidden territory for this sibling. Computers need to appear rational, logical, and unaffected by emotion.

The Distracter

Satir conceptualized the *distracter* as a person who operates from panic mode. Rather than addressing the situation at hand, the distracter works to keep the focus off the problem and may respond in what siblings perceive as a highly irrational manner. Distracters may have a welcome tension-relieving effect on their siblings, as their mode of avoiding conflict is to simply overlook it.

The Leveller

A sibling that is able to respond from this perspective is likely to be the most successful in dealing with stressful situations from childhood throughout adulthood. When confronted with unanticipated challenges, the *leveller* accepts them as simply a part of life with which everyone must cope at some point in time. Levellers want to keep everything and every-one "on the level," as they recognize that this is the best stance to take in response to trouble. The leveller's first thought when faced with a conflict is *"It's okay for all of us to be upset, but we need to cut to the chase and focus on figuring out how to deal."* Levellers are comfortable with emo-tional responses from themselves and others and can tolerate not knowing better than the other types. They don't catastrophize, minimize, or ignore things, they just focus on finding the best solution given the circumstances.

DO BEHAVIOR PATTERNS LAST INTO ADULTHOOD?

A young woman, Maire, reflecting back on her family's roles, unknow-ingly described how she and her siblings responded from the basic four dysfunctional communication stances growing up. Following is her fam-ily typology, with relevant roles included within brackets to point out congruence with the Satir roles: *"I was the one who gave my mother no problems [the placater]. Nicki was the selfish one [the blamer] and Cathy was the bully [another blamer], Pam was the know-it-all [the computer], and Jenny was the crazy one [distracter]."* Maire grew up feeling that she always had to be the family mediator due to her strong dislike for conflict. Being the placater is a heavy role to carry, and Maire now shares that she has taken on the less active aspects of the role. When asked if there was anything that she wished her siblings could understand about who she is today, she replied, *"Nothing . . . my siblings only talk about their own issues . . . which they never seem to resolve. I no longer participate in [their] discussions if I can help it."* Choosing to avoid contact is always an option and, for some, may be the only way to maintain personal well-being. When siblings grow up in a home wracked with conflict, unless there is concerted effort from both sides, the sibling relationship is unlikely to develop into a close, intimate bond, unfortunately.[4]

Beth, now forty-nine, shared that it seemed her younger brother could not move past the blaming role. As she recounted, *"My sister, brother, and I had a huge family argument over my brother choosing to harshly judge my sister's lifestyle, which does not involve or impact his life. He brought up family dynamics from over thirty years ago and is carrying a grudge against me for an incident (not serious or life-threatening, just young sibling stuff) that occurred when I was eight and he was three. He now holds me responsible for all his negative feelings in adulthood. He is transferring his issues with his wife onto me and using our childhood as an excuse."* Some siblings get caught in the past and have difficulty recognizing the futility of clinging to past relational behaviors.

WHAT STANCE REFLECTS YOUR OWN BEHAVIOR RESPONSES?

The specific descriptions of each of the survival stances may suggest that each person falls into only one category. However, healthy adults respond from a variety of modes depending on the specific circumstances of a conflict.[5] It can be important to give yourself permission to acknowledge that others are to blame for problems when they actually are. There are also times when the dispassionate response of the computer role is necessary to cope with overwhelming emotions, such as when making end-of-life decisions for older adult family members. If you find yourself constantly falling into the same role—and that role is not doing you or your siblings any good—it might be useful to explore whether or not you play the same role in your other relationships. If so, then it may be time to work intentionally to expand your response repertoire. Try standing up for yourself if you always accept unfounded blame. If you're always looking for someone else to blame, take an honest inventory of the role that you may play in a problematic situation. Try being more reasonable and logical if you always jump to irrational responses to rational problems. If it is only around your siblings that you fall into particular patterns, you may want to determine what your triggers might be and develop new ways of responding to these situations. Change is never easy, but remember that all it takes for a system to shift is for one member to change.

IT CAN GET BETTER

Among some siblings, it may only take the simple recognition of how unproductive their communication patterns truly are for change to begin. Sometimes it takes a family crisis to provide the urgency that tends to accompany change. As siblings mature, the value of healthy relationships grows in priority.[6] Even seemingly immutable behaviors from childhood can shift. Whitney, a thirty-something middle child between a brother and a sister, addressed the conflicts that she and her siblings had faced in adulthood. She noted, *"Many conflicts are the same as when we were kids—petty stuff. A few years ago, we had a deep discussion about how we fight over petty stuff and don't enjoy each other. That conversation changed everything. We quit fighting about stupid things and enjoy each other's company."* Another respondent shared that the most meaningful experience between her, her brother, and their sister had been *"a discussion with all three of us about how we want to relate to each other as adults."* Whether siblings are able to name the communication problem directly or merely learn to tolerate siblings' behavior for the sake of the relationship, positive change can happen.

TAKING A RISK TO SHARE WITH SIBLINGS

When siblings are able to open up to one another and risk vulnerability, this may reflect a more mature perspective and level of acceptance than childhood memories might predict. As Lisa, fifty-six, shared, *"When I found out my adult son was addicted to drugs . . . I was afraid to tell them, afraid of judgement. The outcome was that they were the opposite of judgmental, they have been supportive and loving."* Unfortunately, not everyone is as fortunate as Lisa. Another woman dealing with her own daughter's addiction shared the following narrative of the fear of relating an addictions secret to a sibling: *"I liked it when my sister and I were pregnant at the same time and the first summers when our children played together. Things have changed now, though. My daughter has been an opiate addict for the past nine years and will be [turning only] twenty-three next month. My sister would be the last person I would confide in about my daughter's issues."* Being unable to discuss this type of heavy burden with siblings can add to the weight of the burden.

Keeping up consistent communication brings satisfaction for many siblings, regardless of the seeming significance of the topics discussed. While Belinda found it somewhat difficult to adjust to her sister's numerous marriages, she felt that the most rewarding aspect of her and her sister's relationship was regular communication, *"when the sister I felt close to would call me every Sunday (or I would call her) no matter where I lived. I would encourage her or we would just listen to the ups and downs of life. We had a trusting, supportive relationship [regardless of] the multiple husbands and the effects of those changes."*

Another woman who had several cut-off relationships from her siblings reported an enhanced relationship with her brother. She related, *"[Unlike most of my sisters], my brother and I do have a 'contact relationship,' and we can talk frankly. Both of us can say what we feel and can express our perspective of family events and dynamics to each other without the other trying to correct or fix [the other's perspective]."* Being able to own your mistakes and being able to forgive the frailties of your siblings can make a significant difference in the lifetime durability and depth of the relationship.

A woman in her fifties, Jess, who longs for greater closeness with her siblings, regretted a great deal in her sibling relationships. She affirmed, *"I envy truly those who are so close to their siblings. My family is very fragmented, and I wish we had different foundations and upbringing. But I accept the way the past is."* Piecing back together a fragmented family can only happen if a family member takes a risk and reaches out to another.

(OVER)DEPENDING ON FAMILY?

While there are a few people who believe they would be better off without their siblings, most people grow to appreciate them more and more over time. Connections with friends can shift as life stages or geographical locations change. Neighbors move. Coworkers leave. Friends' interests may change or the activities you once enjoyed together may lose their appeal. On the other hand, siblingships are pretty difficult to let go. For some sibs, the entanglement runs so deep that the relationship might be considered enmeshment. Referring to the earlier discussion of boundaries in family systems, enmeshment occurs when the boundaries are too diffuse and family members have difficulty individuating from the family.

Describing her regrets related to her sibling relationships, Toni, a midlife woman, shared, "*My regret is that I think I loved them too much. I didn't form too many other relationships in my new hometown because I was always running back home.*" Toni felt that she allowed her sibling identity to become the most prominent aspect of her self-identity as she developed into adulthood. She realizes that she has reinforced her siblings' expectations of her over several decades and is on a challenging path to "reeducate" them. She went on, "*I plan on continuing to reach out to my siblings in positive ways, but at the same time, reaching out less and looking around at forming new friendship opportunities that I have ignored over the years. I will always love my siblings deeply. I am sure of that.*" She also realized that she had been the sibling who took the lead in maintaining relationships and connections between siblings. Admitting this to herself made her "*feel a little rejected in this realization.*" Toni wished for a more even balance in her sibling relationships.

Unfortunately, no relationship—either friendship or family—is ever likely to offer a day-by-day, moment-to-moment balance of give-and-take. In a recent study from MIT, it was suggested that we are only accurate about 50 percent of the time when we assume who our friends actually are.[7] The measure of true friendship rests in mutuality, and not everyone a person believes is his friend would consider that person a friend. However, regarding true friendships, the chronological aspect of mutuality is not set in stone; it can fluctuate as life circumstances change. Sibling relationships are dissimilar to friendships in that our sibs are not chosen or self-selected, as friends are. However, for the sibship to deepen and grow into a valuable and valued commodity, it requires a similar give-and-take as good friendships offer over time. When one sib believes himself to be the one that continues to give in, make allowances for, alter his plans for, or cede control to his siblings, resentment builds over time, just as it will in other relationships. Keeping a check on how you feel about the effort you are investing in your sibships can help you avoid reaching the point where discussions become arguments or where accusations are made that are difficult to take back.

Being able to acknowledge that no one has the power to change the past is an important first step in letting go of the past and building more supportive relationships in adulthood. Earlier in this chapter, the story of Jess was shared. She had allowed herself to take on the placater role in her family and did what was necessary to avoid unpleasant conflict. However, as she matured, Jess was able to leave behind a judgmental perspective that had kept her from truly seeing her siblings for who they were. She went on to note, "*I find I need to be more forceful about my feelings . . . and I decided not to judge my sister in my head. I finally saw her hurt (just like mine) and stopped treating her like she is stupid or an emotional basket case. She is suffering as much as me and just needs a longer path to find herself . . . I need to acknowledge my siblings' pain is real and they are not stupid or [still children]. [They are] people who are just on a different path than me.*"

Although Jess may sound like she has gotten it all together now that a few decades have passed, she admits that she still has some issues with sibling communication. As she concluded, "*I feel guilty avoiding some of them. I simply cannot pick the phone and call them without powering myself for weeks or months at a time. I need to chill my nerves and see if I can keep contact with them more often. When we get together, you would not know the fragmentation, but ooh boy, I bet they feel the same inside.*"

CONCLUSION

Ineffective communication styles can be learned early, but research provides evidence that enhancing these skills can pay off in adulthood. Encouraging your siblings to improve their communication skills may not be as effective as you would like, but remember that when one member in the family system changes, the entire system must shift in response.

In closing, it is worthwhile mentioning a study that explored the development of individuals' social networks over adulthood. It turns out that there are two factors that can predict the status of our social support networks at fifty; these two factors reflect what was going on in our social world at age twenty and again at age thirty. According to researchers Carmichael, Reis, and Duberstein, the higher the number of people in your support network at age twenty combined with the quality of your social interactions at age thirty predict your overall psychological and social well-being at age fifty.[8] While it may be a little late to turn back the clock to re-set your social networks, remember that every rule has its exceptions, and you can create more satisfying relationships and friendships at any age. If you think your siblings would be the best place to start, it may be time to make that call.

FINAL TAKEAWAY: Faulty communication systems cannot improve their functioning unless someone is willing to change it up. If you want to see yours change, be willing to stick at new behaviors even if your siblings are slow to respond to the changes.

Chapter Fifteen

Siblings for Life

Closing the Gaps in the Family Circle

When you pause to think of the most important roles you hold in life, *sibling* might not be the one that first running smothly springs to mind. Many individuals take their sibling relationships for granted when they are first running smoothly or simply write them off when they go off-track. However, it is important to recognize that the deeper you move into adulthood, the greater the potential benefits of efforts to improve your sibling relationships.

There are studies that have tied together experiences in sibships with experiences in later romantic relationships and friendships.[1, 2] According to many individuals interviewed for this book, there can be a satisfyingly positive relationship between the quality of sibships and romantic or platonic relationships; conversely, there are strong hopes that negative outcomes in other relationships can be avoided when early sibships were filled with tension or animosity.

DO OPPOSITE GENDER SIBS INFLUENCE ROMANTIC RELATIONSHIPS?

We learn a lot about anger management, conflict resolution, and relationship maintenance from our early relationships. In fact, the conflict resolution behaviors we practice with our mothers and siblings mediate our romantic-partner conflict behaviors.[3] Good siblings tend to become good partners.

Brothers with Sisters

Perhaps not too surprising is the finding that individuals with opposite sex siblings actually develop stronger romantic relationship competence than adults without opposite sex siblings.[4] Men who participated in the current study shared the belief that growing up with a sister was an asset in terms of understanding women in general. A forty-five-year-old man affirmed that his two sisters had given him an edge over "sisterless" men as he stated, *"I seem to respect women more than my friends who do not have sisters."* Another man noted, *"I got some pretty good insight and relationship advice from my sister, which helped [me in my romantic relationships]."*

While the examples above suggest that early relationships fostered respect for women, Zack, the thirty-five-year-old brother to an older sister, shared his thoughts about how much he admires his sister: *"I always ask myself why I can't just find a version of my sister to date, but maybe the emotionally stable, logical, intelligent women seep into my subconscious as platonic, whereas the emotionally distressed ones—like my mother— I see as mates. I have a problem breaking this pattern on my own."* He summed up, *"Well I'm a really good friend, and my sister was my first friend. I have solid friendships in my life. She's probably a big reason for why."* Zack was fortunate to have received an early entry into the development of friendships with females, although his romantic preferences may hinder the development of stable romantic relationships.

Sisters with Brothers

A good proportion of women with brothers believed these early sister-brother relationships positively influenced their own standards and expectations of romantic partners. For some siblings, their brother or sister may actually be the measure of a potential friend or partner's value. As Morgan, in her late twenties, shared, *"Since my brother and dad have always taken care of me, it helped me recognize what I seek in relationships. My brother is a man of integrity and has an extremely high work ethic. I value these characteristics and made sure that my now-husband had these traits. I also informally sought his approval of my husband because I value his opinion."* A twenty-five-year-old woman believes that her relationship with her brother "*helped a lot with my romantic relationships since my brother is one of the main male figures in my life.*"

Another woman, however, shared a different take on the influence that brothers might have that might not be as beneficial as her partners would like. As she related, "*My siblings and I tend to lay everything out on the table without thinking first. While our initial reaction may be hurt and anger, we are quick to forgive each other and then figure out how to fix things to move forward. This pattern has been toxic in my romantic relationships, as my partners don't understand how I can say exactly what I'm thinking or feeling without censoring it and then expect them to forgive.*"

SIBSHIPS AND NON-ROMANTIC RELATIONSHIPS: GROWING FROM ADVERSITY

The most frequently reported *negative* effects of poor early sibling relationships on adult relationships were difficulties with trusting others and figuring out how to build healthy connections with others. Most children's early social skills development occurs within the family-of-origin. When men reflected on the influence of their sibling relationships on other relationships, beyond the romantic type, many of them mentioned that the presence of siblings helped them feel more confident in themselves and their identities. Unfortunately, respondents whose families-of-origin had been particularly dysfunctional or conflict-saturated frequently reported, sadly, that independence and autonomy were valued more than relationships in adulthood.

Forty-eight-year-old Barb was the youngest child in a family of three girls and three boys where the family relationships and history were filled with turmoil. Barb revealed, "*I really crave deeper connections with friends and I often want more than what's possible. I feel disappointed a lot and I feel alone a lot. I'm embarrassed to admit this, but it's true.*"

One forty-nine-year-old middle child, a family position that often gets a bad rap by many even though criticism is not necessarily warranted,[5] sadly shared, "*I trust no one. Love no one.*" Another middle child acknowledged that dealing with his siblings growing up gave him greater resilience, a quality that often protects middle children from psychological distress.[6] The oldest child in his family, one older brother shared, *"I learned from an early age to deal with conflicts . . . without violence."* He confirmed the earlier noted research finding that conflict resolution skills tend to spill over from one environment to another. The oldest daughter in another family shared, *"I learned how to communicate calmly and forgive without an apology. Though our relationship has been negative, I've gained positive things from it."* Sometimes the most effective learning arises out of the disappointments and adversity we withstand.

For brothers and sisters who did not create enduring positive relationships with their siblings, the development of close social networks of friends often provides the sense of belonging and support they crave, as illustrated by this comment: *"I am very close with friends. I consider them more like family."* Another stated, *"I am very discriminating in choosing my close circle of friends—my friends are my family—[they provide] unconditional love and support [and are] open minded and nonjudgmental."*

SIBSHIPS AND NON-ROMANTIC RELATIONSHIPS: WHEN EARLY RELATIONS WERE GOOD

Sometimes the relationships you enjoyed as a child and young adult do not always serve as the prototype for later relationships. Accommodating differences between family cultures is often necessary when building new friendships. As one fifty-year-old woman noted, *"I was able to be trusting and open with my siblings, so I looked for that as I was developing intimate and non-intimate relationships."* She wanted to replicate the warmth and support that her family provided. Another woman around the same age shared, *"I guess I know how to open up and be chummy . . . I expect to be able to have disagreements with friends without it ruining the relationship, but that hasn't always been the case."* A woman around thirty affirmed that *"the same qualities I display and same actions of love and care that I give to my siblings and learned from interacting with them, I transfer to other adult relationships that I have."* Aimee, the youngest of a family of four, shared, *"My sibling relationships are my strongest adult relationships. They are my closest friends."*

NO BETTER FRIEND THAN A SIBLING?

Being able to turn your sibships into friendships can create an unparalleled type of intimate friendship. The youngest of three siblings, Donna feels strongly that her older sister is truly her best friend. As Donna affirmed, *"My sister and I are 'sisters by birth and friends by choice.' We're not angels by any stretch of the imagination, but we've dedicated our lives to being the best sisters, daughters, aunts we can possibly be. We have great respect for each other and know we can call on one another anytime for anything."*

Another woman, around forty, shared, *"I believe that the closeness my siblings and I shared during our sibling relationships has taught me to keep those who mean the most to you the closest and remain in accord despite the challenging experiences that life can bring."* Another happy sister shared how much she valued *"having my sister as my best friend. I am extremely picky about who I allow in my life, as I have the luxury of having someone I can trust implicitly as my best friend."* Zena, forty-two years old, shared, *"My sister and I are best friends and enjoy so many rewarding experiences together, too many to list. We travel together, vacation together, see each other weekly, and talk daily. She's my best friend. I trust her implicitly."*

APPRECIATING SIBLINGS FOR WHO THEY ARE AND THE BEST THEY CAN OFFER

In some families, children can barely wait to reach adulthood and leave behind any evidence of their youthful lives in their families-of-origin. Autonomy does not preclude the possibility of satisfying time spent with siblings, of course. In a family of three children, Nora, the youngest, reminisced about the unexpected positive developments in her sibling relationships. Around thirty years of age, Nora shared that the most meaningful experience she has shared with her brother and sister has been *"making memories with shared experiences. We began sibling weekends several years ago and would all gather in one of our cities to spend the weekend together going to a concert or on a hike or cooking dinner together. These weekends were fun and rewarding."*

On a more sober note, Nora shared the most challenging, but meaning-ful, experience with her siblings: "*A year ago, my sister broke up with the boyfriend that we had disliked. This was a challenging experience for all of us. Although we were thrilled by her decision, it was heartbreaking to see her go through such a challenging time, move out, file a restraining order, etc. It instantly brought us closer together though, and she sud-denly opened up about everything in the relationship, and I suddenly had permission to be fully honest with her regarding my opinions about her relationship.*" When asked about her hopes for herself and her sibling re-lationships, Nora answered, "*I hope that my siblings and I can continue to be friends in addition to siblings. As we get married and have children of our own—very powerful life experiences—I hope we can grow even closer and continue to support each other.*" Nora knew she and her siblings had a good thing going. Like most relationships, acknowledging and expressing your appreciation for siblings can encourage the positive behaviors that are necessary to maintain them.

THE STRONG BOND BETWEEN SISTERS AND BROTHERS

While women who had only sisters often noted the benefits of their sib-ships, women with brothers often expressed the appreciation they felt for the diverse perspectives and experiences that arose from the gender split between sibs. One woman shared, "*I think I understand men better be-cause of my brother, and vice versa for him. I've noticed that people who only have same-sex siblings have a more difficult time understanding the opposite sex, and I wonder if it's because they've not grown up with the challenge to see things from a different gender perspective.*"

Other women shared that they learned to be more confident from be-ing raised with brothers. Still others noted that they had learned early the importance of standing up for themselves and knowing how to stand their ground. Trina, around twenty, shared her earliest sibling memory; it provides evidence that early experiences can set the stage for how a relationship develops over time:

> *When I was reaching one and my brother was four, we used to enjoy a lot of outdoor time. My mom . . . used to put me on a large folding bed sur-*

rounded by pillows in the middle of the garden. I loved watching the sky.
She used to do her work and watch me simultaneously . . . once, a hawk was
hovering above in the sky, circling prey. I was fascinated by the large bird
and started clapping. My elder brother used to sit and play near me till the
time mom took us inside. He saw the hawk and started shouting at it to go
away. . . . It was flying really high and had started going in the opposite
direction. My mom told my brother that it was fine. But he kept on insisting
that the hawk would take me away. He started crying and asked my mom
to pick me up. In the end, she had to take us inside because my brother
was getting hysterical. I remember throwing a tantrum and him appeasing
me. After that incident, my brother would always watch me "like a hawk"
whenever I lay outside. That is my fondest memory of us.

In some families, sibships can set the friendship bar even higher. The
shared history and potential for intimacy and authenticity can be difficult to find in other relationships. One of three children, all now well
over fifty, Angie described the depth and intensity of the relationship
between her and her brother: *"My brother and I are more than friends*
and always have been . . . I just always remember liking him from my
early life . . . we were playmates even though there was a three-and-a-
half-year age difference . . . my husband is very close with him also . . . I
don't know what to compare it to other than he is as much a part of my
life as my husband and children."

Enduring respect between brother and sister can bring a lifetime of
support, as one sister noted, *"I have less need of approval because I*
have a built-in friend." Another sister, now forty-seven years old, was
grateful to her brother for helping her grow as a person: *"My brother is*
really a creative genius and unique thinker, and he taught me a lot about
carving your own path. I am forever grateful for the unique slant on
the world he showed me." Actually, the wide diversity of the responses
gathered for this study suggests that all sibs enjoy their own unique slant
on the sibling relationship.

Between Sisters

Many women who participated in this study acknowledged the friendship they enjoyed with their sisters. As noted in earlier chapters, sisters
tend to form the closest bonds and the bonds that last the longest between

siblings. Fifty-six-year-old Denise noted, "*As we all got married and had children, our relationships turned to friendships, and as we got older, these friendships grew deeper. My sisters are the only 'friends' I could count on in a crisis.*"

The untimely death of a sister can leave an enduring emptiness for surviving sisters. Wondering about the possibilities of what the relationship might have become can be especially poignant in older adulthood. Violette, a woman in her early sixties, shared a bittersweet reminiscence about her only sister whom she had lost three decades ago:

When my sister was twenty I took her out driving because she still didn't have a driver's license. I told her to come with me and she asked what for. I told her, you'll find out. We went to the lake and I told her to move over, you're driving. She got her driver's license not long afterwards, and my mom took her to practice more.

The most challenging experience we shared was when she had cancer. I called her all the time just to talk to her. I can't even remember what we talked about, just that I needed to talk to her. Her last Christmas she had lost most of her hair to chemotherapy and was embarrassed to go to mom's for Christmas. I told her to wear a Santa hat or a baseball hat, and she was good with that. I remember that we were at her house on New Year's that year. I heard her tell my mom that if she got over her cancer she wanted to go to college. I've always wondered if she regretted her decision to marry and not go to college as I had.

I've wondered how our relationship would be today, me sixty-two and she would have been sixty, if she had lived. How weird is it that I've lost my mother, father, sister, and kicked my only remaining sibling, my brother, to the curb.

Some of the other affirmations of sisterly closeness included the comment of a woman, sixty-one years old, who shared, "*My sister and I have a wonderful relationship and get together often or keep in touch often. My brothers are not as forthcoming in relationships.*" She regretted that her relationships with her brothers were not as open and supportive, but she took great pleasure in the deepening relationship she and her sister shared. The bond of sisterhood can provide intimate friendship as well as some added protection against the loneliness often experienced in older adulthood.

Between Brothers

As noted earlier, sisters usually report being closer to one another than brothers tend to be in adulthood.[7] Researchers Spitze and Trent have explored the relational behaviors of siblings based on gender, and some interesting findings were revealed.[8] In comparing sister dyads with brother dyads, the sisters may have felt closer to one another, but brothers reported more frequent visits with one another. Not only were brothers getting together more frequently than sisters, but brothers also reported more instances of helping out with repairs or chores than sisters did. Not surprisingly, as far as advice-giving goes, sisters reported significantly more of this behavior than brothers did.

Comparing the responses of brothers who participated in this current study with the earlier studies, it appears that brothers still enjoy "action-brothering" rather than more focused "emotionally supportive brothering." Bruce, one of three brothers, admitted that sibling rivalry had continued into adulthood for these men and, not too surprising, that the topic he found most difficult to address with his brothers was sharing emotions. True to the existing literature, Bruce noted that the most meaningful time he and his brothers spent together was while hanging out and working on their cars together. Another man shared that for him and his brothers, *"just hanging out together"* was what he valued most; he followed up and explained, *"The challenging experiences have been when we have disagreements or someone gets too emotional over something minuscule like a sports game or video game."*

Shows of affection and family loyalty were also noted by brothers as particularly meaningful activities. Jordan noted, *"The best experience [between us] was when my younger brother and his wife and my nephew flew to Georgia for my wedding."* Another man, in his thirties, shared his most meaningful brother-to-brother experience. He revealed, *"[It was] my brother taking me in after my girlfriend died. He and his wife made me feel so welcome, and I don't know what I would have done without them."* With brother-to-brother relationships, it is all about *"showing up"* when it comes to generating the most lasting and supportive relationships between men.

GIFTS FROM OUR SIBLINGS

Every life experience and relationship helps to shape an individual's adult identity in some way. Ideally, every relationship will provide some opportunity for personal growth, increased self-awareness, and appreciation for the people and events that have made each person who he or she is today. Not everyone is able to reflect on the ways in which positive and even negative relationship experiences can positively affect their strengths as well as one young woman was able to do: "*My older sister showed me that it's ok to be nerdy and fall in love with a book, movie, or subject, and to share that with other people. My younger sister taught me how to navigate conflict and how to live with people who are difficult, both of which have been valuable.*"

The Gift Is Our Sibling

Most adult siblings are understandably focused on keeping their own lives humming and likely don't take time to recognize that their siblings may have substantially contributed to their development over time. Putting psychological distance between childhood and adulthood is often a natural by-product of maturation. One young woman, though, was able to pause and reflect on just how much she appreciated her brothers and sister. She stated that she had "*no regrets*" when it came to her sibling relationships, and she considers her siblings the "*best gifts*" her parents had ever given her.

BETTER OR WORSE BECAUSE OF YOUR SIBLINGS?

If you were asked to fill in the blanks on a sentence that began, "Because of my siblings, I am . . . ," what words would you choose? The majority of this study's participants noted positive outcomes rather than poor ones. In analyzing the varied responses, it was found that birth order influenced people's responses. Overall, a dozen discernible themes were revealed across the data: appreciative of family, compassionate/kind, confident/strong, happier, independent, take on leadership role, loved/connected/belonging, nurturing, patient, enhanced conflict management/people skills, more resilient, and smarter/wiser. When these characteristics were organized by birth order, the most frequently noted outcomes were as follows:

Youngest	Middle	Oldest
Confident/Strong	Confident/Strong	Loved/Connected/ Belonging
Loved/Connected/ Belonging	People Skills/Conflict Management	Compassionate/Kind
Happier	Appreciative of Family	Confident/Strong
People Skills/Conflict Management	Independent	People Skills/Conflict Management
Smart/Wise	Resilient	Nurturing
Compassionate/Kind	Leader	Patient
Patient	Nurturing	Resilient
Independent	Compassionate/Kind	Leader
	Smart/Wise	Smart/Wise
		Independent

The youngest siblings arrived in families already sibling-populated, and their responses suggested that they were content with the presence of sibs and, perhaps, that they learned how to stand up for themselves early as they interacted with the older children in the home. Only the youngest siblings acknowledged that having siblings left them feeling happier. Middle children also seemed to appreciate their place in the family as they entered adulthood feeling confident about themselves as well as their ability to resolve conflict. Older sibling responses seemed to reflect a sense of being at peace with and connected to their younger sibs. For those participants who felt that little good had come out of their sibling relationships, their responses tended to focus on a tendency toward little trust in others, feelings of abandonment or isolation, and a sense of inferiority or inadequacy in some cases. Negative feelings about early relationships often endure far longer than is beneficial, as noted by the areas of regret shared by the respondents.

ADDRESSING REGRETS AND
MAKING POSITIVE CHANGES

We will close this chapter and the book with a brief exploration of some of the frequently articulated regrets and hopes expressed for sibling relationships. Among respondents who shared regrets, the greatest, for many, was failing to remain close to their siblings as the years passed or failing to develop close, intimate relationships with their siblings over time. Regret for poor behavior toward siblings, regret that the early years had been as difficult or dysfunctional as they had been, and regret over allowing relationships to unravel over the years were the other most often described regrets. The longing for a family and a space where you feel accepted, no matter what, reflects a very basic human need. A sentiment shared by the middle child of a large family illustrates many of the respondents' wishes: "*I always hope for the next family gathering that we are able to laugh together and soak up that fun feeling that emerges when one is among kin.*"

Ten Lessons to Take Away from the Regrets of Others

1. You cannot redo or undo the past, but you can acknowledge and release the pain it may have caused and now let yourself focus on the present.
2. If you have given and lost more than you could afford to a sibling—whether the investment was time, money, self-respect, or other finite resources—be willing to admit this and communicate this knowledge to your sibling. If circumstances require, take a break from the relationship until you and your sibling are in a better position to relate in a mutually rewarding way.
3. Siblings show their best and their worst to one another; own the shadows that *your own* past mistakes have cast on your siblings and your relationships.
4. Siblings do not always fight fair, and they almost always know your weaknesses. If they try to engage you in verbal conflict, choose your responses carefully in adulthood; how you respond will speak volumes about who you have become as an adult.
5. Life is short, and losing a sibling before past conflicts can be resolved can leave regrets that may follow you throughout adulthood.

6. Critical moments in life, such as medical emergencies and death, have a seldom-replicated success rate in bringing siblings and families back together with less drama or discord than in earlier years; don't wait for your own or a family member's health crisis to make the effort to reach out to siblings.

7. As people grow older, they increasingly long to reconnect with family; do not let pride or "being in the right" keep you from making a tangible difference in the life of a sibling, or in your own life.

8. If a sibling makes the effort to reach out to you, do not be too proud to pick up the phone, return the text, or reply to the email. Would anyone want their youthful errors to be the measure of their merit as an adult?

9. Overlooking the shortcomings of a sibling—even one who has caused you and your family grief—is sometimes worth the effort. The ability to move beyond the past takes a significant level of maturity.

10. Carrying resentment or unexpressed rage about another's poor behavior takes away from your own happiness and colors your own attitudes and interactions in ways that you likely cannot realize. Never allow adult siblings the power to make you feel bad about your choices or who you have become. Every sibling must follow their own journey through life.

It is not always easy to let go of hard feelings from the past or realign our fantasized sibling relationships with what is actually possible, but these are definitely achievable goals. The desire to grow closer to or to connect with adult siblings are frequently expressed hopes. Small steps, such as cards or calls, are the hope for some, and larger steps, such as frequent visits, are the hopes of others. One woman shared that there are a couple of things she would like for her and her two brothers to accomplish: "*Go places together and get matching tattoos!*" Another woman simply stated, "*Hopefully, they'll get their [own lives] together and realize how frickin' awesome I am.*" Regardless of whom you expect to do the changing, a sibling or yourself, remember that change is one of the hardest things for people to do—unless sufficient motivation is present. Be prepared to be the best sibling that you can be, too, if you want to make you or your sib's changes worth the effort. Before you give up on any wayward sibs, bear in mind that you might someday need them in your life in ways that you never thought would happen.

Appendix A

PARTICIPANT DATA AND SURVEY QUESTIONNAIRE

Participants

Participants for this study were recruited via word-of-mouth, professional listservs, and the online *Psychology Today* magazine blog site of the author. In addition to face-to-face interviews with eleven individuals, an online survey was also made available to potential participants. A total of 440 participants completed the online open-ended questionnaire. Approximately 11 percent of the sample were men, 89 percent were women, and one participant identified as trans*.

In Table A1, a comprehensive compilation of the demographic data and quantitative responses of the electronic survey participants is presented:

Appendix A

Table A1. Participant Demographic Data

Demographic Characteristic	Frequency	Percent
Age Range		
18–24 years of age	41	9.3%
25–34 years of age	93	21.1%
35–44 years of age	83	18.9%
45–59 years of age	132	30.0%
60 years and over	52	11.8%
Missing	39	8.9%
Total	440	100.0%
Birth Order		
Youngest	130	29.5%
Middle	125	28.4%
Oldest	133	30.2%
Only Child	8	1.8%
Missing	44	10.0%
Total	440	100.0%
Participants' Number of Sisters		
1	171	38.9%
2	69	15.7%
3	40	9.1%
4 or more	22	5.0%
None	89	20.2%
Missing	49	11.1%
Total	440	100.0%
Participants' Number of Brothers		
1	177	40.2%
2	73	16.6%
3	29	6.6%
4 or more	22	5.0%
None	94	21.4%
Missing	45	10.2%
Total	440	100.0%

Table A2. Sibling Friendship Data

Sibling Friendships	Frequency	Percent	Percent of Qualifying Respondents
Friends with Older Siblings			
Yes	113	25.7%	**44.8%**
No	139	31.6%	**55.1%**
Not Applicable	123	28.0%	
Missing	65	14.8%	
Total	440	100.0%	
Friends with Younger Siblings			
Yes	140	31.8%	**54.1%**
No	119	27.0%	**45.9%**
Not Applicable	118	26.8%	
Missing	63	14.3%	
Total	440	100.0%	

SIBLING RELATIONSHIPS IN ADULTHOOD SURVEY QUESTIONS

1. Age
2. Gender
3. Place in the family birth order? (e.g., youngest child, middle child, only child, etc.)
4. How much of a role do you feel birth order plays in your sibling relationships?
5. How many sisters? How many brothers?
6. Were you also a twin?
7. Did you experience the death of a sibling when you were a child? If so, how does this loss continue to influence you and your family-of-origin?
8. Have you experienced the death of a sibling during your adult years? If yes, how does this loss continue to influence you and your family-of-origin?
9. Did your family have any family secrets that you and your sibling(s) were not supposed to share? If so, what did they concern? How are they dealt with today?

10. How would you complete these sentences: *"Without my siblings, I would . . ."* and *"Because of my siblings, I am . . ."*

11. Oftentimes, parents will refer to children by a specific quality, such as *"Tom is the athletic one"* or *"Maddie is the funny one."* If this happened in your family, what adjectives were used to describe you? Your sibling(s)?

12. If you were an only child, please describe what you believe were the most positive and negative aspects of not having siblings.

13. What were the most significant conflicts you have had with your sibling(s) as an adult?

14. What has been the most difficult issue you have had to discuss with your sibling(s)? Please describe the issue and the outcome.

15. What are the things that you wish your sibling(s) understood about you or that you wish you could tell or could have told your sibling(s) without fear of negative repercussions?

16. What do you most wish that your sibling(s) would say to you today? If you have a sibling who is now deceased, please share about any unresolved issues that you wish had been addressed before the loss.

17. To which parent did you feel closest? Briefly share a little bit about that relationship as it was when you were a child and how it is (or was) for you as an adult.

18. Would you describe your current relationship with your sibling(s) as friendship?

19. Please share how your relationship(s) with your sibling(s) have changed over time.

20. Please describe any sibling rivalry experienced during childhood. Has it been resolved? Has it continued into adulthood?

21. What were the most meaningful sibling experiences you have had as an adult? Please share both the challenging and the rewarding experiences.

22. How did your sibling relationships shape your adult relationships?

23. Share any regrets you have regarding your sibling relationships.

24. Share any hopes you have for enhancing your sibling relationships.

Notes

INTRODUCTION

1. Goetting, A. (1986). The developmental tasks of siblingship over the life cycle. *Journal of Marriage and Family* 48, 703–14.
2. Ibid.
3. Ibid., 711.
4. Ibid., 711–12.
5. Ibid., 712.

CHAPTER 1. BIRTH ORDER AND FAMILY CONSTELLATIONS

1. Ansbacher, H. L., and Ansbacher, R. R. (1956). *The Individual Psychology of Alfred Adler*. New York: Basic Books.
2. Kennedy, S., and Ruggles, S. (2014). Breaking up is hard to count: The rise of divorce in the United States, 1980-2010. *Demography* 51, 587–98.
3. Adler, A. (1929). Position in family influences lifestyle. *International Journal of Individual Psychology* 3, 211–27.
4. Sulloway, F. J. (1996). *Born to Rebel*. New York: Pantheon.
5. Damian, R. I., and Roberts, B. W. (2015). The associations of birth order with personality and intelligence in a representative sample of U.S. high school students. *Journal of Research in Personality* 58, 96–105.
6. Zajonc, R. B., and Sulloway, F. J. (2007). The confluence model: Birth order as a within-family or between-family dynamic? *Personality & Social Psychology Bulletin* 33, 1187–94.
7. Holmgren, S., Molander, B., and Nilsson, L. (2007). Episodic memory in adult age and effects of sibship size and birth order: Longitudinal data. *Journal of Adult Development* 14, 37–46.

8. Hotz, V. J., and Pantano, J. (2015). Strategic parenting, birth order, and school performance. *Journal of Population Economics* 28, 911–36.

9. Black, Sandra E., Devereux, Paul J., and Salvanes, Kjell G. (2007). From the cradle to the labor market? The effect of birth weight on adult outcomes. *Quarterly Journal of Economics* 122(1), 409–39.

10. Savage, T., Derraik, J. G., Miles, H. L., Mouat, F., Cutfield, W. S., and Hofman, P. L. (2013). Birth order progressively affects childhood height. *Clinical Endocrinology* 79, 379–85.

11. Ayyavoo, A., Savage, T., Derraik, J. G. B., Hofman, P. L., and Cutfield, W. S. (2013). First-born children have reduced insulin sensitivity and higher daytime blood pressure compared to later born children. *Journal of Clinical Endocrinology & Metabolism* 98, 1248–53.

12. Ponzo, M., and Scoppa, V. Trading height for education in the marriage market. *American Journal of Human Biology* 27, 164–74.

13. Ibid.

14. Ayyavoo et al. (2013).

15. Black, S. E., Devereux, P. J., and Salvanes, K. G. (July 2015). Healthy (?), wealthy and wise: Birth order and adult health. NBER working Paper No. w21337. Available at SSRN: http://ssrn.com/abstract=2629942.

16. Barclay, K., and Kolk, M. (2015). Birth order and morality: A population-based cohort study. *Demography* 52, 613–39.

17. Adler, A. (1929).

18. Dinkmeyer, D., and Sperry, L. (2000). *Counseling and Psychotherapy: An Integrated, Individual Psychology Approach.* Upper Saddle River, NJ: Merrill/ Prentice Hall.

19. McGuire, K. T. (2013). The psychological origins of a constitutional revolution: The Supreme Court, birth order, and nationalizing the Bill of Rights. *Political Research Quarterly* 66, 441–53.

20. Adler, A. (1929).

21. Sulloway (1996).

22. Kerr, M., and Bowen, M. (1988). *Family Evaluation: An Approach Based on Bowen Theory.* New York: Norton.

CHAPTER 2. CULTURAL INFLUENCES
ON SIBLING RELATIONSHIPS

1. Cicirelli, V. G. (1994). Sibling relationships in cross-cultural perspective. *Journal of Marriage and Family* 56, 7–20.

2. U.S. Census Bureau, Current Population Survey, Annual Social and Economic Supplements, 1955, 1960, 1965, and 1970 to 2015.

3. U.S. Census Bureau, Current Population Survey, 2014 Annual Social and Economic Supplement.

4. Watson-Gegeo, K. A., and Gegeo, D. W. (1989). The role of sibling interaction in child socialization. In P. G. Zukow (ed.), *Sibling Interaction Across Cultures: Theoretical and Methodological Issues* (pp. 54–76). New York: Springer-Verlag.

5. Ervin-Tripp, S. (1989). Sisters and brothers. In P. G. Zukow (ed.), *Sibling Interaction Across Cultures: Theoretical and Methodological Issues* (pp. 105–48). Lanham, MD: University Press of America.

6. Cicirelli (1994).

7. Pew Research Center. (2015). Family size, by race and ethnicity. Pew Research Center analysis of 1986, 1988, 1990, 1992, 1994, 1995, 2012, and 2014 Current Population Survey June Supplements. Retrieved from http://www.pewsocialtrends.org/2015/05/07/childlessness-falls-family-size-grows-among-highly-educated-women/st_2015-05-07_childlessness-12/.

8. Cicirelli (1994).

9. Haines, Michael. "Fertility and Mortality in the United States." EH.Net Encyclopedia, edited by Robert Whaples. March 19, 2008.

10. Gao, G. (2015). Americans' ideal family size is small than it used to be. Fact Tank: News in the Numbers. Pew Research Center. Data retrieved from http://www.pewresearch.org/fact-tank/2015/05/08/ideal-size-of-the-american-family/.

11. Pew Research Center. May 12, 2015. America's changing religious landscape.

12. Ibid.

13. Loshny, H. (2004). From birth control to menstrual control: The launch of the extended oral contraceptive, Seasonale. *Canadian Women's Studies* 24, 63–67.

14. Pew Research Center. (2015). Among highly educated moms, families are getting bigger. Pew Research Center analysis of 1986, 1988, 1990, 1992, 1994, 1995, 2012, and 2014 Current Population Survey June Supplements. Retrieved from http://www.pewsocialtrends.org/2015/05/07/childlessness-falls-family-size-grows-among-highly-educated-women/st_2015-05-07_childlessness-12/.

15. Ibid.

16. Last, Jonathan. (2013). *What to Expect When No One's Expecting: America's Coming Demographic Disaster*. New York: Encounter Books.

17. Kramer, L., and Baron, L. A. (1995). Intergenerational linkages: How experiences with siblings relate to the parenting of siblings. *Journal of Social and Personal Relationships* 12(1), 67–87.

18. Lynch, R. F. (2016). Parents face quantity-quality trade-offs between reproduction and investment in offspring in Iceland. *Royal Society Open Science.* doi:10.1098/rsos.160087.

19. Hetherington, E. M. (1988). Parents, children, and siblings: Six years after divorce. In R. A. Hinde and J. Stevenson-Hinde (eds.), *Relationships within Families: Mutual Influences* (pp. 311–31). New York: Oxford University Press.

20. Downey, D. B., Condron, D. J., and Yucel, D. (2015). Number of siblings and social skills revisited among American fifth graders. *Journal of Family Issues* 38(2), 273–96.

21. Keynes, M. (2015). Being a "middle seat child" can spell success in later life. SKODA.UK press release. Retrieved from http://www.skoda.co.uk/news/being-a-middle-seat-child-can-spell-success-in-later-life.

22. Yang, J., Hou, X., Wei, D., Wang, K., Li, Y., and Qiu, J. (2016). Only-child and non-only-child exhibit differences in creativity and agreeableness: Evidence from behavioral and anatomical structural studies. *Brain Imaging and Behavior*, 1–10.

23. Mosli, R. H., Kaciroti, N., Corwyn, R. F., Bradley, R. H., and Lumeng, J. C. (2016). Effect of sibling birth on BMI trajectory in the first 6 years of life. *Pediatrics* 137(4). doi:http://dx.doi.org/10.1542/peds.2015-2456.

24. Garcia, S. N. (2011). Ecological perspectives of adult Latina only children: A qualitative study. *Dissertation Abstracts International: Section B: The Sciences and Engineering* 72(3-B), 1779.

25. Gao (2015).

26. Tyler, K. M., Boykin, A. W., Boelter, C. M., and Dillihunt, M. L. (2005). Examining mainstream and Afro-cultural value socialization in African American households. *Journal of Black Psychology* 31, 291–311.

27. Soli, A. R., McHale, S. M., and Feinberg, M. E. (2009). Risk and protective effects of sibling relationships among African American adolescents. *Family Relations* 58, 578–92.

28. Ibid.

29. Budak, D., and Chavajay, P. (2012). Cultural variation in the social organization of problem solving among African American and European American siblings. *Cultural Diversity and Ethnic Minority Psychology* 18(3), 307–11.

30. Buist, K. L., and Vermande, M. (2014). Sibling relationship patterns and their associations with child competence and problem behavior. *Journal of Family Psychology* 28(4), 529–37.

31. Kim, B. S. K., Yang, P. H., Atkinson, D. R., Wolfe, M. M., and Hong, S. (2001). Cultural value similarities and differences among Asian American ethnic groups. *Cultural Diversity and Ethnic Minority Psychology* 7(4), 343–61.

32. Feng, W., Gu, B., and Cai, Y. (2016). The end of China's one-child policy. *Studies in Family Planning* 47(1), 83–86.

33. Kim et al. (2001).

34. Fuligni, A., and Masten, C. L. (2010). Daily family interactions among young adults in the United States from Latin American, Filipino, East Asian, and European backgrounds. *International Journal of Behavioral Development* 34(6), 491–99.

35. Pyke, K. (2005). "Generational deserters" and "black sheep": Acculturative differences among siblings in Asian immigrant families. *Journal of Family Issues* 26(4), 491–517.

36. Fuligni and Masten (2010).

37. Budak and Chavajay (2012).

38. Rapoza, K. A., Cook, K., Zaveri, T., and Malley-Morrison, K. (2010). Ethnic perspectives on sibling abuse in the United States. *Journal of Family Issues* 31(6), 808–29.

39. Fuligni and Masten (2010).

40. Campos, B., Ullman, J. B., Aguilera, A., and Dunkel Schetter, C. (2014). Familism and psychological health: The intervening role of closeness and social support. *Cultural Diversity and Ethnic Minority Psychology* 20(2), 191–201.

41. Killoren, S. E., Thayer, S. M., and Updegraff, K. A. (2008). Conflict resolution between Mexican origin adolescent siblings. *Journal of Marriage and Family* 70(5), 1200–12.

42. Wheeler, L., Killoren, S., Whiteman, S., Updegraff, K., McHale, S., and Umana-Taylor, A. (2016). Romantic relationship experiences from late adolescence to young adulthood: The role of older siblings in Mexican-origin families. *Journal of Youth & Adolescence* 45(5), 900–15.

43. Killoren, S. E., Alfaro, E. C., Lindell, A. K., and Streit, C. (2014). Mexican American college students' communication with their siblings. *Family Relations* 63, 513–25.

44. Skierkowski, D., and Wood, R. M. (2012). To text or not to text? The importance of text messaging among college-aged youth. *Computers in Human Behavior* 28(2), 744–56.

45. Wan He, Daniel Goodkind, and Paul Kowal. U.S. Census Bureau, International Population Reports, P95/16-1, An Aging World: 2015, U.S. Government Publishing Office, Washington, DC, 2016.

CHAPTER 3. SIBLING LOSS IN CHILDHOOD AND ADOLESCENCE

1. Xu, J. Q., Murphy, S. L., Kochanek, K. D., and Bastian, B. A. (2016). Deaths: Final data for 2013. *National Vital Statistics Reports* 64(2). Hyattsville, MD: National Center for Health Statistics.

2. Worden, J. W. (1999). Comparing parent loss with sibling loss. *Death Studies* 23(1), 1–15.

3. Kirwin, K. M., and Hamrin, V. (2005). Decreasing the risk of complicated bereavement and future psychiatric disorders in children. *Journal of Child Adolescent Psychiatric Nursing* 18(2), 62–78.

4. Fletcher, J., Mailick, M., Song, J., and Wolfe, B. (2013). A sibling death in the family: Common and consequential. *Demography* 50, 803–26.

5. Rogers, C. H., Floyd, F. J., Seltzer, M. M., Greenberg, J. S., and Hong, J. (2008). Long-term effects of the death of a child on parents' adjustment in midlife. *Journal of Family Psychology* 22, 203–11.

6. Song, J., Floyd, F. J., Seltzer, M. M., Greenberg, J. S., and Hong, J. (2010). Long-term effects of child death on parents' health-related quality of life: A dyadic analysis. *Family Relations* 59, 269–82.

7. Torbic, H. (2011). Children and grief: But what about the children? *Home Healthcare Nurse* 29(2), 67–79.

8. Erikson, E. (1959). *Identity Development and the Life Cycle: Selected Papers, with a Historical Introduction by David Rapaport*. New York: International University Press.

9. Dyregrov, A. (1990). *Grief in Children: A Handbook for Adults*. London: Jessica Kingsley Publishers.

10. Wang, Q., and Peterson, C. (2014). Your earliest memory may be earlier than you think: Prospective studies of children's dating of earliest childhood memories. *Developmental Psychology* 50, 1680–86.

11. Decinque, N., Monterosso, L., Dadd, G., Sidhu, R., Macpherson, R., and Aoun, S. (2006). Bereavement support for families following the death of a child from cancer: Experience of bereaved parents. *Journal of Psychosocial Oncology* 24(2), 65–83. doi:10.1300=J077v24n02_05.

12. Panfile, T. M., Laible, D. J., and Eye, J. L. (2012). Conflict frequency within mother-child dyads across contexts: Links with attachment and security. *Early Childhood Research Quarterly* 27, 78–106.

13. Dyregrov (1990).

14. Kempson, D., and Murdock, V. (2010). Memory keepers: A narrative study on siblings never known. *Death Studies* 34(8), 738–56.

15. Ibid.

16. Dyregrov (1990).

17. Steinberg, L. (2008). A social neuroscience perspective on adolescent risk-taking. *Developmental Review* 28, 78–106.

18. Bingham, C. R., Shope, J. T., Zakrajsek, J., and Raghunathan, T. E. (2008). Problem driving behavior and psychosocial maturation in young adulthood. *Accident Analysis & Prevention* 40, 1758–64.

19. Morris, A. T., Gabert-Quillen, C., Friebert, S., Carst, N., and Delahanty, D. L. (2016). The indirect effect of positive parenting on the relationship between parent and sibling bereavement outcomes after the death of a child. *Journal of Pain & Symptom Management* 51, 60–70.

20. Machajewski, K. (2013). Childhood grief related to the death of a sibling. *Journal for Nurse Practitioners* 9, 443–48.

21. Kempson, D., Conley, V. M., and Murdock, V. (2008). Unearthing the construct of transgenerational grief: The "ghost" of the sibling never known. *Illness, Crisis & Loss* 16(4), 271–84.

CHAPTER 4. FAMILY COMMUNICATION AND ENGAGEMENT

1. Adler, R. B., and Proctor II, R. F. (2014). *Looking Out, Looking In* (15th ed.). Boston: Cengage.

2. McLeod, J. M., and Chaffee, S. H. (1972). The construction of social reality. In J. Tedeschi (ed.), *The Social Influence Processes* (pp. 50–59). Chicago: Aldine-Atherton.

3. Fitzpatrick, M. A. (2004). Family communication patterns theory: Observations on its development and application. *Journal of Family Communications* 4(3&4), 167–79.

4. Olson, D. H., Sprenkle, D. H., and Russell, C. S. (1979). Circumplex Model of marital and family systems. *Family Process* 18(1), 3–28.

5. Fitzpatrick, M. A., Ritchie, L. D., and Koerner, A. F. (1994). Communication schemata within the family: Multiple perspectives on family interaction. *Human Communication Research* 20, 275–301.

6. Huang, L. N. (1999). Family communication patterns and personality characteristics. *Communication Quarterly* 47(2), 230–43.

7. Lyon, M. L. (2006). The relation of managers' perceptions of their leadership styles to parenting styles in their families of origin. *Dissertation Abstracts International* 67(3-B). (University Microfilms No. AAI3209590).

8. Olson, Sprenkle, and Russell (1979).

9. Ibid.

10. Bank, S., and Kahn, M. D. (1982). *The Sibling Bond*. New York: Basic Books.

11. Hesketh, T., Zhou, X., and Wang, Y. (2015). The end of the one-child policy: Lasting implications for China. *Journal of the American Medical Association* 314(24), 2619–20.

12. Gustafson, K., and Baofeng, H. (2014). Elderly care and the one-child policy: Concerns, expectations and preparations for elderly life in a rural Chinese township. *Journal of Cross-Cultural Gerontology* 29(1), 25–36.

13. Tifferet, S., Pollet, T., Bar, A., and Efrati, H. (2016). Predicting sibling investment by perceived sibling resemblance. *Evolutionary Based Sciences* 10(1), 64–70.

14. Widdig, A., Nürnberg, P., Krawczak, M., Streich, W. J., and Bercovitch, F. B. (2001). Paternal relatedness and age proximity regulate social relationships among adult female rhesus macaques. PNAS Proceedings of the National Academy of Sciences of the United States of America, 98, 13769–773. 10.1073/pnas.241210198 1.

15. Pollet, T. V. (2007). Genetic relatedness and sibling relationship characteristics in a modern society. *Evolution and Human Behavior* 28, 176–85. 10.1016/j.evolhumbehav.2006.10.001.

16. Pollet, T. V., and Nettle, D. (2009). Dead or alive? Knowledge about a sibling's death varies by genetic relatedness in a modern society. *Evolutionary Psychology*, 7, 57–65.

17. Degges-White, S., and Borzumato-Gainey, G. (2011). *Friends Forever: How Girls and Women Forge Lasting Relationships*. Lanham, MD: Rowman & Littlefield.

18. Rocca, K. A., Martin, M. M., and Dunleavy, K. N. (2010). Siblings' motives for talking to each other. *The Journal of Psychology* 144(2), 205–19.

19. Gilligan, C. (1993). *In a Different Voice: Psychological Theory and Women's Development*. Boston: Harvard University Press.

20. Kim, J., McHale, S. M., Osgood, D. W., and Crouter, A. C. (2006). Longitudinal course and family correlates of sibling relationships from childhood through adolescence. *Child Development* 77(6), 1746–61.

21. Salmon, C. (2003). Birth order and relationships. *Human Nature* 14, 73–88.

22. Salmon, C., Cuthbertson, A. M., and Figueredo, A. J. (2016). The relationship between birth order and prosociality: An evolutionary perspective. *Personality and Individual Differences* 96, 18–22.

23. Fischer, C. S., and Beresford, L. (2014). Changes in support networks in late middle age: The extension of gender and educational differences. *Journals of Gerontology Series B: Psychological Sciences and Social Sciences* 70, 123–31 gbu057.

CHAPTER 5. SIBLING RIVALRY IN ADULTHOOD

1. Bedford, V. H., Volling, B. L., and Avioli, P. S. (2000). Positive consequences of sibling conflict in childhood and adulthood. *International Journal of Aging and Human Development* 51(1), 53–69.

2. Ibid.

3. Abuhatoum, S., and Howe, N. (2013). Power in sibling conflict during early and middle childhood. *Social Development* 22(4), 738–54.

4. Wang, Y. N. (2015). Authenticity and relationship satisfaction: Two distinct ways of directing power to self-esteem. *PLoS ONE* 10(12): e0146050. doi:10.1371/journal.pone.0146050.

5. Erol, R. Y., and Orth, U. (2013). Actor and partner effects of self-esteem on relationship satisfaction and the mediating role of secure attachment between the partners. *Journal of Research in Personality* 47(1), 26–35.

6. Yeh, H., and Lempers, J. D. (2004). Perceived sibling relationships and adolescent development. *Journal of Youth and Adolescence* 33(2), 133–47.

7. Kramer, L., and Baron, L. A. (1995). Intergenerational linkages: How experiences with siblings relate to the parenting of siblings. *Journal of Social and Personal Relationships* 12(1), 67–87.

8. Volling, B., and Bedford, V. H. (1998, July). Sibling relationships in childhood and adulthood: Contributions from a life-span perspective. In V. H. Bedford and K. Fingerman (chairs), *Lessons from the Later Years: What Child Development Can Learn from Gerontology about Social Relationships.* Symposium presented at the XVth Biennial Meetings of the International Society for the Study of Behavioral Development, Berne, Switzerland.

9. Okudaira, H., Kinari, Y., Mizutani, N., Ohtake, F., and Kawaguchi, A. (2015). Older sisters and younger brothers: The impact of siblings on preference for competition. *Personality and Individual Differences* 82, 81–89.

10. Gilligan, M., Suitor, J. J., and Nam, S. (2015). Maternal differential treatment in later life families and within-family variations in adult sibling closeness. *Journals of Gerontology, Series B: Psychological Sciences and Social Sciences* 70(1), 167–77. doi:10.1093/geronb/gbu148.

11. Tillman, K. H. (2007). "Non-traditional" siblings and the academic outcomes of adolescents. *Social Science Research* 37(1), 88–108.

12. Becker, O. A., Salzburger, V., Lois, N., and Nauck, B. (2013). What narrows the stepgap? Closeness between parents and adult (step)children in Germany. *Journal of Marriage and Family* 75(5), 1130–48.

13. Ibid.

14. Mikkelson, A. C., Myers, S. A., and Hannawa, A. F. (2011). The differential use of relational maintenance behaviors in adult sibling relationships. *Communication Studies* 62(3), 258–71.

15. de Shazer, S., and Dolan, Y. (2007). *More than Miracles: The State of the Art of Solution-Focused Brief Therapy*. New York: Routledge Publishing.

CHAPTER 6. FAMILY ROLES

1. Fortuna, K., Roisman, G. I., Haydon, K. C., Groh, A. M., and Holland, A. S. (2011). Attachment states of mind and the quality of young adults' sibling relationships. *Developmental Psychology* 47, 1366–73.

2. Leung, A. K. D., and Robson, L. M. (1991). Sibling rivalry. *Clinical Pediatrics* 30, 314–17. doi:10.1177/00099 2289103000510.

3. Jensen, A. C., Whiteman, S. D., Fingerman, K. L., and Birditt, K. S. (2013). "Life still isn't fair": Parental differential treatment of young adult siblings. *Journal of Marriage and Family* 75(2), 438–52.

4. Vivona, J. M. (2010). Siblings, transference, and the lateral dimension of psychic life. *Psychoanalytic Psychology* 27(1), 8–26.

5. Satir, V. (1967). *Conjoint Family Therapy: A Guide to Theory and Technique*. Palo Alto, CA: Science & Behavior Books.

6. Satir, V. (1972). *Peoplemaking*. Palo Alto, CA: Science & Behavior Books.

7. Wegscheider, S. (1976). *The Family Trap: No One Escapes from a Chemical Dependent Family*. St. Paul: Nurturing Networks.

8. Wegscheider-Cruse, S. (1986). *Understanding Me*. Pompano Beach, FL: Health Communications.

9. Fischer, J. L., and Wampler, R. S. (1994). Abusive drinking in young adults: Personality type and family role moderators of family-of-origin influences. *Journal of Marriage and Family* 56(2), 469–79.

10. Samuel, I. S., Mahmood, Z., and Saleem, S. (2014). The development of the Role Identification Scale for adult children of alcoholic fathers. *Pakistan Journal of Social and Clinical Psychology* 12(1), 3–11.

11. Littrell, J. (1991). *Understanding and Treating Alcoholism: Volume I: An Empirically Based Clinician's Handbook for the Treatment of Alcoholism*. Hillsdale, NJ: Laurence Erlbaum Press.

12. Ungar, M. (2013). Resilience, trauma, context, and culture. *Trauma Violence Abuse* 14(3), 255–66.

13. Vernig, P. M. (2011). Family roles in homes with alcohol-dependent parents: An evidence-based review. *Substance Use & Misuse* 46, 535–42.

14. Erikson, E. (1959). *Identity Development and the Life Cycle: Selected Papers, with a Historical Introduction by David Rapaport*. New York: International University Press.

15. Sherman, A. M., Lansford, J. E., and Volling, B. L. (2006). Sibling relationships and best friendships in young adulthood: Warmth, conflict, and well-being. *Personal Relationships* 13(2), 151–65.

16. Jewsbury Conger, K., and Little, W. M. (2010). Sibling relationships during the transition to adulthood. *Child Development Perspectives* 4(2), 87–94. doi:10.1111/j.1750-8606.2010.00123.x.

17. Milevsky, A., and Heerwagen, M. (2013). A phenomenological examination of sibling relationships in emerging adulthood. *Journal of Marriage & Family Review* 49(3), 251–63. doi:http://dx.doi.org/10.1080/01494929.2012.7 62444.

18. Tibbetts, G., and Scharfe, E. (2015). Oh, brother (or sister)!: An examination of sibling attachment, conflict, and cooperation in emerging adulthood. *Journal of Relationships Research* 6(e8). doi:10.1017/jrr.2015.4.

19. Spitze, G., and Trent, K. (2006). Gender differences in adult sibling relations in two-child families. *Journal of Marriage & Family* 68(4), 977–92.

20. Degges-White, S., and Borzumato-Gainey, C. (2011). *Friends Forever: How Girls and Women Forge Lasting Relationships*. Lanham, MD: Rowman & Littlefield.

21. Cicirelli, V. G. (1995). *Sibling Relationships across the Life Span*. New York: Plenum.

22. Merz, E., and De Jong Gierveld, J. (2016). Childhood memories, family ties, sibling support and loneliness in ever-widowed older adults: Quantitative and qualitative results. *Ageing & Society* 36(3), 534–61.

CHAPTER 7. FAMILY SECRETS

1. Orgad, Y. (2015). The culture of family secrets. *Culture & Psychology* 21(1), 59–80.

2. Hadjiosif, M. (2013). From strategy to process: Validation in Dialectical Behavior Therapy. *Counseling Psychology Review* 28(1), 72–80.

3. Perls, F. (1969). *Gestalt Therapy Verbatim*. Moab, UT: Real People Press.

4. White, M., and Epston, D. (1990). *Narrative Means to Therapeutic Ends*. New York: Norton.

5. Kiser, L. J., Baumgardner, B., and Dorado, J. (2010). Who we are, but for the stories we tell: Family stories and healing. *Psychological Trauma* 2(3), 223–49.

6. Selvini-Palazzoli, M., Boscolo, L., Cecchin, G., and Prata, G. (1978). *Paradox and Counterparadox: A New Model in the Therapy of the Family in Schizophrenic Transaction*. New York: Jason Aronson.

7. Selvini-Palazzoli, M., Boscolo, L., Cecchin, G., and Prata, G. (1980). Hypothesizing-circularity-neutrality: Three guidelines for the conductor of the session. *Family Process* 19, 3–12.

8. Hamilton-Giachritsis, C. E., and Browne, K. D. (2005). A retrospective study of risk to siblings in abusing families. *Journal of Family Psychology* 19(4), 619–24.

9. Ibid.

10. Nelson, E. C., Heath, A. C., Madden, P. A. F., Cooper, L., Dinwiddie, S. H., Bucholz, K. K., and Martin, N. G. (2002). Association between self-reported childhood sexual abuse and adverse psychosocial outcomes. Results from a twin study. *Archives of General Psychiatry* 59, 139–45.

11. Cloitre, M., Rosenberg, A., Follette, V. M., and Ruzek, J. I. (eds.) (2006). *Cognitive Behavioral Therapies for Trauma*. New York: The Guilford Press.

12. Simonelli, C. J., Mullis, T., Elliott, A. N., and Pierce, T. W. (2002). Abuse by siblings and subsequent experiences of violence within the dating relationship. *Journal of Interpersonal Violence* 17(2), 103–21.

13. Tucker, C. J., Finkelhor, D., Turner, H., and Shattuck, A. M. (2014). Family dynamics and young children's sibling victimization. *Journal of Family Psychology* 28(5), 625–33.

14. Goffman, E. (1963). *Stigma: Notes on the Management of Spoiled Identity*. Englewood Cliffs, NJ: Prentice-Hall.

15. Widemalm, M., and Hjarthag, F. (2015). The forum as a friend: Parental mental illness and communication on open Internet forums. *Social Psychiatry and Psychiatric Epidemiology* 50(1), 1601–7.

16. Sharp, M., Fear, N. T., Rona, R. J., Wessley, S., Greenberg, N., Jones, N., and Goodwin, L. (2015). Stigma as a barrier to seeking health care among military personnel with mental health problems. *Epidemiological Review* 37, 144–62. doi:10.1093/epirev/mxu012.

17. Mantovani, N., Pizzolati, M., and Edge, D. (2016). Exploring the relationship between stigma and help-seeking for mental illness in African-descended faith communities in the UK. *Health Expectations* (April 28) doi:10.1111/hex.12464.

18. Staiger, T., Waldmann, R., Krumm, S., and Rusch, N. (2016). Stigma and poor mental health literacy as barriers to service use among unemployed people with mental illness: A qualitative study. *European Psychiatry* 33S, S487.

19. Mahoney, D. M., Rickspoone, L., and Hull, J. C. (2016). Narcissism, parenting, complex trauma: The emotional consequences created for children by narcissistic parents. *The Practitioner Scholar: Journal of Counseling and Professional Psychology* 5, 45–59.

20. Ibid.

21. Summers, D. M., and Summers, C. C. (2006). Unadulterated arrogance: Autopsy of the narcissistic parental alienator. *American Journal of Family Therapy* 34, 399–428.

22. Shaw, D. (2010). Enter ghosts: The loss of intersubjectivity in clinical work with adult children of pathological narcissists. *Psychoanalytic Dialogues* 20(1), 46–59.

23. Park, S., Schepp, K. G., and Park, D. (2016). Living with appending a scarlet letter: The lifelong suffering of children of alcoholics in South Korea. *Journal of Ethnicity in Substance Abuse* (May 2016). doi:10.1080/15332640.20 16.1175989.

24. Tony, A. (1978). The Laundry List. Retrieved from http://www.adultchil dren.org/lit-Laundry_List.

25. Harter, S. L. (2000). Psychosocial adjustment of adult children of alcoholics: A review of the recent empirical literature. *Clinical Psychology Review* 20(3), 311–37.

26. Hall, C. W., and Webster, R. E. (2002). Traumatic symptomatology characteristics of adult children of alcoholics. *Journal of Drug Education* 32(3), 195–211.

27. Park, S., and Schepp, K. G. (2015). A systematic review of research on children of alcoholics: Their inherent resilience and vulnerability. *Journal of Child and Family Studies* 24, 1222–31.

28. Caya, M., and Liem, J. H. (1998). The role of sibling support in high-conflict families. *American Journal of Orthopsychiatry* 68(2), 327–33.

29. Abbey, C. (2004). The experience of the impact of divorce on sibling relationships: A qualitative study. *Clinical Child Psychology & Psychiatry* 9(2), 241–59.

30. Poortman, A., and Voorpostel, M. (2009). Parental divorce and sibling relationships: A research note. *Journal of Family Issues* 30(1), 74–91.

CHAPTER 8. TABOO TOPICS

1. Ojeda, C., and Hatemi, P. K. (2015). Accounting for the child in the transmission of party identification. *American Sociological Review* 80(6), 1150–74.

2. Campbell, A., Converse, P. E., Miller, W. E., and Stokes, D. E. (1960). *The American Voter*. New York: Wiley.

3. Iyengar, S., and Westwood, S. J. (2015). Fear and loathing across party lines: New evidence on group polarization. *American Journal of Political Science* 59(3), 690–707.

4. Pew Research Center. April 2015. A deep dive into party affiliation.

5. Ojeda and Hatemi (2015).

6. Shea, D. M. (2015). Young voters, declining trust and the limits of "service politics." *The Forum: A Journal of Applied Research in Contemporary Politics* 13(3), 459–79. doi: http://dx.doi.org/10.1515/for-2015-0036.

7. Pew Research Center. November 3, 2015. U.S. public becoming less religious.

8. Alsemgeest, L. (2014). Family communication about money: Why the taboo? *Mediterranean Journal of Social Sciences* 5(16), 516–23.

9. Atwood, J. D. (2012). Couples and money: The last taboo. *The American Journal of Family Therapy* 40, 1–19.

10. Ibid.

11. Chan-Brown, K., Douglass, A., Halling, S., Keller, J., and McNabb, M. (2016). What is money? A qualitative study of money as experienced. *The Humanistic Psychologist* 44(2), 190–209.

12. Ibid.

13. Pew Research Center. May 12, 2016. Public opinion on same-sex marriage. Survey conducted March 17–27, 2016.

14. Ballantine, M. W. (2012). Sibling incest dynamics: Therapeutic themes and clinical challenges. *Clinical Social Work Journal* 40(1), 56–65.

15. Abrahams, J., and Hoey, H. (1994). Sibling incest in a clergy family: A case study. *Child Abuse and Neglect* 18, 1029–35.

16. Morrill, M. (2014). Sibling sexual abuse: An exploratory study of long-term consequences for self-esteem and counseling considerations. *Journal of Family Violence* 29, 205. doi:10.1007/s10896-013-9571-4.

17. Meyers, A. (2016). Trauma and recovery: Factors contributing to resiliency of survivors of sibling abuse. *The Family Journal: Counseling and Therapy for Couples and Families* 24(2), 147–56.

18. Romo, L. K. (2015). Family secrets. In *The International Encyclopedia of Interpersonal Communication*. John Wiley & Sons, Inc.

CHAPTER 9. VALUES CONFLICTS BETWEEN SIBLINGS

1. Schwartz, S. H. (1992). Universals in the content and structure of values: Theoretical advances and empirical tests in 20 countries. *Advances in Experimental Social Psychology* 25, 1–65.

2. Haste, H. (2010). Citizenship education: A critical look at a contested field. In Sherrod, L. R., Torney-Purta, J., and Flanagan, C. A. (eds.), *Handbook of Research on Civic Engagement in Youth* (Ch. 7, pp. 161–88). New York: Wiley. doi:http://dx.doi.org/10.1002/9780470767603.

3. Ram, A., and Ross, H. (2008). "We got to figure it out": Information-sharing and siblings' negotiations of conflicts of interests. *Social Development* 17(3), 512–27.

4. Aslan, S., and Gelbal, S. (2016). Separation-individuation of late adolescents: A longitudinal study. *Educational Research and Reviews* 11(1), 1–15. DOI: 10.5897/ERR2015.2570.

5. Prioste, A., Narciso, I., Goncalves, M., and Pereira, C. (2016). Adolescent parents' values: The role played by retrospective perceptions of the family-of-origin. *Journal of Child & Family Studies* 25(1), 224–31.

6. Ricky Finzi-Dottan, D., and Cohen, O. (2010) Young adult sibling relations: The effects of perceived parental favoritism and narcissism. *The Journal of Psychology* 145, 1–22. doi:10.1080/00223980.2010.528073.

7. Kimura, D. (2000). *Sex and Cognition*. Cambridge, MA: A Bradford Book/The MIT Press.

8. Berninger, V. W., Nielsen, K. H., Abbott, R. D., Wijsman, E., and Raskind, W. (2008). Gender differences in severity of writing and reading disabilities. *Journal of School Psychology 46*, 151–72.

9. Kimura (2000).

10. Phillips, M., Lowe, M., Lurito, J. T., Dzemidzic, M., and Matthews, V. (2001). Temporal lobe activation demonstrates sex-based differences during passive listening. *Radiology* 220, 202–7.

11. Rosen-Grandon, J. R., Myers, J. E., and Hattie, J. A. (2004). The relationship between marital characteristics, marital interaction processes, and marital satisfaction. *Journal of Counseling & Development* 82(1), 58–68.

12. Gaunt, R. (2006). Couple similarity and marital satisfaction: Are similar spouses happier? *Journal of Personality* 74(5), 1401–20.

13. Kretschmer, T., and Pike, A. (2010). Associations between adolescent siblings' relationship quality and similarity and differences in values. *Journal of Family Psychology* 24(4), 411–18.

14. Degner, J., and Dalege, J. (2013). The apple does not fall far from the tree or does it? A meta-analysis of parent-child similarity in intergroup attitudes. *Psychological Bulletin* 139(6), 1270–1304.

15. Killoren, S. E., Wheeler, L. A., Updegraff, K. A., Rodreiguez de Jesus, S. A., and McHale, S. M. (2015). Longitudinal associations among parental acceptance, familism values, and sibling intimacy in Mexican-origin families. *Family Process* 54(2), 217–31.

16. Prioste, A., Narciso, I., Goncalves, M., and Pereira, C. (2015). Family relationships and parenting practices: A pathway to adolescents' collectivist and individualist values? *Journal of Child & Family Studies* 24(11), 3258–67.

17. Nordqvist, P., and Smart, C. (2014). Troubling the family: Coming out as lesbian and gay. *Families, Relationships and Societies* 3(1), 97–112.

18. Hilton, A. N., and Szymanski, D. M. (2014). Predictors of heterosexual siblings' acceptance of their lesbian sister or gay brother. *Journal of LGBT Issues in Counseling* 8(2), 164–88. doi:10.1080/15538605.2014.895664.

19. Bogaert, A. F. (2004). Asexuality: Prevalence and associated factors in a national probability sample. *The Journal of Sex Research* 41, 279–87.

20. Ono, M., and Devilly, G. J. (2013). The role of childhood and adulthood trauma and appraisal of self-discrepancy in overgeneral memory retrieval. *Cognition and Emotion* 27(6), 979–94.

CHAPTER 10. DEALING WITH SIBLING SHORTCOMINGS

1. Voorpostel, M., van der Lippe, T., and Flap, H. (2012). For better or worse: Negative life events and sibling relationships. *International Sociology* 27(3), 330–48.

2. Kann, L., McManus, T., Harris, W. A., et al. (2016). Youth risk behavior surveillance—United States, 2015. *MMWR Surveillance Summaries* 65, 6.

3. Gorka, S. M., Liu, H., Klein, D., Daughters, S. B., and Shankman, S. A. (2015). Is risk-taking propensity a familial vulnerability factor for alcohol use? An examination in two independent samples. *Journal of Psychiatric Research* 68, 54–60.

4. Seglem, K. B., Waaktaar, T., Ask, H., and Torgersen, S. (2016). Sex differences in genetic and environmental contributions to alcohol consumption from early adolescence to young adulthood. *Addiction* 111, 1188–95.

5. Webb, J. R., Hirsch, J. K., and Toussaint, L. (2015). Forgiveness as a positive psychotherapy for addiction and suicide: Theory, research, and practice. *Spirituality in Clinical Practice* 2(1), 48–60.

6. Jennison, K. M., and Johnson, K. A. (2001). Parental alcoholism as a risk factor for DSM-IV-defined alcohol abuse and dependence in American women: The protective benefits of dyadic cohesion in marital communication. *The American Journal of Drug and Alcohol Abuse* 27(2), 349–74.

7. Corrigan, P. W., Watson, A. C., and Miller, F. E. (2006). Blame, shame, and contamination: The impact of mental illness and drug dependence stigma on family members. *Journal of Family Psychology* 20(2), 239–46. doi:10.1037/0893-3200.20.2.239.

8. Selvini-Palazzoli, M., Boscolo, L., Cecchin, G., and Prata, G. (1978). *Paradox and Counterparadox: A New Model in the Therapy of the Family in Schizophrenic Transaction.* New York: Jason Aronson.

9. Selvini-Palazzoli, M., Boscolo, L., Cecchin, G., and Prata, G. (1980). Hypothesizing-circularity-neutrality: Three guidelines for the conductor of the session. *Family Process* 19, 3–12.

10. Voorpostel, van der Lippe, and Flap (2012).

11. Breslin, K. A., Kumar, V. K., Ryan, R. B., Browne, J., and Porter, J. (2016). Effect of apology on interpersonal forgiveness and distancing within familial relationships. *Current Psychology* 1, 1–12. doi:10.1007/s12144-016-9450-2.

CHAPTER 11. SIBLINGS AND THEIR PARTNERS

1. Minuchin, S. (1996). *Families and Family Therapy*. Cambridge, MA: Harvard University Press.

2. Ibid.

3. Ibid.

4. Erikson, E. (1980). *Identity Development and the Life Cycle: Selected Papers, with a Historical Introduction by David Rapaport*. New York: International University Press.

5. Nichols, M. P., and Davis, S. (2016). *Family Therapy: Concepts and Methods* (11th ed.). Saddlebrook, NJ: Pearson.

6. Biegler, R., and Kennair, L. E. O. (2016). Sisterly love: Within-generation differences in ideal partner for sister and self. *Evolutionary Behavioral Sciences* 10(1), 29–42.

7. Kennair, L. E. O., and Biegler, R. (in press). Conflicting tastes: Conflicts between female family members in choice of romantic partners. In M. L. Fisher (ed.), *The Oxford Handbook of Women and Competition*. New York: Oxford University Press.

8. Sarkisian, N., and Gerstel, N. (2016). Does singlehood isolate or integrate? Examining the link between marital status and ties to kin, friends, and neighbors. *Journal of Social & Personal Relationships* 33(3), 361–84.

9. Carpenter, E. N. (2014). Romantic relationship conflict management techniques of adult only children and adults with siblings. Thesis submitted to Texas Woman's University. http://hdl.handle.net/11274/4898.

CHAPTER 12. HEALTH AND WELL-BEING CONCERNS OF SIBLINGS

1. Namkung, E. H., Greenberg, J. S., and Mailick, M. R. (2016). Well-being of sibling caregivers: Effects of kinship relationship and race. *The Gerontologist* 10.1093. doi:10.1093/geront/gnw008.

2. Cuskelly, M. (2016). Contributions to adult sibling relationships and intention to care of siblings of individuals with Down Syndrome. *American Journal on Intellectual and Developmental Disabilities* 121(3), 204–18.

3. Burke, M. M., Fish, T., and Lawton, K. (2015). A comparative analysis of adult siblings' perceptions toward caregiving. *Intellectual and Developmental Disabilities* 53(2), 143–57.

4. Bassuk, E. L., Mickelson, K. D., Bissell, H. D., and Perloff, J. N. (2002). Role of kin and nonkin support in the mental health of low-income women. *American Journal of Orthopsychiatry* 72, 39–49.

5. Center for Behavioral Health Statistics and Quality. (2015). Behavioral health trends in the United States: Results from the 2014 National Survey on Drug Use and Health. HHS Publication No. SMA 15-4927, NSDUH Series H-50. Retrieved from http://www.samhsa.gov/ data/.

6. Smith, M. J., Greenberg, J. S., and Mailick Seltzer, M. (2007). Siblings of adults with schizophrenia: Expectations about future caregiving roles. *American Journal of Orthopsychiatry* 77(1), 29–37.

7. Seltzer, M. M., Greenberg, J. S., Krauss, M. W., Gordon, R. M., and Judge, K. (1997). Siblings of adults with mental retardation or mental illness: Effects on lifestyle and psychological well-being. *Family Relations* 46(4), 395–405.

CHAPTER 13. CARING FOR AGING PARENTS

1. Suitor, J. J., and Pillemer, K. (2006). Choosing daughters: Exploring why mothers favor adult daughters over sons. *Sociological Perspectives* 49(2), 139–61.

2. Spitze, G., Ward, R., Deane, G., and Zhuo, Y. (2012). Cross-sibling effects in parent-adult child exchanges of socioemotional support. *Research on Aging* 34(2), 197–221.

3. Degges-White, S., and Borzumato-Gainey, C. (2011). *Friends Forever: How Girls and Women Forge Lasting Relationships*. Lanham, MD: Rowman & Littlefield.

4. Fischer, C. S., and Beresford, L. (2015). Changes in support networks in late middle age: The extension of gender and educational differences. *Journals of Gerontology Series B: Psychological Sciences and Social Science* 70, 123–31. doi:10.1093/geronb/gbu057.

5. Kahn, J. R., McGill, B. S., and Bianchi, S. M. (2011). Help to families and friends: Are there gender differences at older ages? *Journal of Marriage and Family* 73(1), 77–92.

6. Collins, C. R. (2014). Men as caregivers of the elderly: Support for the contributions of sons. *Journal of Interdisciplinary Healthcare* 7, 525–31. doi:22813-10.2147/JMDH.S6835.

7. Dawson, A., Pike, A., and Bird, L. (2015). Parental division of household labor and sibling relationship quality: Family relationships mediators. *Infant & Child Development* 24(4), 379–93.

8. MetLife. (2004). Miles away: The MetLife study of long-distance caregiving: Findings from a national study. Available from http://www.metlife.com/WP SAssets/1266552904116064686V1FLongDistaneCaregiving.pdf.

9. Caregiving in the U.S. (2004). National Alliance for Caregiving and AARP, funded by the MetLife Foundation.

10. Douglas, S. L., Mazanec, P., Lipson, A., and Leuchtag, M. (2016). Distance caregiving a family member with cancer: A review of the literature on distance caregiving and recommendations for future research. *World Journal of Clinical Oncology* 7(2), 214–19.

11. Rogers, C. (1961). *On Becoming a Person: A Therapist's View of Psychotherapy*. Boston: Houghton Mifflin.

12. Amaro, L. M., and Miller, K. I. (2016). Discussion of care, contribution, and perceived (in)gratitude in the family caregiver and sibling relationship. *Personal Relationships* 23(1), 98–110.

13. Hayslip Jr., B., Pruett, J. H., and Caballero, D. M. (2015). The "how" and "when" of parental loss in adulthood: Effects on grief and adjustment. *Omega (Westport)* 71(1), 3–18.

14. Ibid.

15. Carmon, A. F., Western, K. J., Miller, A. N., Pearson, J. C., and Fowler, M. R. (2010). Grieving those we've lost: An examination of family communication patterns and grief reactions. *Communication Research Reports* 27, 253–62.

16. Greif, G. L., and Woolley, M. E. (2015). Patterns in adult sibling relationships after the death of one or both parents. *Journal of Social Work in End-of-Life & Palliative Care* 11(1), 74–89.

17. Lashewicz, B. (2014). Sibling resentments and alliances during the parent care years: Implications for social work practice. *Journal of Evidence-Based Social Work* 11(5), 460–67.

18. Spitze, G. D., and Trent, K. (2016). Changes in individual sibling relationships in response to life events. *Journal of Family Issues*. doi:10.1177/0192513X16653431.

CHAPTER 14. DECONSTRUCTING
UNPRODUCTIVE COMMUNICATION PATTERNS

1. Satir, V. (1972). *Peoplemaking*. Palo Alto, CA: Science & Behavior Books.

2. Satir, V., Bandler, R., and Grinder, J. (1976). *Changing with Families*. Palo Alto, CA: Science & Behavior Books.

3. Satir (1972).

4. Pauldine, M. R., Snyder, J., Bank, L., and Owen, L. D. (2015). Predicting sibling relationship quality from family conflict: A longitudinal study from early adolescence to young adulthood. *Journal of Child and Adolescent Behavior* 3(4), 231. doi:10.4172/2375-4494.1000231.

5. Satir (1972).

6. Van Volkom, M. (2006). Sibling relationships in middle and older adulthood: A review of the literature. *Marriage & Family Review* 40(2/3), 151–70.

7. Almaatouq, A., Radaelli, L., Pentland, A., and Shmueli, E. (2016). Are you your friends' friend? Poor perception of friendship ties that limits the ability to promote behavioral change. *PLoS ONE* 11(3). E0151588. doi:10.1371/journal. pone.0151588.

8. Carmichael, C. L., Reis, H. T., and Duberstein, P. R. (2015). In your 20s it's quantity, in your 30s it's quality: The prognostic value of social activity across 30 years of adulthood. *Psychology & Aging* 30(1), 95–105.

CHAPTER 15. SIBLINGS FOR LIFE: CLOSING THE GAPS IN THE FAMILY CIRCLE

1. Doughty, S. E., McHale, S. M., and Feinberg, M. E. (2015). Sibling experiences as predictors of romantic relationship qualities in adolescence. *Journal of Family Issues* 35(5), 589–608.

2. Schulte, H. A. (2006). Family of origin and sibling influence on the experience of social support in adult friendships. *Dissertation Abstracts International: Section B: The Sciences and Engineering* 67(6-5), 3510.

3. Reese-Weber, M., and Kahn, J. H. (2005). Familial predictors of sibling and romantic-partner conflict resolution: Comparing late adolescents from intact and divorced families. *Journal of Adolescence* 28(4), 479–93.

4. Doughty, S., Lam, C., Stadnik, C., and McHale, S. (2015). Links between sibling experiences and romantic competence from adolescence through young adulthood. *Journal of Youth & Adolescence* 44(11), 2054–66.

5. Carballo, J., Garcia-Neito, R., Alvarez-Garcia, R., Caro-Cañuzares, I., López-Castromán, J., Muñoz-Lorenzo, L., de Leon-Martinez, V., and Baca-Garcia, E. (2013). Sibship size, birth order, family structure and childhood mental disorders. *Social Psychiatry & Psychiatric Epidemiology* 48(8), 1327–33.

6. Ibid.

7. Spitze, G., Ward, R., Deane, G., and Zhuo, Y. (2012). Cross-sibling effects in parent-adult child exchanges of socioemotional support. *Research on Aging* 34(2), 197–221.

8. Spitze, G., and Trent, K. (2006). Gender differences in adult sibling relations in two-child families. *Journal of Marriage and Family* 68(4), 977–92.

Bibliography

Abbey, C. (2004). The experience of the impact of divorce on sibling relationships: A qualitative study. *Clinical Child Psychology & Psychiatry* 9(2), 241–59.

Abrahams, J., and Hoey, H. (1994). Sibling incest in a clergy family: A case study. *Child Abuse and Neglect* 18, 1029–35.

Abuhatoum, S., and Howe, N. (2013). Power in sibling conflict during early and middle childhood. *Social Development* 22(4), 738–54.

Adler, A. (1929). Position in family influences lifestyle. *International Journal of Individual Psychology* 3, 211–27.

Adler, R. B., and Proctor II, R. F. (2014). *Looking Out, Looking In* (15th ed.). Boston: Cengage.

Almaatouq, A., Radaelli, L., Pentland, A., and Shmueli, E. (2016). Are you your friends' friend? Poor perception of friendship ties that limits the ability to promote behavioral change. *PLoS ONE* 11(3). E0151588. doi:10.1371/journal.pone.0151588.

Alsemgeest, L. (2014). Family communication about money: Why the taboo? *Mediterranean Journal of Social Sciences* 5(16), 516–23.

Amaro, L. M., and Miller, K. I. (2016). Discussion of care, contribution, and perceived (in)gratitude in the family caregiver and sibling relationship. *Personal Relationships* 23(1), 98–110.

Ansbacher, H. L., and Ansbacher, R. R. (1956). *The Individual Psychology of Alfred Adler*. New York: Basic Books.

Aslan, S., and Gelbal, S. (2016). Separation-individuation of late adolescents: A longitudinal study. *Educational Research and Reviews* 11(1), 1–15. doi:10.5897/ERR2015.2570.

Atwood, J. D. (2012). Couples and money: The last taboo. *The American Journal of Family Therapy* 40, 1–19.

Ayyavoo, A., Savage, T., Derraik, J. G. B., Hofman, P. L., and Cutfield, W. S. (2013). First-born children have reduced insulin sensitivity and higher daytime blood pressure compared to later born children. *Journal of Clinical Endocrinology & Metabolism* 98, 1248–53.

Ballantine, M. W. (2012). Sibling incest dynamics: Therapeutic themes and clinical challenges. *Clinical Social Work Journal* 40(1), 56–65.

Bank, S., and Kahn, M. D. (1982). *The Sibling Bond.* New York: Basic Books.

Barclay, K., and Kolk, M. (2015). Birth order and morality: A population-based cohort study. *Demography* 52, 613–39.

Bassuk, E. L., Mickelson, K. D., Bissell, H. D., and Perloff, J. N. (2002). Role of kin and nonkin support in the mental health of low-income women. *American Journal of Orthopsychiatry* 72, 39–49.

Becker, O. A., Salzburger, V., Lois, N., and Nauck, B. (2013). What narrows the stepgap? Closeness between parents and adult (step)children in Germany. *Journal of Marriage and Family* 75(5), 1130–48.

Bedford, V. H., Volling, B. L., and Avioli, P. S. (2000). Positive consequences of sibling conflict in childhood and adulthood. *International Journal of Aging and Human Development* 51(1), 53–69.

Berninger, V. W., Nielsen, K. H., Abbott, R. D., Wijsman, E., and Raskind, W. (2008). Gender differences in severity of writing and reading disabilities. *Journal of School Psychology 46*, 151–72.

Biegler, R., and Kennair, L. E. O. (2016). Sisterly love: Within-generation differences in ideal partner for sister and self. *Evolutionary Behavioral Sciences* 10(1), 29–42.

Bingham, C. R., Shope, J. T., Zakrajsek, J., and Raghunathan, T. E. (2008). Problem driving behavior and psychosocial maturation in young adulthood. *Accident Analysis & Prevention* 40, 1758–64.

Black, S. E., Devereux, Paul J., and Salvanes, Kjell, G. (2007). From the cradle to the labor market? The effect of birth weight on adult outcomes. *Quarterly Journal of Economics* 122(1), 409–39.

Black, S. E., Devereux, P. J., and Salvanes, K. G. (July 2015). Healthy (?), wealthy and wise: Birth order and adult health. NBER Working Paper No. w21337. Available at SSRN: http://ssrn.com/abstract=2629942.

Bogaert, A. F. (2004). Asexuality: Prevalence and associated factors in a national probability sample. *The Journal of Sex Research* 41, 279–87.

Breslin, K. A., Kumar, V. K., Ryan, R. B., Browne, J., and Porter, J. (2016). Effect of apology on interpersonal forgiveness and distancing within familial relationships. *Current Psychology* 1, 1–12. doi:10.1007/s12144-016-9450-2.

Budak, D., and Chavajay, P. (2012). Cultural variation in the social organization of problem solving among African American and European American siblings. *Cultural Diversity and Ethnic Minority Psychology* 18(3), 307–11.

Buist, K. L., and Vermande, M. (2014). Sibling relationship patterns and their associations with child competence and problem behavior. *Journal of Family Psychology* 28(4), 529–37.

Burke, M. M., Fish, T., and Lawton, K. (2015). A comparative analysis of adult siblings' perceptions toward caregiving. *Intellectual and Developmental Disabilities* 53(2), 143–57.

Campbell, A., Converse, P. E., Miller, W. E., and Stokes, D. E. (1960). *The American Voter*. New York: Wiley.

Campos, B., Ullman, J. B., Aguilera, A., and Dunkel Schetter, C. (2014). Familism and psychological health: The intervening role of closeness and social support. *Cultural Diversity and Ethnic Minority Psychology* 20(2), 191–201.

Carballo, J., Garcia-Neito, R., Alvarez-Garcia, R., Caro-Cañuzares, I., López-Castromán, J., Muñoz-Lorenzo, L., de Leon-Martinez, V., and Baca-Garcia, E. (2013). Sibship size, birth order, family structure and childhood mental disorders. *Social Psychiatry & Psychiatric Epidemiology* 48(8), 1327–33.

Caregiving in the U.S. (2004). National Alliance for Caregiving and AARP, funded by the MetLife Foundation.

Carmichael, C. L., Reis, H. T., and Duberstein, P. R. (2015). In your 20s it's quantity, in your 30s it's quality: The prognostic value of social activity across 30 years of adulthood. *Psychology & Aging* 30(1), 95–105.

Carmon, A. F., Western, K. J., Miller, A. N., Pearson, J. C., and Fowler, M. R. (2010). Grieving those we've lost: An examination of family communication patterns and grief reactions. *Communication Research Reports* 27, 253–62.

Carpenter, E. N. (2014). Romantic relationship conflict management techniques of adult only children and adults with siblings. Thesis submitted to Texas Woman's University. URI: http://hdl.handle.net/11274/4898.

Caya, M., and Liem, J. H. (1998). The role of sibling support in high-conflict families. *American Journal of Orthopsychiatry* 68(2), 327–33.

Center for Behavioral Health Statistics and Quality. (2015). Behavioral health trends in the United States: Results from the 2014 National Survey on Drug Use and Health. HHS Publication No. SMA 15-4927, NSDUH Series H-50. Retrieved from http://www.samhsa.gov/data/.

Chan-Brown, K., Douglass, A., Halling, S., Keller, J., and McNabb, M. (2016). What is money? A qualitative study of money as experienced. *The Humanistic Psychologist* 44(2), 190–209.

Cicirelli, V. G. (1994). Sibling relationships in cross-cultural perspective. *Journal of Marriage and Family* 56, 7–20.

Cicirelli, V. G. (1995). *Sibling Relationships across the Life Span*. New York: Plenum.

Cloitre, M., Rosenberg, A., Follette, V. M., and Ruzek, J. I. (eds.) (2006). *Cognitive Behavioral Therapies for Trauma*. New York: The Guilford Press.

Collins, C. R. (2014). Men as caregivers of the elderly: Support for the contributions of sons. *Journal of Interdisciplinary Healthcare* 7, 525–31. doi:2281310.2147/JMDH.S6835.

Corrigan, P. W., Watson, A. C., and Miller, F. E. (2006). Blame, shame, and contamination: The impact of mental illness and drug dependence stigma on family members. *Journal of Family Psychology* 20(2), 239–46. doi:10.1037/08933200.20.2.239.

Cuskelly, M. (2016). Contributions to adult sibling relationships and intention to care of siblings of individuals with Down Syndrome. *American Journal on Intellectual and Developmental Disabilities* 121(3), 204–18.

Damian, R. I., and Roberts, B. W. (2015). The associations of birth order with personality and intelligence in a representative sample of U.S. high school students. *Journal of Research in Personality* 58, 96–105.

Dawson, A., Pike, A., and Bird, L. (2015). Parental division of household labor and sibling relationship quality: Family relationships mediators. *Infant & Child Development* 24(4), 379–93.

de Shazer, S., and Dolan, Y. (2007). *More than Miracles: The State of the Art of Solution-Focused Brief Therapy*. New York: Routledge Publishing.

Decinque, N., Monterosso, L., Dadd, G., Sidhu, R., Macpherson, R., and Aoun, S. (2006). Bereavement support for families following the death of a child from cancer: Experience of bereaved parents. *Journal of Psychosocial Oncology* 24(2), 65–83. doi:10.1300=J077v24n02_05.

Degges-White, S., and Borzumato-Gainey, C. (2011). *Friends Forever: How Girls and Women Forge Lasting Relationships*. Lanham, MD: Rowman & Littlefield.

Degner, J., and Dalege, J. (2013). The apple does not fall far from the tree or does it? A meta-analysis of parent-child similarity in intergroup attitudes. *Psychological Bulletin* 139(6), 1270–1304.

Dinkmeyer, D., and Sperry, L. (2000). *Counseling and Psychotherapy: An Integrated, Individual Psychology Approach*. Upper Saddle River, NJ: Merrill/Prentice Hall.

Doughty, S. E., McHale, S. M., and Feinberg, M. E. (2015). Sibling experiences as predictors of romantic relationship qualities in adolescence. *Journal of Family Issues* 35(5), 589–608.

Doughty, S., Lam, C., Stadnik, C., and McHale, S. (2015). Links between sibling experiences and romantic competence from adolescence through young adulthood. *Journal of Youth & Adolescence* 44(11), 2054–66.

Douglas, S. L., Mazanec, P., Lipson, A., and Leuchtag, M. (2016). Distance caregiving a family member with cancer: A review of the literature on distance caregiving and recommendations for future research. *World Journal of Clinical Oncology* 7(2), 214–19.

Downey, D. B., Condron, D. J., and Yucel, D. (2015). Number of siblings and social skills revisited among American fifth graders. *Journal of Family Issues* 38(2), 273–96.

Dyregrov, A. (1990). *Grief in Children: A Handbook for Adults*. London: Jessica Kingsley Publishers.

Erikson, E. (1959). *Identity Development and the Life Cycle*. New York: International University Press.

Erikson, E. (1980). *Identity Development and the Life Cycle: Selected Papers, with a Historical Introduction by David Rapaport*. New York: International University Press.

Erol, R. Y., and Orth, U. (2013). Actor and partner effects of self-esteem on relationship satisfaction and the mediating role of secure attachment between the partners. *Journal of Research in Personality* 47(1), 26–35.

Ervin-Tripp, S. (1989). Sisters and brothers. In P. G. Zukow (ed.), *Sibling Interaction Across Cultures: Theoretical and Methodological Issues* (pp. 105–48). New York: Springer-Verlag.

Feng, W., Gu, B., and Cai, Y. (2016). The end of China's one-child policy. *Studies in Family Planning* 47(1), 83–86.

Fischer, C. S., and Beresford, L. (2014). Changes in support networks in late middle age: The extension of gender and educational differences. *Journals of Gerontology Series B: Psychological Sciences and Social Sciences* 70, 123–31. doi:10.1093/geronb/gbu057.

Fischer, J. L., and Wampler, R. S. (1994). Abusive drinking in young adults: Personality type and family role moderators of family-of-origin influences. *Journal of Marriage and Family* 56(2), 469–79.

Fitzpatrick, M. A. (2004). Family communication patterns theory: Observations on its development and application. *Journal of Family Communications* 4(3&4), 167–79.

Fitzpatrick, M. A., Ritchie, L. D., and Koerner, A. F. (1994). Communication schemata within the family: Multiple perspectives on family interaction. *Human Communication Research* 20, 275–301.

Fletcher, J., Mailick, M., Song, J., and Wolfe, B. (2013). A sibling death in the family: Common and consequential. *Demography* 50, 803–26.

Fortuna, K., Roisman, G. I., Haydon, K. C., Groh, A. M., and Holland, A. S. (2011). Attachment states of mind and the quality of young adults' sibling relationships. *Developmental Psychology* 47, 1366–73.

Fuligni, A., and Masten, C. L. (2010). Daily family interactions among young adults in the United States from Latin American, Filipino, East Asian, and

European backgrounds. *International Journal of Behavioral Development* 34(6), 491–99.

Gao, G. (2015). Americans' ideal family size is smaller than it used to be. Fact Tank: News in the Numbers. Pew Research Center. Data retrieved from http://www .pewresearch.org/fact-tank/2015/05/08/ideal-size-of-the-american-family/.

Garcia, S. N. (2011). Ecological perspectives of adult Latina only children: A qualitative study. *Dissertation Abstracts International: Section B: The Sciences and Engineering* 72(3-B), 1779.

Gaunt, R. (2006). Couple similarity and marital satisfaction: Are similar spouses happier? *Journal of Personality* 74(5), 1401–20.

Gilligan, C. (1993). *In a Different Voice: Psychological Theory and Women's Development.* Boston: Harvard University Press.

Gilligan, M., Suitor, J. J., and Nam, S. (2015). Maternal differential treatment in later life families and within-family variations in adult sibling closeness. *Journals of Gerontology, Series B: Psychological Sciences and Social Sciences* 70(1), 167–77. doi:10.1093/geronb/gbu148.

Goetting, A. (1986). The developmental tasks of siblingship over the life cycle. *Journal of Marriage and Family* 48, 703–14.

Goffman, E. (1963). *Stigma: Notes on the Management of Spoiled Identity.* Englewood Cliffs, NJ: Prentice-Hall.

Gorka, S. M., Liu, H., Klein, D., Daughters, S. B., and Shankman, S. A. (2015). Is risk-taking propensity a familial vulnerability factor for alcohol use? An examination in two independent samples. *Journal of Psychiatric Research* 68, 54–60.

Greif, G. L., and Woolley, M. E. (2015). Patterns in adult sibling relationships after the death of one or both parents. *Journal of Social Work in End-of-Life & Palliative Care* 11(1), 74–89.

Gustafson, K., and Baofeng, H. (2014). Elderly care and the one-child policy: Concerns, expectations and preparations for elderly life in a rural Chinese township. *Journal of Cross-Cultural Gerontology* 29(1), 25–36.

Hadjiosif, M. (2013). From strategy to process: Validation in Dialectical Behavior Therapy. *Counseling Psychology Review* 28(1), 72–80.

Haines, Michael. "Fertility and Mortality in the United States." EH.Net Encyclopedia, edited by Robert Whaples. March 19, 2008.

Haley, J., and Richeport-Haley, M. (2003). *The Art of Strategic Therapy.* Hove, East Sussex: Brunner-Routledge.

Hall, C. W., and Webster, R. E. (2002). Traumatic symptomatology characteristics of adult children of alcoholics. *Journal of Drug Education* 32(3), 195–211.

Hamilton-Giachritsis, C. E., and Browne, K. D. (2005). A retrospective study of risk to siblings in abusing families. *Journal of Family Psychology* 19(4), 619–24.

Harter, S. L. (2000). Psychosocial adjustment of adult children of alcoholics: A review of the recent empirical literature. *Clinical Psychology Review* 20(3), 311–37.

Haste, H. (2010). Citizenship education: A critical look at a contested field. In Sherrod, L. R., Torney-Purta, J., and Flanagan, C. A. (eds.), *Handbook of Research on Civic Engagement in Youth* (Ch. 7, pp. 161–88). New York: Wiley. doi:http://dx.doi.org/10.1002/9780470767603.

Hayslip Jr., B., Pruett, J. H., and Caballero, D. M. (2015). The "how" and "when" of parental loss in adulthood: Effects on grief and adjustment. *Omega (Westport)* 71(1), 3–18.

Hesketh, T., Zhou, X., and Wang, Y. (2015). The end of the one-child policy: Lasting implications for China. *Journal of the American Medical Association* 314(24), 2619–20.

Hetherington, E. M. (1988). Parents, children, and siblings: Six years after divorce. In R. A. Hinde and J. Stevenson-Hinde (eds.), *Relationships within Families: Mutual Influences* (pp. 311–31). New York: Oxford University Press.

Hilton, A. N., and Szymanski, D. M. (2014). Predictors of heterosexual siblings' acceptance of their lesbian sister or gay brother. *Journal of LGBT Issues in Counseling* 8(2), 164–88. doi:10.1080/15538605.2014.895664.

Holmgren, S., Molander, B., and Nilsson, L. (2007). Episodic memory in adult age and effects of sibship size and birth order: Longitudinal data. *Journal of Adult Development* 14, 37–46.

Hotz, V. J., and Pantano, J. (2015). Strategic parenting, birth order, and school performance. *Journal of Population Economics* 28, 911–36.

Huang, L. N. (1999). Family communication patterns and personality characteristics. *Communication Quarterly* 47(2), 230–43.

Israelstam, K. (1988). Contrasting four major family therapy paradigms: Implications for family therapy training. *Journal of Family Therapy* 10, 179–96.

Iyengar, S., and Westwood, S. J. (2015). Fear and loathing across party lines: New evidence on group polarization. *American Journal of Political Science* 59(3), 690–707.

Jennison, K. M., and Johnson, K. A. (2001). Parental alcoholism as a risk factor for DSM-IV-defined alcohol abuse and dependence in American women: The protective benefits of dyadic cohesion in marital communication. *The American Journal of Drug and Alcohol Abuse* 27(2), 349–74

Jensen, A. C., Whiteman, S. D., Fingerman, K. L., and Birditt, K. S. (2013). "Life still isn't fair": Parental differential treatment of young adult siblings. *Journal of Marriage and Family* 75(2), 438–52.

Jewsbury Conger, K., and Little, W. M. (2010). Sibling relationships during the transition to adulthood. *Child Development Perspectives* 4(2), 87–94. doi:10.1111/j.1750-8606.2010.00123.x.

Kahn, J. R., McGill, B. S., and Bianchi, S. M. (2011). Help to families and friends: Are there gender differences at older ages? *Journal of Marriage and Family* 73(1), 77–92.

Kann, L., McManus, T., Harris, W. A., et al. (2016). Youth risk behavior surveillance—United States, 2015. *MMWR Surveillance Summaries* 65, 6.

Kempson, D., and Murdock, V. (2010). Memory keepers: A narrative study on siblings never known. *Death Studies* 34(8), 738–56.

Kempson, D., Conley, V. M., and Murdock, V. (2008). Unearthing the construct of transgenerational grief: The "ghost" of the sibling never known. *Illness, Crisis & Loss* 16(4), 271–84.

Kennair, L. E. O., and Biegler, R. (in press). Conflicting tastes: Conflicts between female family members in choice of romantic partners. In M. L. Fisher (ed.), *The Oxford Handbook of Women and Competition*. New York: Oxford University Press.

Kennedy, S., and Ruggles, S. (2014). Breaking up is hard to count: The rise of divorce in the United States, 1980-2010. *Demography* 51, 587–98.

Kerr, M., and Bowen, M. (1988). *Family Evaluation: An Approach Based on Bowen Theory*. New York: Norton.

Keynes, M. (2015). Being a "middle seat child" can spell success in later life. SKODA.UK press release. Retrieved from http://www.skoda.co.uk/news/being-a-middle-seat-child-can-spell-success-in-later-life.

Killoren, S. E., Alfaro, E. C., Lindell, A. K., and Streit, C. (2014). Mexican American college students' communication with their siblings. *Family Relations* 63, 513–25.

Killoren, S. E., Thayer, S. M., and Updegraff, K. A. (2008). Conflict resolution between Mexican origin adolescent siblings. *Journal of Marriage and Family* 70(5), 1200–12.

Killoren, S. E., Wheeler, L. A., Updegraff, K. A., Rodreiguez de Jesus, S. A., and McHale, S. M. (2015). Longitudinal associations among parental acceptance, familism values, and sibling intimacy in Mexican-origin families. *Family Process* 54(2), 217–31.

Kim, B. S. K., Yang, P. H., Atkinson, D. R., Wolfe, M. M., and Hong, S. (2001). Cultural value similarities and differences among Asian American ethnic groups. *Cultural Diversity and Ethnic Minority Psychology* 7(4), 343–61.

Kim, J., McHale, S. M., Osgood, D. W., and Crouter, A. C. (2006). Longitudinal course and family correlates of sibling relationships from childhood through adolescence. *Child Development* 77(6), 1746–61.

Kimura, D. (2000). *Sex and Cognition*. Cambridge, MA: A Bradford Book/The MIT Press.

Kirwin K. M, and Hamrin, V. (2005). Decreasing the risk of complicated bereavement and future psychiatric disorders in children. *Journal of Child Adolescent Psychiatric Nursing* 18(2), 62–78.

Kiser, L. J., Baumgardner, B., and Dorado, J. (2010). Who we are, but for the stories we tell: Family stories and healing. *Psychological Trauma* 2(3), 243–49.

Kramer, L., and Baron, L. A. (1995). Intergenerational linkages: How experiences with siblings relate to the parenting of siblings. *Journal of Social and Personal Relationships* 12(1), 67–87.

Kretschmer, T., and Pike, A. (2010). Associations between adolescent siblings' relationship quality and similarity and differences in values. *Journal of Family Psychology* 24(4), 411–18.

Lashewicz, B. (2014). Sibling resentments and alliances during the parent care years: Implications for social work practice. *Journal of Evidence-Based Social Work* 11(5), 460–67.

Last, Jonathan. (2013). *What to Expect When No One's Expecting: America's Coming Demographic Disaster*. New York: Encounter Books.

Leung, A. K. D., and Robson, L. M. (1991). Sibling rivalry. *Clinical Pediatrics* 30, 314–17. doi:10.1177/00099 2289103000510.

Littrell, J. (1991). *Understanding and Treating Alcoholism: Volume I: An Empirically Based Clinician's Handbook for the Treatment of Alcoholism*. Hillsdale, NJ: Laurence Erlbaum Press.

Loshny, H. (2004). From birth control to menstrual control: The launch of the extended oral contraceptive, Seasonale. *Canadian Women's Studies* 24, 63–67.

Lynch, R. F. (2016). Parents face quantity-quality trade-offs between reproduction and investment in offspring in Iceland. *Royal Society Open Science*. doi:10.1098/rsos.160087.

Lyon, M. L. (2006). The relation of managers' perceptions of their leadership styles to parenting styles in their families of origin. *Dissertation Abstracts International* 67(3-B). (University Microfilms No. AAI3209590).

Machajewski, K. (2013). Childhood grief related to the death of a sibling. *Journal for Nurse Practitioners* 9, 443–48.

Mahoney, D. M., Rickspoone, L., and Hull, J. C. (2016). Narcissism, parenting, complex trauma: The emotional consequences created for children by narcissistic parents. *The Practitioner Scholar: Journal of Counseling and Professional Psychology* 5, 45–59.

Mantovani, N., Pizzolati, M., and Edge, D. (2016). Exploring the relationship between stigma and help-seeking for mental illness in African-descended faith communities in the UK. *Health Expectations*. doi:10.1111/hex.12464.

McGuire, K. T. (2013). The psychological origins of a constitutional revolution: The Supreme Court, birth order, and nationalizing the Bill of Rights. *Political Research Quarterly* 66, 441–53.

McLeod, J. M., and Chaffee, S. H. (1972). The construction of social reality. In J. Tedeschi (ed.), *The Social Influence Processes* (pp. 50–59). Chicago: Aldine-Atherton.

Merz, E., and De Jong Gierveld, J. (2016). Childhood memories, family ties, sibling support and loneliness in ever-widowed older adults: Quantitative and qualitative results. *Ageing & Society* 36(3), 534–61.

MetLife. (2004). Miles away: The MetLife study of long-distance caregiving: Findings from a national study. Available from http://www.metlife.com/WPS Assets/1266552904116064686V1FLongDistaneCaregiving.pdf.

Meyers, A. (2016). Trauma and recovery: Factors contributing to resiliency of survivors of sibling abuse. *The Family Journal: Counseling and Therapy for Couples and Families* 24(2), 147–56.

Mikkelson, A. C., Myers, S. A., and Hannawa, A. F. (2011). The differential use of relational maintenance behaviors in adult sibling relationships. *Communication Studies* 62(3), 258–71.

Milevsky, A., and Heerwagen, M. (2013). A phenomenological examination of sibling relationships in emerging adulthood. *Journal of Marriage and Family Review* 49(3), 251–63. doi: http://dx.doi.org/10.1080/01494929.2012.762444.

Minuchin, S. (1996). *Families and Family Therapy*. Cambridge, MA: Harvard University Press.

Morrill, M. (2014). Sibling sexual abuse: An exploratory study of long-term consequences for self-esteem and counseling considerations. *Journal of Family Violence* 29, 205. doi:10.1007/s10896-013-9571-4.

Morris, A. T., Gabert-Quillen, C., Friebert, S., Carst, N., and Delahanty, D. L. (2016). The indirect effect of positive parenting on the relationship between parent and sibling bereavement outcomes after the death of a child. *Journal of Pain & Symptom Management* 51, 60–70.

Mosli, R. H., Kaciroti, N., Corwyn, R. F., Bradley, R. H., and Lumeng, J. C. (2016). Effect of sibling birth on BMI trajectory in the first 6 years of life. *Pediatrics* 137(4). doi:http://dx.doi.org/10.1542/peds.2015-2456.

Namkung, E. H., Greenberg, J. S., and Mailick, M. R. (2016). Well-being of sibling caregivers: Effects of kinship relationship and race. *The Gerontologist* 10.1093. doi:10.1093/geront/gnw008.

Nelson, E. C., Heath, A. C., Madden, P. A. F., Cooper, L., Dinwiddie, S. H., Bucholz, K. K., and Martin, N. G. (2002). Association between self-reported childhood sexual abuse and adverse psychosocial outcomes: Results from a twin study. *Archives of General Psychiatry* 59, 139–45.

Nichols, M. P., and Davis, S. (2016). *Family Therapy: Concepts and Methods* (11th ed.). Saddlebrook, NJ: Pearson.

Nordqvist, P., and Smart, C. (2014). Troubling the family: Coming out as lesbian and gay. *Families, Relationships and Societies* 3(1), 97–112.

Ojeda, C., and Hatemi, P. K. (2015). Accounting for the child in the transmission of party identification. *American Sociological Review* 80(6), 1150–74.

Okudaira, H., Kinari, Y., Mizutani, N., Ohtake, F., and Kawaguchi, A. (2015). Older sisters and younger brothers: The impact of siblings on preference for competition. *Personality and Individual Differences* 82, 81–89.

Olson, D. H., Sprenkle, D. H., and Russell, C. S. (1979). Circumplex Model of marital and family systems. *Family Process* 18(1), 3–28.

Ono, M., and Devilly, G. J. (2013). The role of childhood and adulthood trauma and appraisal of self-discrepancy in overgeneral memory retrieval. *Cognition and Emotion* 27(6), 979–94.

Orgad, Y. (2015). The culture of family secrets. *Culture & Psychology* 21(1), 59–80.

Panfile, T. M., Laible, D. J., and Eye, J. L. (2012). Conflict frequency within mother-child dyads across contexts: Links with attachment and security. *Early Childhood Research Quarterly* 27, 78–106.

Park, S., and Schepp, K. G. (2015). A systematic review of research on children of alcoholics: Their inherent resilience and vulnerability. *Journal of Child and Family Studies* 24, 1222–31.

Park, S., Schepp, K. G., and Park, D. (2016). Living with appending a scarlet letter: The lifelong suffering of children of alcoholics in South Korea. *Journal of Ethnicity in Substance Abuse* (May 2016). doi:10.1080/15332640.2016.1175989.

Pauldine, M. R., Snyder, J., Bank, L., and Owen, L. D. (2015). Predicting sibling relationship quality from family conflict: A longitudinal study from early adolescence to young adulthood. *Journal of Child and Adolescent Behavior* 3(4), 231. doi:10.4172/2375-4494.1000231.

Perls, F. (1969). *Gestalt Therapy Verbatim*. Moab, UT: Real People Press.

Pew Research Center. April 2015. A deep dive into party affiliation.

Pew Research Center. May 12, 2015. America's changing religious landscape.

Pew Research Center. May 12, 2016. Public opinion on same-sex marriage. Survey conducted March 17–27, 2016.

Pew Research Center. November 3, 2015. U.S. public becoming less religious.

Pew Research Center. (2015). Among highly educated moms, families are getting bigger. Pew Research Center analysis of 1986, 1988, 1990, 1992, 1994, 1995, 2012, and 2014 Current Population Survey June Supplements. Retrieved from http://www.pewsocialtrends.org/2015/05/07/childlessness-falls-family-size -grows-among-highly-educated-women/st_2015-05-07_childlessness-12/.

Pew Research Center. (2015). Family size, by race and ethnicity. Pew Research Center analysis of 1986, 1988, 1990, 1992, 1994, 1995, 2012, and 2014 Current Population Survey June Supplements. Retrieved from http://www.pew socialtrends.org/2015/05/07/childlessness-falls-family-size-grows-among -highly-educated-women/st_2015-05-07_childlessness-12/.

Phillips, M., Lowe, M., Lurito, J. T., Dzemidzic, M., and Matthews, V. (2001). Temporal lobe activation demonstrates sex-based differences during passive listening. *Radiology* 220, 202–7.

Pollet, T. V. (2007). Genetic relatedness and sibling relationship characteristics in a modern society. *Evolution and Human Behavior* 28, 176–85. 10.1016/j. evolhumbehav.2006.10.001.

Pollet, T. V., and Nettle, D. (2009). Dead or alive? Knowledge about a sibling's death varies by genetic relatedness in a modern society. *Evolutionary Psychology*, 7, 57–65.

Ponzo, M., and Scoppa, V. Trading height for education in the marriage market. *American Journal of Human Biology* 27, 164–74.

Poortman, A., and Voorpostel, M. (2009). Parental divorce and sibling relationships: A research note. *Journal of Family Issues* 30(1), 74–91.

Prioste, A., Narciso, I., Goncalves, M., and Pereira, C. (2015). Family relationships and parenting practices: A pathway to adolescents' collectivist and individualist values? *Journal of Child & Family Studies* 24(11), 3258–67.

Prioste, A., Narciso, I., Goncalves, M., and Pereira, C. (2016). Adolescent parents' values: The role played by retrospective perceptions of the family-of-origin. *Journal of Child & Family Studies* 25(1), 224–31.

Pyke, K. (2005). "Generational deserters" and "black sheep": Acculturative differences among siblings in Asian immigrant families. *Journal of Family Issues* 26(4), 491–517.

Ram, A., and Ross, H. (2008). 'We got to figure it out': Information-sharing and siblings' negotiations of conflicts of interests. *Social Development* 17(3), 512–27.

Rapoza, K. A., Cook, K., Zaveri, T., and Malley-Morrison, K. (2010). Ethnic perspectives on sibling abuse in the United States. *Journal of Family Issues* 31(6), 808–29.

Reese-Weber, M., and Kahn, J. H. (2005). Familial predictors of sibling and romantic-partner conflict resolution: Comparing late adolescents from intact and divorced families. *Journal of Adolescence* 28(4), 479–93.

Ricky Finzi-Dottan, D., and Cohen, O. (2010) Young adult sibling relations: The effects of perceived parental favoritism and narcissism. *The Journal of Psychology* 145, 1–22. doi:10.1080/00223980.2010.528073.

Rocca, K. A., Martin, M. M., and Dunleavy, K. N. (2010). Siblings' motives for talking to each other. *The Journal of Psychology* 144(2), 205–19.

Rogers, C. (1961). *On Becoming a Person: A Therapist's View of Psychotherapy.* Boston: Houghton Mifflin.

Rogers, C. H., Floyd, F. J., Seltzer, M. M., Greenberg, J. S., and Hong, J. (2008). Long-term effects of the death of a child on parents' adjustment in midlife. *Journal of Family Psychology* 22, 203–11.

Romo, L. K. (2015). Family secrets. In *The International Encyclopedia of Interpersonal Communication.* John Wiley & Sons, Inc.

Rosen-Grandon, J. R., Myers, J. E., and Hattie, J. A. (2004). The relationship between marital characteristics, marital interaction processes, and marital satisfaction. *Journal of Counseling & Development* 82(1), 58–68.

Salmon, C. (2003). Birth order and relationships. *Human Nature* 14, 73–88.

Salmon, C., Cuthbertson, A. M., and Figueredo, A. J. (2016). The relationship between birth order and prosociality: An evolutionary perspective. *Personality and Individual Differences* 96, 18–22.

Samuel, I. S., Mahmood, Z., and Saleem, S. (2014). The development of the Role Identification Scale for adult children of alcoholic fathers. *Pakistan Journal of Social and Clinical Psychology* 12(1), 3–11.

Sarkisian, N., and Gerstel, N. (2016). Does singlehood isolate or integrate? Examining the link between marital status and ties to kin, friends, and neighbors. *Journal of Social & Personal Relationships* 33(3), 361–84.

Satir, V. (1967). *Conjoint Family Therapy: A Guide to Theory and Technique.* Palo Alto, CA: Science & Behavior Books.

Satir, V. (1972). *Peoplemaking.* Palo Alto, CA: Science & Behavior Books.

Satir, V., Bandler,. R., and Grinder, J. (1976). *Changing with Families.* Palo Alto, CA: Science & Behavior Books.

Savage, T., Derraik, J. G., Miles, H. L., Mouat, F., Cutfield, W. S., and Hofman, P. L. (2013). Birth order progressively affects childhood height. *Clinical Endocrinology* 79, 379–85.

Schulte, H. A. (2006). Family of origin and sibling influence on the experience of social support in adult friendships. *Dissertation Abstracts International: Section B: The Sciences and Engineering* 67(6-5), 3510.

Schwartz, S. H. (1992). Universals in the content and structure of values: Theoretical advances and empirical tests in 20 countries. *Advances in Experimental Social Psychology* 25, 1–65.

Seglem, K. B., Waaktaar, T., Ask, H., and Torgersen, S. (2016). Sex differences in genetic and environmental contributions to alcohol consumption from early adolescence to young adulthood. *Addiction* 111, 1188–95.

Seltzer, M. M., Greenberg, J. S., Krauss, M. W., Gordon, R. M., and Judge, K. (1997). Siblings of adults with mental retardation or mental illness: Effects on lifestyle and psychological well-being. *Family Relations* 46(4), 395–405.

Selvini-Palazzoli, M., Boscolo, L., Cecchin, G., and Prata, G. (1978). *Paradox and Counterparadox: A New Model in the Therapy of the Family in Schizophrenic Transaction.* New York: Jason Aronson.

Selvini-Palazzoli, M., Boscolo, L., Cecchin, G., and Prata, G. (1980). Hypothesizing-circularity-neutrality: Three guidelines for the conductor of the session. *Family Process* 19, 3–12.

Sharp, M., Fear, N. T., Rona, R. J., Wessley, S., Greenberg, N., Jones, N., and Goodwin, L. (2015). Stigma as a barrier to seeking health care among military personnel with mental health problems. *Epidemiological Review*. doi:10.1093/epirev/mxu012.

Shaw, D. (2010). Enter ghosts: The loss of intersubjectivity in clinical work with adult children of pathological narcissists. *Psychoanalytic Dialogues* 20(1), 46–59.

Shea, D. M. (2015). Young voters, declining trust and the limits of "service politics." *The Forum: A Journal of Applied Research in Contemporary Politics* 13(3), 459–79. doi: http://dx.doi.org/10.1515/for-2015-0036.

Sherman, A. M., Lansford, J. E., and Volling, B. L. (2006). Sibling relationships and best friendships in young adulthood: Warmth, conflict, and well-being. *Personal Relationships* 13(2), 151–65.

Simonelli, C. J., Mullis, T., Elliott, A. N., and Pierce, T. W. (2002). Abuse by siblings and subsequent experiences of violence within the dating relationship. *Journal of Interpersonal Violence* 17(2), 103–21.

Skierkowski, D. and Wood, R. M. (2012). To text or not to text? The importance of text messaging among college-aged youth. *Computers in Human Behavior* 28(2), 744–56.

Smith, M. J., Greenberg, J. S., and Mailick Seltzer, M. (2007). Siblings of adults with schizophrenia: Expectations about future caregiving roles. *American Journal of Orthopsychiatry* 77(1), 29–37.

Soli, A. R., McHale, S. M., and Feinberg, M. E. (2009). Risk and protective effects of sibling relationships among African American adolescents. *Family Relations* 58, 578–92.

Song, J., Floyd, F. J., Seltzer, M. M., Greenberg, J. S., and Hong, J. (2010). Long-term effects of child death on parents' health-related quality of life: A dyadic analysis. *Family Relations* 59, 269–82.

Spitze, G. D., and Trent, K. (2016). Changes in individual sibling relationships in response to life events. *Journal of Family Issues*. doi:10.1177/0192513X16653431.

Spitze, G., and Trent, K. (2006). Gender differences in adult sibling relations in two-child families. *Journal of Marriage and Family* 68(4), 977–92.

Spitze, G., Ward, R., Deane, G., and Zhuo, Y. (2012). Cross-sibling effects in parent-adult child exchanges of socioemotional support. *Research on Aging* 34(2), 197–221.

Staiger, T., Waldmann, R., Krumm, S., and Rusch, N. (2016). Stigma and poor mental health literacy as barriers to service use among unemployed people with mental illness: A qualitative study. *European Psychiatry* 33S, S487.

Steinberg, L. (2008). A social neuroscience perspective on adolescent risk-taking. *Developmental Review* 28, 78–106.

Suitor, J. J., and Pillemer, K. (2006). Choosing daughters: Exploring why mothers favor adult daughters over sons. *Sociological Perspectives* 49(2), 139–61.

Sulloway, F. J. (1996). *Born to Rebel*. New York: Pantheon.

Summers, D. M., and Summers, C. C. (2006). Unadulterated arrogance: Autopsy of the narcissistic parental alienator. *American Journal of Family Therapy* 34, 399–428.

Tibbetts, G., and Scharfe, E. (2015). Oh, brother (or sister)!: An examination of sibling attachment, conflict, and cooperation in emerging adulthood. *Journal of Relationships Research* 6(e8). doi:10.1017/jrr.2015.4.

Tifferet, S., Pollet, T., Bar, A., and Efrati, H. (2016). Predicting sibling investment by perceived sibling resemblance. *Evolutionary Based Sciences* 10(1), 64–70.

Tillman, K. H. (2007). "Non-traditional" siblings and the academic outcomes of adolescents. *Social Science Research* 37(1), 88–108.

Tony, A. (1978). The Laundry List. Retrieved from http://www.adultchildren.org/lit-Laundry_List.

Torbic, H. (2011). Children and grief: But what about the children? *Home Healthcare Nurse* 29(2), 67–79.

Tucker, C. J., Finkelhor, D., Turner, H., and Shattuck, A. M. (2014). Family dynamics and young children's sibling victimization. *Journal of Family Psychology* 28(5), 625–33.

Tyler, K. M., Boykin, A. W., Boelter, C. M., and Dillihunt, M. L. (2005). Examining mainstream and Afro-cultural value socialization in African American households. *Journal of Black Psychology* 31, 291–311.

U.S. Census Bureau, Current Population Survey, Annual Social and Economic Supplements, 1955, 1960, 1965, and 1970 to 2015.

Ungar, M. (2013). Resilience, trauma, context, and culture. *Trauma Violence Abuse* 14(3), 255–66.

Van Volkom, M. (2006). Sibling relationships in middle and older adulthood: A review of the literature. *Marriage & Family Review* 40(2/3), 151–70.

Vernig, P. M. (2011). Family roles in homes with alcohol-dependent parents: An evidence-based review. *Substance Use & Misuse* 46, 535–42.

Vivona, J. M. (2010). Siblings, transference, and the lateral dimension of psychic life. *Psychoanalytic Psychology* 27(1), 8–26.

Volling, B., and Bedford, V. H. (1998, July). Sibling relationships in childhood and adulthood: Contributions from a life-span perspective. In V. H. Bedford and K. Fingerman (chairs), *Lessons from The Later Years: What Child Development Can Learn from Gerontology about Social Relationships.* Symposium presented at the XVth Biennial Meetings of the International Society for the Study of Behavioral Development, Berne, Switzerland.

Voorpostel, M., van der Lippe, T., and Flap, H. (2012). For better or worse: Negative life events and sibling relationships. *International Sociology* 27(3), 330–48.

Wan He, Goodkind, Daniel, and Kowal, Paul. U.S. Census Bureau, International Population Reports, P95/16-1, An Aging World: 2015, U.S. Government Publishing Office, Washington, DC, 2016.

Wang, Q., and Peterson, C. (2014). Your earliest memory may be earlier than you think: Prospective studies of children's dating of earliest childhood memories. *Developmental Psychology* 50, 1680–86.

Wang, Y. N. (2015). Authenticity and relationship satisfaction: Two distinct ways of directing power to self-esteem. *PLoS ONE* 10(12): e0146050. doi:10.1371/journal.pone.0146050.

Watson-Gegeo, K. A., and Gegeo, D. W. (1989). The role of sibling interaction in child socialization. In P. G. Zukow (ed.), *Sibling Interaction Across Cultures: Theoretical and Methodological Issues* (pp. 54–76). New York: Springer-Verlag.

Webb, J. R., Hirsch, J. K., and Toussaint, L. (2015). Forgiveness as a positive psychotherapy for addiction and suicide: Theory, research, and practice. *Spirituality in Clinical Practice* 2(1), 48–60.

Wegscheider, S. (1976). *The Family Trap: No One Escapes from a Chemical Dependent Family.* St. Paul: Nurturing Networks.

Wegscheider-Cruse, S. (1986). *Understanding Me.* Pompano Beach, FL: Health Communications.

Wheeler, L., Killoren, S., Whiteman, S., Updegraff, K., McHale, S., and Umana-Taylor, A. (2016). Romantic relationship experiences from late adolescence to young adulthood: The role of older siblings in Mexican-origin families. *Journal of Youth & Adolescence* 45(5), 900–15.

White, M., and Epston, D. (1990). *Narrative Means to Therapeutic Ends.* New York: Norton.

Widdig, A., Nürnberg, P., Krawczak, M., Streich, W. J., and Bercovitch, F. B. (2001). Paternal relatedness and age proximity regulate social relationships among adult female rhesus macaques. PNAS Proceedings of the

National Academy of Sciences of the United States of America, 98, 13769–773. 10.1073/pnas.241210198 1.

Widemalm, M., and Hjarthag, F. (2015). The forum as a friend: Parental mental illness and communication on open Internet forums. *Social Psychiatry and Psychiatric Epidemiology* 50(1), 1601–7.

Worden, J. W. (1999). Comparing parent loss with sibling loss. *Death Studies* 23(1), 1–15.

Xu, J. Q., Murphy, S. L., Kochanek, K. D., and Bastian, B. A. (2016). Deaths: Final data for 2013. *National Vital Statistics Reports* 64(2). Hyattsville, MD: National Center for Health Statistics.

Yang, J., Hou, X., Wei, D., Wang, K., Li, Y., and Qiu, J. (2016). Only-child and non-only-child exhibit differences in creativity and agreeableness: Evidence from behavioral and anatomical structural studies. *Brain Imaging and Behavior*, 1–10.

Yeh, H., and Lempers, J. D. (2004). Perceived sibling relationships and adolescent development. *Journal of Youth and Adolescence* 33(2), 133–47.

Zajonc, R. B., and Sulloway, F. J. (2007). The confluence model: Birth order as a within-family or between-family dynamic? *Personality & Social Psychology Bulletin* 33, 1187–94.

Index